T0285226

THE MOTH PRESENTS

A POINT
OF
BEAUTY

TRUE STORIES OF HOLDING ON
AND LETTING GO

THE MOTH
PRESENTS

A POINT OF BEAUTY

TRUE STORIES OF HOLDING ON AND LETTING GO

CROWN
NEW YORK

CURATED AND EDITED BY

Meg Bowles
Catherine Burns
Emily Couch
Suzanne Rust
Chloe Salmon

WITH ADDITIONAL
EDITING BY

Jenifer Hixson
Michelle Jalowski
Sarah Austin Jenness
Jodi Powell
Larry Rosen

LIBRARY OF CONGRESS CATALOGING-IN-PUBLICATION DATA
Names: Moth (Organization), editor.
Title: The Moth presents a point of beauty / by The Moth.
Other titles: Point of beauty | Moth radio hour (Radio program)
Description: First edition. | New York : Crown, 2024.
Identifiers: LCCN 2023048682 (print) | LCCN 2023048683 (ebook) |
ISBN 9780593139035 (hardcover ; acid-free paper) | ISBN 9780593139042 (ebook)
Subjects: LCSH: Moth (Organization) | Moth radio hour (Radio program) |
United States—Social life and customs—20th century—Anecdotes. |
Popular culture—United States—Anecdotes. | United States—Biography—
Anecdotes. | LCGFT: Anecdotes.
Classification: LCC PN1991.77.M675 M6826 2017 (print) |
LCC PN1991.77.M675 (ebook) | DDC 808.88/20973—dc23/eng/20231211
LC record available at https://lccn.loc.gov/2023048682
LC ebook record available at https://lccn.loc.gov/2023048683

Printed in the United States of America on acid-free paper

crownpublishing.com

2 4 6 8 9 7 5 3 1

FIRST EDITION

Editor: Matt Inman • Editorial assistant: Fariza Hawke •
Production editor: Loren Noveck • Text designer: Elizabeth Rendfleisch •
Production manager: Sandra Sjursen • Managing editors: Allison Fox and
Sally Franklin • Copyeditor: Melissa Churchill • Proofreader(s): Deborah Bader
and Liz Carbonell • Publicist: Gwyneth Stansfield • Marketer: Mason Eng

CONTENTS

Foreword   xiii

Introduction   xvii

YOU EAT THAT CAKE. *NOW.*

Eye Spy   MICHAELA MURPHY   5

Danger Zone   WILL MACKIN   13

Chasing Grandma   MORGAN GIVENS   21

Sandwiches and Neighbors   OANH NGO USADI   27

The Best Medicine   MICHAEL FISCHER   34

UNTIL THE LION LEARNS TO WRITE

When the Truth Pops Out   LIN-MANUEL MIRANDA   43

My Knight in Shining Side Curls   FRIMET GOLDBERGER   49

Standing as 10,000   BRIGETTE JANEA JONES   56

Don't Call Me Young Lady!   CAROLYN MEYER   64

Lucky Numbers   BRIDGETT M. DAVIS   70

Loving Grace   ROBIN UTZ   76

YOU KNOW WHO YOU ARE

Meeting Tony Blair   JEREMY JENNINGS   85

So Much, and Enough   ANAÏS BORDIER   91

Angry   AMBER ABUNDANCE   98

A Thpoonful of Thugar   PHIL WANG   104

Blue Genes   CARMEN RITA WONG   112

Do We Know How to Grieve?   FRANCINE LOBIS WHEELER   118

I WILL LIFT MY EYES TO THE HILLS

Nowhere to Run   MONTE MONTEPARE   127

Abuelos, Apples, and Me   LUNA AZCURRAIN   134

That's My Shirt   GEORGE SUMNER   138

A Bratz Life   TALAYA MOORE   145

Swimming Through It   PARVATHY ANANTNARAYAN   151

Being a Foot Soldier   DR. SYBIL JORDAN HAMPTON   156

IT WAS BRUTAL. AND IT WAS BEAUTIFUL.

El Conquistador   SHAUN LEONARDO   165

The Alpha Wolf   ELIZABETH GILBERT   171

If the Suit Fits   PHILL BRANCH   181

Survivor's Guilt   DAVID GASKIN   187

Expecting   TRYSTAN REESE   194

A LIGHT SHINING THROUGH

Operation: Bruin Escape and Rescue (BEAR)
ELANA DUFFY   203

Knockoffs   EDGAR RUIZ JR.   211

Survive, Then Live   PATIENCE MURRAY   217

Dancing in the Bazaar   MANIZA NAQVI   223

It's Your Job to Hold Your Baby   WARREN HOLLEMAN   230

YOU BETTER GET THESE CATTLE OUT OF THE KITCHEN

Finding My Place   IVAN MCCLELLAN   239

A Violin's Life   FRANK ALMOND   246

Meeting Miles   ANDREA KING COLLIER   254

Is Love Wild, Is Love Real?   SARFRAZ MANZOOR   260

Ms. Mary   TIQ MILAN   268

Feedlot Calves   JACKIE ANDREWS   275

THIS PLACE WAS HOME

Little Pink General Lee   SAMUEL JAMES   285

A Complete, Correct Human   JOHN ELDER ROBISON   291

Rich City Skater   JACOBY COCHRAN   299

The Day Tyler Perry Called Me   BRITTNEY COOPER   305

Keeping the Faith . . . and the Feminism
BLESSING OMAKWU   312

The Sky Is the Limit   QURATULAIN FATIMA   319

A HUSHED KIND OF AWE

Between the Rock and a Heart Place
MARGUERITE MARIA RIVAS   327

Chasing the Good Notes   QUIARA ALEGRÍA HUDES   333

Swimmer Girl   HASNA MUHAMMAD   341

Don't Give Up on the Baby   NICK ULLETT   348

Home   ALISTAIR BANE   354

About the Directors/Editors   363

Acknowledgments   369

About The Moth   373

In 2003, I was asked to perform at the US Comedy Arts Festival in Aspen, Colorado. Coincidentally, so was The Moth. At the time, The Moth was simply a storytelling series. There was no radio show. No podcast. No books. The Moth was a small-time operation with a big heart.

Catherine Burns, who was then The Moth's sole producer, asked me if I would be interested in telling a story in Aspen. Up until then I had never told a long-form story on stage, and I would later find out this was the first story Catherine had ever directed. So, we were both a little new. I had always thought about storytelling as something I wanted to do, but whenever I tried to tell stories in a stand-up comedy format, I felt insecure, or it seemed like I was losing the audience's attention. So this seemed like an exciting invitation. What I didn't realize was that it would fundamentally change the way I perform for the rest of my career.

That year in Aspen I told an early version of a story that would end up being the title story from my solo show and Netflix special *My Girlfriend's Boyfriend*. It was about my first girlfriend in high school and how she told me not to tell anyone that she was my girlfriend because she actually had *another* boyfriend. It was a pride-swallowing event in my life that I had never told anyone about, never mind a group of strangers.

I was so nervous when I told the story on stage in Aspen that I was literally trembling. I sometimes tell people who want to try storytelling that being nervous about telling the story might be a good sign. It was for me. If it makes you very uncomfortable to tell it—if you want to bail out at many stages—you might just be going in the right direction.

I was scared in part because storytelling is very personal. If the audience doesn't respond, it feels like a very specific type of rejection. When people don't like your personal story, sometimes it feels like they're saying, "We don't like *you*. Y'know. Your personality." Which is not true, by the way. It can just feel like that.

After performing at The Moth for the first time, I remember thinking, *I think I'm better at this than traditional stand-up comedy. I think this is what I'm meant to do.*

Fifteen years later, this is what I do.

I tell long-form stories that form a narrative arc. I've written and performed five autobiographical shows on and off Broadway. The Moth played a pivotal role in putting me on a path to do just that. My most recent show, *The Old Man and the Pool* at Lincoln Center, is all about life, death, and mortality but more than anything, laughter—my favorite ingredients of a great night at The Moth, and ones you'll find when reading the wide range of stories in this collection.

I owe a huge debt to The Moth for giving me a chance to try telling a story on stage. They taught me how to be vulnerable, how to take my time, and how to listen to someone else's story and share in their moments of triumph, laughter, or, yes, sometimes embarrassment, with an open heart.

It's been twenty years since I met my friends at The Moth.

They've come a long way. The Moth is now a radio show. A hit podcast. Has bestselling books. But also, still, and most important, they have a big heart. My deepest gratitude to The Moth, and I hope you enjoy this book.

—Mike Birbiglia

INTRODUCTION

On a chilly November evening in 2021, a crowd gathered under the cathedral ceiling of the gorgeous St. Ann & the Holy Trinity Church in Brooklyn Heights where, for the first time in nearly two years, we were able to safely hold an in-person indoor event. St. Ann's is an active house of worship that makes ends meet by moonlighting as a live-event space. There was a crackling energy in the room. We were thrilled to be gathering again, even though we were a bit anxious—not just about the risk of another Covid surge but also about making conversation after being isolated for so long. People made nervous jokes about how they'd forgotten how to make small talk. Everyone was wearing masks (many matched to their outfits), and a venue that pre-pandemic would have been packed shoulder to shoulder had been sold to just half capacity, to be as safe as possible.

We sat in candlelight watching the show, and it was such a relief to hear stories told live again—to be in the room with the storytellers and the audience, feel the energy flowing between them, and hear the applause. While we were grateful for the technology that had allowed us to produce online shows from our collective living rooms during the darkest months, we had deeply longed to be back together.

That Brooklyn night, Maniza Naqvi told her moving story about resuscitating a seventy-year-old bookstore in Karachi, Pakistan. In the story she says, "When the noise and ugliness got so loud, I focused in on a point of beauty." That phrase, "a point of beauty," stuck in our heads because that night, and those stories, were a point of beauty after coming through one of the most challenging periods the world had faced in recent memory.

A year later, when we sat down to compile this collection, we wanted to bring that feeling of electricity in the room to the page. So many remarkable stories had been told since our last book (we read more than four hundred Moth stories as we narrowed them down to these fifty!). It can be difficult to find a cohesive title for a collection that spans time, place, and people with wildly different experiences. The nature of a title is to pull everything together, and The Moth pulls stories from every corner of humanity. But we kept coming back to Maniza's story.

The phrase "a point of beauty" speaks to seeing potential, hope, and possibility, the diamond in the rough: Maniza seeing how a dusty, neglected bookstore could become a beautiful literary hub; an elite navy instructor believing that his student could be a "Top Gun" pilot in spite of a very rough initial landing; a future Lucha Libre star getting his butt handed to him during his first match.

It also shines light on moments of grace that might be missed if we move too quickly or let ourselves become distracted: neighbors finally finding a way to connect after living next door for decades; a woman in her eighties optimistically buying fancy new underwear for her first date in years; a prison inmate taking responsibility for his own worth after being treated kindly by a nurse; a teen assuming the reins of a family tradition from her dying grandfather.

It's also about how improbable, ridiculous, and whimsical the world can be: a 23andMe genetic test taken for fun revealing painful family secrets; a culture critic panicking when the famous filmmaker she's publicly rebuked calls her on the phone to talk about it; or a distraught mother processing unexpected family news in a big-box store because "you can work out *a whole lot of shit* in the aisles of Target."

The subtitle "True Stories of Holding On and Letting Go" resonated with all of us. These stories help us see how we may find beauty in strengthening frayed bonds but also in having the courage to walk away from things that no longer feed our spirit; in admitting that some things may just not be meant for us, and at times it's essential to prune dead branches if a tree is going to bloom again in the spring. Certainly the last few years have taught us so much about what's worth holding on to: our relationships with those we love the most, our understanding of ourselves, and of course gathering, listening to, and telling stories.

But it takes strength and bravery to explore your story and share it with the world. And by reading this book, you also become an important part of the process. The Moth's longtime Board co-chair Ari Handel put it well when he spoke at The Moth's 25th Anniversary celebration: "There's the stage, and there's the seats. And if telling stories can change lives, listening to stories [editor's note: or reading them!] is just as important—it can change minds. Too often we talk past each other, through each other, too separated by experience and belief and tribe and predisposition to even hear each other's arguments . . . but stories are different. When you listen to a person's story told from their vulnerable heart, those walls of difference and indifference crumble just a bit, and our basic common humanity shines through."

These stories show us that even on the darkest of days there is usually something beautiful to observe or discover if you're open to it. A soldier finding friendship while working as a guard in one of the world's most notorious prisons. A homeless child taking unexpected solace in her collection of Bratz dolls. Or a mother remembering a tender moment with her son Ben that happened in a Starbucks in Connecticut less than an hour before he was murdered.

These stories help us process what can often feel like an overwhelming stream of sad news that comes at us like a fire hose through our phones, televisions, and radios. Ari continued, "I thought about the Moth show at St. Ann's where a Sandy Hook mom told a story about her son that made me cry in a way I never did when faced with the numbing impersonal magnitude of it all."

That Connecticut mom, Francine Lobis Wheeler, told her story the same night Maniza spoke of her magical bookstore in Pakistan. Even though her story was devastating, Francine wanted to let some light in as well. The audience laughed with her as she recounted the many sweet, funny things that Ben said on that terrible morning. We were thrilled that her humor—a foundational part of who she is—came through, and her radiance and wit allowed the audience to take in that day in a new way. She showed us that it's possible to find tiny moments of brightness and beauty—moments that are worth holding on to—in a world that can sometimes feel brutal.

It has been a joy putting this collection together, and we hope that these stories will open your world as they have ours.

With love,

—Catherine Burns, on behalf of the Moth editing team:
Meg Bowles, Emily Couch, Suzanne Rust, and
Chloe Salmon

THE MOTH PRESENTS

A POINT
OF
BEAUTY

TRUE STORIES OF HOLDING ON
AND LETTING GO

YOU EAT THAT CAKE. *NOW.*

EYE SPY

MICHAELA MURPHY

I grew up in Providence, Rhode Island, and for my entire childhood we were never more than twenty miles away from the core of our universe: the Kennedys.

We were Irish, they were Irish.

We were Catholic, they were Catholic.

They were family. We were like the relatives that they never got to see. But we knew they were busy, and that they loved us.

Anything that was happening to them was also happening to us. So, their tragedy plus our own tragedy was *a lot*.

This one Thanksgiving after dinner and a family fight at Grandma's house, we were driving home, and the radio was playing this story about the tenth anniversary of the JFK assassination. I'm sitting in the backseat, and I start to cry.

My sister, Erin, says, "Hey, Dad, Michaela is cryin'."

My father pulls that car right over to the shoulder of I-95.

He stops, he turns around, he looks at us, and with tears in his own eyes, he says, "Don't you ever be ashamed to cry for that man."

My parents grew up near Newport, and they got married in the same exact church as Jack and Jackie, St. Mary's, and my father gave my mother jewelry that were exact replications of the jewelry that Jack gave to Jackie. Every Saturday night after mass, my family would be in the living room, and we'd be happily ever after listening to the original Broadway soundtrack of *Camelot*.

Every year during the seventies, my four aunts would take me and my two cousins on their dream vacation—a rented beach house in Hyannis—on the very cove, sharing beachfront with the Kennedy compound.

Every day, for an entire week, my Aunt Pat would roll up her sisters' hair. My aunts would apply sunscreen to the back of their necks, the backs of the hands, and the tops of their feet. And then they would drag their beach chairs down to the beach, and they would set them up perfectly.

Not facing the water.

Not into the sun for tanning.

But perfectly for spying on the Kennedys.

They would sit there all day in the broiling sun with high-powered binoculars and keep constant surveillance. Every year, they'd have the same conversations.

Around mid-morning, the first sighting would be made, usually by my Aunt Pat; she'd be, "Ah, they got Rose out—walkin'. Ethel looks drawn."

And then about an hour later, my Aunt Gert would say, "How old is Rose now?"

Aunt Momo would make the calculations.

"Well, let's see. Jack died in '63 when she was seventy-four. And Rose's birthday was two weeks last Thursday, and Joe died in '69, makin' her a widow at eighty-one. So, eighty-five."

And then they'd break for lunch.

After lobster and drawn butter and hosing us down, they'd all hustle back to their posts, and they'd watch.

Every now and then, there'd be someone they didn't know: "Hey, who's that? *Who's that?*"

So, they'd draw out the family tree in the sand. They'd analyze it. They'd come up with a profile, and they'd crack the code:

"It's one of Bobby's."

Now, any mention of Bobby would always bring up the inevitable, "Oh, I just pray to God they don't tell poor senile Rose about Bobby. It'll break her."

Then, the long afternoon stretch would end with the inevitable annual observation, "You don't see Jackie much here," and then all of my aunts would drop their binoculars and look at each other meaningfully.

Now, all of this meant that no one was paying any attention to me and my cousins in the water. And the summer when we were nine years old, we found something washed up on the beach that caught our eye.

Now, had an aunt, perhaps in an effort to ease a cramp in her prying neck, just sort of glanced toward the water, she might have seen us climbing into this tiny, plastic, half-inflated boat.

She might have cried out in alarm at the lack of oars and life vests.

She might have had a conniption fit to see us shove off and drift into the violent riptide that would sweep us, within five minutes, out to the open sea and into the path of a Nantucket-bound ferry.

But an aunt *didn't,* and we *did.*

It all happened so fast, and it wasn't until we realized that we could make out the specific features of the ferry passengers that we knew we were really far from shore. We were *so* far from shore that my aunts were now reduced to four hopping dots. Uh-oh. It was like *Gilligan's Island* for real.

An Atlantic swell crashes over our heads. But as soon as the water clears out of our eyes, a powerboat pulls up out of nowhere. In this powerboat are . . . David and Michael Kennedy.

David and Michael pull us up into the boat, and we're like, "Oh my God! We are saved by . . . a powerboat!"

The powerboat sends us back to shore, and we're psyched because we're saved, until we start to watch the four hopping dots morph back into our four crazed, livid aunts.

We are *so* going to get it.

Now, when we are in huge trouble, my aunts, under any circumstances, each has their own weird thing about yelling.

My Aunt Gert, she gets so freaked out that all she can do is yell out our addresses, like, "EILEEN AND KEVIN, 275 HOOPER STREET! MICHAELA, 280 ASYLUM ROAD!"

I swear to God, I grew up on *Asylum Road*. A very telling piece of my childhood.

Then, my Aunt Pat would do this thing where she would say things that were, like, actually kind of nice things, but she'd say them like they were death threats.

She'd be like, "Yeah, I'll save you from drowning. You get on that beach towel, and you lie in that sun. Now!"

Or, she'd say, "I'm going to buy you a birthday present. You eat that cake. *Now.*"

We knew that this is what was coming; the Kennedy boys didn't. So, they're vivaciously tanned, and they pull up to the shoreline, and we brace ourselves.

Now what happens is, our aunts are out of their minds. They're ready to flay us. But when they see us in the same boat as the Kennedys, it's like they don't have the emotional capacity to handle it.

They kind of snap. They're freaking out, ready to yell at us, but they start fake smiling and trying to act all normal. My Aunt Momo, she just takes on this Kennedy-esque way of speaking, which is sort of halfway between Katharine Hepburn and the Queen of England.

We're looking at them like, *What are you guys doing?*

And they're smiling the smile, but when they smile at us, it's like, "You just wait."

But then they're like, "Oh, David. Oh, Michael, thank you. Thank you, thank you."

And they're not mad at us for almost drowning. They're mad at us because the Kennedys had to save us.

Like, "Don't those people have enough trouble? Now you?" As if our almost drowning was yet another Kennedy tragedy.

These poor boys finally pry themselves away from my aunts.

They get back in the boat, and my Aunt Momo's going, "*Please give our best to your grandmother!*"

And now, it's time for our real punishment, which was that we, for the rest of vacation, had to stay on the beach, because we did not have any respect for the water.

It's a hundred degrees out, and after about a half hour of whining and fighting and emptying out all the Coppertone and kicking sand, we break my Aunt Pat's last nerve, and she says, "All right, you can go in the water, but only up to your knees."

We're happy for a minute until we get in the water and realize how boring "up to your knees" is. And then, we get the great idea of having chicken fights. We start to have chicken fights, but it's weird because there are only three of us.

But we're doing the best we can to have a chicken fight and knock each other off into the water, so we get fully immersed.

And then, my Uncle Al, who never, *ever* played with us, ever, comes into the water to play chicken fights with us. He puts his daughter, my cousin Eileen, up on his shoulders, and then I get up on my cousin Kevin's shoulders, and we're having chicken fights, and it's like actual family fun for a moment. We're hitting each other, falling in the water.

And then I take my foot, and I accidentally kick the side of my Uncle Al's head *really, really* hard.

And his eyeball pops out of his head, falls into the water, and sinks.
It pops out of his head,
And it sinks.
Eileen, Kevin, and I are in instant complete shock.

Right this minute, there is still a part of me that is on that beach screaming.

It's like, *Oh my God*. We had no idea that he had a fake eye! We didn't even know that you *could* have a fake eye! Why would you have a fake eye?

They didn't tell us that Uncle Al had a fake eye because they didn't want us bragging to all the neighbors. They didn't tell us, so we didn't know. Later on, there was Columbo and Sandy Duncan, but this was way before that. We had no idea.

So, we're all standing there, and it's so horrible. I'm like, *Oh my God*.

My cousins, Eileen and Kevin, are staring at me with complete hate, like, "You broke our dad." My Uncle Al is standing there, and he's got the lid open. So, you can see inside the socket where now it's just like skin, and the eyeball—gone!

You cannot just say "I'm sorry" to someone whose eye you just knocked out.

My Aunt Pat is hysterically screaming because that eyeball cost top dollar. It was a special magnetized eye so it could keep up with the other one. And now vacation was over, and I had just better pray that they got that deposit back, because they're going to have to buy a brand-new top-dollar eye, and that was not in the budget.

So, I just didn't know what to do. I was like, *My life is over. I am no longer Michaela, I am now Herb's girl who kicked Al's eye out at the Cape*. And it's awful, and everybody's just crying and pointing at me.

Now my other aunts are getting in on it, and the "who's to blame" part of the conversation is happening.

So, I just kind of back off into the water. I'm going back to where life as I once knew it had ended. I stand there, and I kind of wish I had drowned, that the Kennedys hadn't saved me.

I bend over into the waves. I start sifting through sand and shells and pebbles. It's totally ridiculous, but I will never stop looking for this eye. I'm going to look forever. I keep looking and looking, and I'm sifting through, and then all of a sudden, there is an eyeball in my palm staring right at me.

And I scream, and I drop it.

It sinks back into the water.

But now, we know it's possible. Everybody gets back into the water, and now we're *all* sifting through. I pray to God for no more future happiness until we find this eye. I also pray that it will not be me who finds it this time.

After an hour, my Cousin Kevin finds the eye, and he holds it up in triumph, and he does not let go!

My Uncle Al takes the eye, washes it off, and just pops it back in. And then, he tests it, and it's keeping up with the other one, so it's working still. It's the weirdest thing because now that we know it's a fake eye, it totally looks like a fake eye. I can't believe that I never noticed it was a fake eye before.

Now vacation's back on. Everybody gets back into their beach chairs, and they start to settle down to begin telling the story over and over a million times about what I just did.

But I have not really fully reintegrated back into the family yet. I'm standing apart, and I notice that there actually has been a group of people who've been watching this whole thing.

And then, I see something that I didn't notice—that no one noticed.

And that's that two of the Kennedy kids, David and Michael, had taken a walk on the beach. I can tell, just by the look on their faces, that they had stood there and seen the entire episode.

That they had been there, watching *us*.

＊ ⊙ ＊

MICHAELA MURPHY is a writer, playwright, storyteller, producer, and teacher. Her one-woman show *Something Blue* was performed at the US Comedy Arts Festival in Aspen, the Improv Theatre (Los Angeles), and Off-Broadway (Second Stage Theater). Her stories have been featured on NPR, The Moth Mainstage (NYC and national tours) and Peabody Award–winning *The Moth Radio Hour;* at the Nantucket Film Festival, the Whitney Museum (NYC), On the Boards (Seattle), Seattle Repertory Theatre (Seattle), the cruise ship *Origin* (Galapagos Islands), *The Liar Show, RISK!,* Word of Mouth (Bucks County Playhouse), TEDx, the Clinton White House; and in *The New Yorker* and the Moth book *How to Tell a Story.* She was formerly the director of education at Second Stage Theater and was a guest artistic director for the 52nd Street Project replications (Navajo and Chippewa Nations, and Yale University). Michaela is a co-founder of "L!FE: Leadership Fueled by Entrepreneur–ISM" (Detroit, NYC), an education leadership platform for high school students. Michaela continues to tell stories and helps others to tell their own.

This story was told on April 16, 2004, at The Players in New York City. The theme of the evening was Star Struck. Director: Catherine Burns.

DANGER ZONE

WILL MACKIN

June 1986, I had just graduated high school. I was working in a parking lot on the Jersey Shore. By working, I mean I was playing stickball with my friends. I was surfing when the waves were good. And I was perfectly happy to continue doing that for the rest of my days.

Then one night, I went to the movies, and I saw *Top Gun*. And my life changed forever.

From that moment on, I wanted to fly jets. Not only did I want to fly jets, I wanted to be Maverick, because Maverick was *cool*. So, I joined ROTC, I graduated college, I went to the U.S. Navy Flight School in Pensacola, Florida.

And there I classed up with a group of thirty young men and women, all of whom had seen *Top Gun*.

All of whom wanted to be Maverick.

But only the top three of our graduating class would get their choice of aircraft; everyone else would do whatever the navy wanted us to do.

The thirty of us emerged from ground school ranked more or less the same. Next was the flight phase of training. And here was where we separated the cream from the cream, the best from the best, the puppies from the small dogs. And it was critically important which instructor was assigned to you during flight phase, because the instructor will grade your flights, and the grades will determine your class rank.

And so, on the spectrum of instructors, the easiest by far was a lieutenant I'll call Howdy Doody, who, just like the puppet from the 1950s children's show, had a permanent smile on his face. He had freckles on his apple cheeks. He walked around like strings were attached to his hands and feet. And he was a genuinely nice guy. He would call you by your first name instead of your rank. And when he asked you how you were, you thought he really wanted to hear the answer.

On the other end of the spectrum was Major Small, who never smiled. And who never spoke a word to anybody about anything. He walked around like he carried the weight of the world on his shoulders. And the reason for that probably was because Major Small had been shot down over Iraq in the first Gulf War, and he'd been taken prisoner. And so, he'd gone from being a POW to being an instructor at Pensacola. And there he earned a reputation as the toughest grader.

Also, as someone who is out to break your soul.

We all knew the story of the guy a class ahead of mine who, after a bad flight with Major Small, not only quit flight school, but quit the navy and started selling Amway. When he invited me to his house to listen to his Ponzi scheme presentation, I went. And I bought a giant box of soap because I didn't want the karma wheel to spin against me.

The day of my first flight, I'm driving into the squad, and I'm really hoping for a good instructor. I park in the parking lot, I enter the hangar, and climb the stairs to the ready room. I check the status board.

I find my name, and written in the instructor box next to my name is Lieutenant Howdy Doody. I can't believe my luck. But because I'd never flown a plane before, and even though the T-34 was more toy than a plane—it was mostly plastic, painted orange and white like a Big Wheel, and had a little motor like a Weedwacker—I was still a little bit nervous.

So, fast-forward to the end of the runway. I am preparing for my very first takeoff and going through my procedures that I've memorized. My feet are on the brakes; I go to full power on the engine; I check all the engine gauges; I wipe out the controls. Everything looks and feels good. I check the rearview mirror, and behind me is Lieutenant Howdy Doody, and he's smiling.

I say, "Sir, are you ready to go?"

And he detects the nervousness in my voice, and he says, "Will, relax. Everything is going to be fine."

And he was right. I took my feet off the brakes, rolled down the runway; we took off into the clear blue sky, out over the Gulf of Mexico, took a right turn, and went over Mobile Bay. Then over the woods of southern Alabama we found a deserted runway where I could practice my landings.

In a maneuver called a touch and go, I descended to pattern altitude; I dropped the flaps; I dropped the gear; I went through the landing checklist; I turned to line up with the runway. And from that point on, it's just a matter of controlling my descent, all the way down, down, down, until the wheels touched the pavement. Then full power, back up in the air to pattern altitude, and do it again.

I did that about eight times. We flew back to the squadron; I met up with Howdy in the debrief room; he had a grade sheet, and he was smiling.

He said, "Will, you're a natural."

He gave me good grades. That pattern repeated itself for the next six flights. Me and Howdy out in Alabama, doing touch and goes. I was starting to feel in control of the aircraft. I was starting to feel confident like, *This is something I can actually do.*

And Howdy was grading me accordingly, giving me really good

grades. I was moving up the ranks in my class. I went from sixteen out of thirty to twelve, from twelve to nine, from nine to six.

And that's where I was on the night of my last flight. I drove into the squadron under a full moon, which was a good sign, and I parked in the lot outside the hangar.

I entered the hangar and climbed the stairs to the ready room. I checked the status board—there's my name, Lieutenant Howdy Doody's is next to mine, but something's wrong.

Howdy's name had been crossed out in red marker and underneath had been written *Major Small*. I thought, *I was so close.*

It turns out, Howdy had a case of the sniffles; Major Small was filling in for him. I found the major in the briefing room. He was frowning.

True to form, he didn't say a word during the flight brief. He didn't say a word as we walked out to the plane, as we started up, as we taxied to the runway. And there on the runway I'm going through my procedures, feet on the brakes, full power. Wiping out the controls, checking the gauges; everything looks good. I look in the rearview mirror; and there is Major Small, pissed off.

I said, "Sir, are you ready to go?"

He didn't answer me. He just opened the canopy, put a cigarette in his mouth, and he lit it.

And to say that smoking was prohibited in a navy aircraft is an understatement. The nearest place that you were allowed to smoke was on the other side of the hangar across the parking lot, across the street, past the softball fields, where the dumpsters were. And I suppose what I should have done is ask Major Small to put the cigarette out.

Instead I asked myself, *What would Maverick do?*

You all know. Maverick is dangerous, right?

Maverick busted the hard deck to shoot down Jester.

Maverick did an unauthorized flyby of the control tower and made everyone spill their coffee on their uniforms.

Maverick jumped up and down on Oprah's couch.

So, feet off the brakes, I rolled down the runway, and took off into the night sky with Major Small smoking in the backseat.

Somewhere over Mobile Bay, he flicked out his first cigarette, lit a second. Over the woods of Alabama, I found my favorite runway, descended to pattern altitude, dropped the flaps, dropped the wheels, did the landing checklist, turned to final.

And I thought I was controlling my rate of descent. But something felt off. It was too late before I realized that we were dropping like shit off a tall moose.

That's a technical term.

But we hit the runway so hard, my helmet popped off my head, and Major Small's cigarette flew up from the backseat, over my shoulder, under the instrument panel, and buried itself in the floorboards right by the firewall. And that's where it remained as we literally bounced back up in the air, cigarette glowing and burning.

As I was climbing back up to pattern altitude, Major Small spoke his first words to me.

He said, "Can you reach it?"

So, I unstrapped from my parachute, I bent over and reached as far as I could, but it was no use.

"No, sir," I said.

And in the silence that followed, I imagined in the worst-case scenario, that cigarette was going to catch the airplane on fire, we would have to bail out of a burning aircraft, parachute into the pitch-black woods; I would get snagged in a tree; I'd have to cut myself down, that I'd break my leg when I hit the dirt.

And then I heard Major Small's voice, very calm, very patient: "Here's what we're going to do."

And he talked me through a maneuver called a zero-G bunt. Zero G meaning zero gravity, or weightlessness. Bunt meaning like, not a full swing; it's a very gentle maneuver. Almost fun, like riding a fast roller coaster over a really big hill. And so imagine, I've got the stick between my knees. I hold it in my right hand. I grip the throttles with my left.

Small says, "Go to full power."

I push the throttles all the way forward.

"Now pull back on the stick."

I pull back, and we start climbing.

"Pull harder," Small says.

When I do, the G force spikes. It drags my face down. It drains the blood out of my head, and my vision goes grayscale.

Small says, "Good."

He was happy, which made me happy.

Next, Small wants me to push the stick forward without dipping the wings one way or the other. Just a smooth forward push.

"Stick forward and neutral laterally" is the way he put it.

So, I did that; he's like, "More."

I push the stick forward a little bit more.

And that's when the magic happened. We went weightless; I floated up in my seat. All of the dirt, the dust that had been in the floorboards for years, floated up into the canopy and sparkled in the moonlight like a snow globe.

And then the cigarette *pops* out. It was still lit. It floats in the middle of the cockpit, and it turns these little orange circles right in front of my face.

So, I reached up with my free hand—everything was slow motion—and I grabbed it.

I put it out in my hand.

And it hurt like a son of a bitch.

I wanted to scream, but I didn't, because Major Small had been through worse.

I was done doing touch and goes that night—we were a little afraid I broke the plane; the nose wheel was shimmying like a bum wheel on a shopping cart. The wings kind of felt bent, and the engine sputtered a little bit, so we flew back to the squadron.

I met up with Major Small up in the debrief room, and he had the grade sheet. He was looking at it like it couldn't possibly contain his disgust.

He said to me, "That's the worst landing I've ever seen." (And keep in mind, he'd ejected from a flaming aircraft over Iraq and parachuted into enemy hands.)

Somehow my landing was worse than that.

So, he gave me the worst possible grade for landings.

But then he said, "But that was a really good catch."

And he smiled at me. He gave me a good grade for airmanship. And I left with an even grade sheet; I went into selection ranked six out of thirty. And lucky for me that week, the navy needed more than three jet pilots. And so, I was selected to fly jets.

But by then I no longer wanted to be Maverick.

Because I knew that Maverick was a Hollywood hero. The danger that he had faced was make-believe.

Major Small, on the other hand, had survived very real danger. And here he was teaching young people like myself how to survive it too.

And I wanted to be more like him.

* ✦ *

WILL MACKIN is a veteran of the U.S. Navy. His work has appeared in *The New Yorker, GQ, Tin House,* and *The New York Times Magazine.* His debut collection of short stories, *Bring Out the Dog,* won the 2019 PEN/Robert W. Bingham Prize.

This story was recorded at a live performance at Alice Tully Hall at Lincoln Center for the Performing Arts in New York City on March 22, 2019. The theme of the evening was Occasional Magic. Director: Catherine Burns.

CHASING GRANDMA

MORGAN GIVENS

My grandmother pulled me to the side and waited until I met her eyes before she said, "Now, Morgan, if you ever have an interaction with the police, you keep your hands where they can see them. You telegraph your movements and tell them everything you're going to do *before* you do it. Do you understand me?"

I nodded and said I did, because my grandmother and I have been having that same conversation for years.

The fact that we talked about it so much didn't make it any less confusing, because my grandmother? She *was* the police. She was literally a cop. The woman had a badge, a uniform, a police car, everything. And her friends? The people who were always up in our house for cookouts and barbecues, the ones who helped us move, loading boxes into the back of pickup trucks? They were the police too.

As a kid, I didn't really understand because at that time, in my mind, cops were heroes. But I was also being taught to fear them.

My grandma, she's one of those Black women they write inspirational novels and movies about because she was one of the first Black women through the Charlotte Police Academy, and she was excellent. She was exceptional.

She was perfection because she had no choice. She knew that

everything she did would be used to judge every Black woman who came up behind her. In the inspirational movie of my grandmother's life, some well-meaning white person would show up to take all the credit in the end. But if I'm keeping it completely 100 with you all, white folks weren't looking out for my grandma like that. She had to sue to get the job she had already earned when she graduated from the police academy, as if she didn't have the highest academic marks in her class, as if she weren't running laps around her training instructors.

But in the end, she prevailed, and her life turned out a bit like a fairy tale. But one with some baggage, particularly for me, because it's already hard enough to live up to the expectations of our parents and our grandparents. But when your grandmother is literally *Superwoman,* it gets just a little bit harder. But I'm not going to stand up here and front like I don't appreciate everything she did in her path to success, or that I don't appreciate how I can trace it like a thread of hope from her, to my mother, right down to me.

My grandmother spent thirty years in the Charlotte Police Department. When she retired, we had to rent a banquet hall because of how respected she was. The chief of police himself showed up.

But I still had questions. I didn't really get how some cops could end up like my grandma and some could be like the ones I read about in history books—still read about today—and see on TV, the ones who appear to be on the wrong side of history.

I never thought I'd actually get an answer to that question, but then I graduated in the middle of the worst recession in recent memory, and I needed a job. So I looked to my grandma like, *You know what? If Grandma can do this and be successful, maybe I can too.* And could I have gone to the Charlotte Police Academy like my grandma did? I *could* have, but my grandmother casts a long shadow. The last thing I needed was for some snitching instructor to call her up and let her know I couldn't do a single doggone push-up. It's true. I ain't proud of it, but it's true.

So, I found myself at the Washington, D.C., police academy, joining a class of thirty other recruits ready to do anything and everything we could to become officers in the nation's capital. But something weird was happening. When we started the academy, everybody was always staring at us, looking at us, but not *just* looking at us. It was almost like they were trying to look *through* us. These people would be peering around the hallways, staring in through the window of our classroom doors. As we got further and further along, I was like, *What the heck is going on?* For a minute, I thought, *They* did *say part of the training was making you more observant, but this is ridiculous.*

We couldn't figure out what was going on.

And then one day, I sat down in the cafeteria next to one of my classmates, and he looked at me and went, "Hey, man, I know why everybody is staring at us! It's because they think there's a transgender person in our class. Where on Earth could they be?"

Look, y'all, I almost choked on my lunch. And after a second, I jumped up and ran to the bathroom, where I barricaded myself in a stall, reliving some of the worst memories from high school because . . . I'm transgender. The trans person they were looking for was *me*.

The call was literally coming from inside the house!

After I calmed down, I made my way back to the cafeteria and sat back down.

The guy looks back at me again, and he goes, "I figured out who it is! It's Everett. And you know how I know it's him? Because he's always talking with his hands, putting them on his hips and things—very feminine qualities."

My name is not Everett, so my secret was safe for a little longer. I eventually wanted to tell my class, but I wanted to wait just a little while so they could get to know me as a person first. But my plans were thrown into disarray because someone high up in the police department thought it'd be a good idea to tell everybody and their mama that a trans person was going to be in the next class and that if anybody messed with them, they're going to get fired.

To an extent, I get it. I was never going to be *just another recruit*. But the problem was, I was now going to have to out myself way sooner than I intended. I was scared. And I was afraid, particularly of this one cat in my class named Winston. Winston was the conservative oil to my liberal water. That man smoked cigarettes and chewed tobacco *at the same time*. On more than one occasion, he tried to convince me that the Civil War wasn't about slavery, as if history books do not exist, but I was going to have to speak regardless.

Eventually, I stood in front of my class and said, "All right, y'all, *it's me*. The trans person everybody is searching for is me. Can we just quit this game of hide-and-seek and move on?"

I should have known that ain't going to be the case. I was the first openly trans person through the Washington, D.C., police academy. The path for me was going to be a little different. I would have to be excellent. I would have to be perfection because they were going to judge every trans person who came after me by the standard I set. Thank God my grandmother laid out a path—because I was going to have to walk the same tightrope to perfection that she had all those decades ago when *she* was the first.

So, I worked my ass off. I stayed up all night studying to make sure I got A's on all my exams. I crushed myself in physical training just to prove that I could do it.

Over time, I could see the change in my classmates and my instructors. I could see the moment they began seeing me as a person first. And then, my class surprised me by voting for me to give the graduation speech in front of the chief, the assistant chief, and hundreds of our family and friends.

After graduation, I got another surprise, and it came from Winston of all people, who walked up to me, and held out his hand, and waited for me to take it.

And when I did, he looked me square in my eyes, the same way my grandmother had when I was small, and said, "Hey, man. Anybody messes with you when you get out on them streets, you let me know, and we're going to handle it."

I couldn't have been more shocked if I had been struck by a bolt of lightning. Here was this man I had been seeing in nothing but hues of black and white, showing me that I needed to see the gray in him—the same gray that I so often demanded that others see in me. Winston, in his own way, was showing me just a piece of his heart, and I got it. The heart of the officer does matter, because all that badge does is exacerbate and project whoever they are at that core of their person. That's the power of being a cop.

But it wasn't a power that I really wanted. I eventually left the Washington, D.C., police department—but not before I made some changes because the chief of police tasked me and a small group of other officers with rewriting the entire training curriculum. And I rewrote *the hell* out of that curriculum.

Understanding unconscious bias and intersectionality?

Oh, you're going to get that today.

Learning how not to be homophobic, transphobic, or misogynistic?

I wrote *all* of that down.

Because here's what happens when officers get in trouble for excessive force: The courts and the lawyers pull their training records. The old refrain was often, "Oh, I wasn't trained in that. I didn't know."

They can't say that no more.

And the officers that I met, most of them when they hear that, will now put that lie to rest because they know the truth and that the heart of the officer *does* matter.

And I had seen their heart, and they had also seen mine.

＊ ⊙ ＊

MORGAN GIVENS is a storyteller, writer, journalist, editor, and audio pro-ducer originally from Charlotte, North Carolina. He's the creator of the award-winning hopepunk fiction podcast *Flyest Fables* and spends most of his time hanging out with his favorite person: his wife, Catherine Hendrix.

This story was told on April 4, 2019, at the Lobero Theatre in Santa Barbara. The theme of the evening was Occasional Magic. Director: Jenifer Hixson.

SANDWICHES AND NEIGHBORS

OANH NGO USADI

We had just arrived in America, to this small town in southeast Texas called Port Arthur. It was 1984, and I was twelve years old. My family and I were immigrants from Vietnam. We were boat refugees.

We moved into this ranch house that belonged to our landlord, who lived just next door, across the yard. Before we even finished unpacking, my father said our whole family, the seven of us—me, my parents, my two older sisters, my two older teenage brothers—should go over and introduce ourselves.

We walked across the yard and saw our landlord out on his back porch. He was this heavyset, gruff-looking older man. He was sitting in a wheelchair, puffing on a cigarette, while watching us. He did not look happy.

My father had warned us that our landlord might be upset. My parents had been trying for weeks to find a place for our family to live, with a very limited budget. In the end, they fudged the number of people in our family. Our landlord had expected only five, not seven of us.

When we got closer, he abruptly turned away from us and shouted something through the screen door into his house. I had no idea what he said. His thick Texas drawl, in this heavy smoker's voice, was nothing like the English I had been learning in a refugee camp just a few weeks earlier.

The screen door opened, and this friendly woman stepped down. She didn't seem upset at all, and she was really talkative.

She introduced herself as Loretta and her husband as Walter.

Walter, with an *l*.

I had been learning English for only a few months. I could barely make out that tiny *l* sound wedged in the middle of the name Walter. I was pretty sure my parents didn't even hear it. So, the rest of us copied my father and called our landlord "Mr. Water."

"Mr.," because it was unthinkable for any of us to refer to an adult without a title, and as for Loretta, her name was just too hard. So, we called her "Mrs. Water."

Neither of them corrected us.

After we moved in, I was somehow the go-between for our two families. My job was to deliver rent and home repair questions. I didn't mind the rent deliveries because I didn't have to say very much. But I dreaded the home repair questions. I had to use my limited English to talk to Mr. Water.

I couldn't understand a lot of what he said, and to be honest, Mr. Water terrified me. Everything about him scared me. And the more scared I got, the more my English sounded like Vietnamese with a lot of hand waving mixed in.

I kept thinking he was going to lose it. He was going to explode, like that time he was in the backyard screaming at my brothers and me. My older brother had dumped leftover hot charcoal from our barbecue in different parts of our yard to kill fire ants.

Mr. Water yelled, "In AMERICA you don't BURN GRASS. You CUT IT!"

I thought, *Why so much yelling? It's just grass. It will grow back.*

Growing up in Vietnam, I didn't even know what a lawn was. I thought of grass only as weeds. In Vietnamese, grass and weeds are called the same thing. I used to wonder why people in America, this land of riches and wealth, would choose to live in homes surrounded by weeds.

But I got why Mr. Water was upset. I mean, our yard looked like some kind of lunar landscape with all these black patches. But his anger seemed so out of proportion. I just thought he hated us. I didn't know if his feelings would ever change, or if we could ever feel at home here.

In our new hometown, my parents decided to open a family business—a Vietnamese bánh mì sandwich shop. A bánh mì sandwich is a French baguette, with a thin, crispy crust. Inside it is spread with paté and homemade mayonnaise, then filled with roasted meats and topped with all kinds of vegetables—pickled carrots, daikons, slices of cucumber, cilantro, fresh chili peppers, and a few dashes of soy sauce.

It's really delicious.

But back then, in our small town, few people had ever heard of, much less tasted, a bánh mì. But somehow, my father was convinced that he was going to give McDonald's a run for its money.

He named the shop *Budget Sandwiches*. He had seen the word *budget* on the side of some trucks and thought it would make a great name for a food place. We all thought it was a great idea too.

After the shop opened, my parents worked twelve hours a day, seven days a week. My siblings and I all helped out.

After school, I often came to the shop to stay with my father, taking over my mother's shift, so she could rest a little because, at night, there was still a lot more work to do at home. But despite these long hours, we barely scraped by.

As it turned out, the McDonald's down the street had nothing to fear.

But then, one beautiful spring afternoon, I was at the shop doing homework when the phone rang. My father picked it up. Right away, I could tell he was really excited.

I heard my father repeating in English that the customer wanted fifty bánh mì. *Fifty?*

This was the biggest order we had ever had. But the fact that the order came from a customer who spoke English was even more amazing. Until then, most of our customers had come from the Vietnamese community. It looked like the American public had started to discover bánh mì. This was something my father had always hoped for. It felt like times were changing.

Right away, we went to work. My father joked that McDonald's had no idea what was about to come.

Finally, the sandwiches were done. We couldn't wait to see who this customer was.

But then half an hour passed, and then an hour, and then more time . . . and no one showed up.

I opened my notebook, and started doing homework again, and that's when I saw the date in the margin.

April 1st.

April Fools' Day.

My heart sank.

I didn't know where to begin explaining to my father this holiday that I didn't fully understand myself.

More than that, I didn't know if this heartless prank might just finally crush his spirit. The spirit that had been tested time and time again, in a life filled with turbulence.

In Vietnam, my father had been imprisoned by French forces occupying Vietnam for taking part in the resistance. Then later, under communism, he had survived multiple attempts on his life before he finally organized our family's dangerous escape, inside a small fishing boat, across the South China Sea.

In all these desperate situations, somehow he stayed optimistic.

It was the same optimism that made him open the sandwich shop.

My siblings and I understood that the sandwich shop was my parents' last big gamble. It was a chance for him and my mother to experience a little bit of the American dream, instead of just living in the service of that dream for their children.

When I explained April Fools' to my father, he didn't say anything. He just stayed quiet for a long time. But I could tell he was disappointed.

I could see the disappointment in his eyes.

We never found out who placed the order. But from that incident we learned to take down contact information anytime an order came over the phone. And with each setback, our footing in America became a little more steady.

We learned to decorate to match the festivities of Halloween, Thanksgiving, and Christmas.

We learned to close our shop a little earlier on a certain Sunday, in the dead of winter, because everyone was at home, watching some football game on TV.

Even though our shop never did much better, it did provide us with a living and put me and my siblings through school. And then, one by one, my siblings started leaving home for college, or for their jobs.

Seven years after we moved into Mr. Water's house, I was the only one left at home with my parents. By then, my English had improved to where I could easily pronounce the *l* in Walter.

But we never stopped calling our landlords Mr. and Mrs. Water— because it was familiar, and because it was who they were to us.

One day, I was again delivering the rent. I was a senior in high school and would soon be leaving home for college.

Mr. Water said he had something to tell my parents, but he wouldn't tell just me.

Later, when I came back with my parents, I saw that Mrs. Water had set up this nice pitcher of pink lemonade, with five glasses, on a small table on their back porch. This was the first time our families had sat down for something to drink.

After we had taken a sip of the lemonade, Mr. Water started to speak.

Speaking really slowly, something I had never witnessed, he told us that he had recently found out that he was very sick. His doctor wouldn't say how much time he had left, but he suspected it wasn't very long.

He said he wanted his wife to be near good folks after he passed. So, he offered to sell my parents the house we had been living in, his rental house, for what he had paid for it—minus all the rent my parents had paid him over the years.

My parents were stunned and saddened. But they were especially sad because they couldn't grant Mr. Water his wish.

It had always been their plan to retire to Houston, to be near my oldest sister and her family, when I finished high school. In fact, they had already been trying to find a buyer for the shop.

Mr. Water died a few months later, and sometime after the funeral my mom asked me to go check on Mrs. Water.

I remember waiting by the screen door, only that time, I had no rent payment or home repair questions to ask.

When Mrs. Water saw me, she hugged me for a long time, then invited me to come inside.

I saw Mr. Water's wheelchair folded and leaned against the wall.

Mrs. Water talked about life without her husband and how lonely she felt.

She asked about me and my siblings.

She said Mr. Water might have yelled at us sometimes, but he always thought we were good kids. He missed my brothers when they moved away to college.

I never would have guessed that.

As I left, I couldn't help thinking that, after all these years, the only thing that had really changed was our understanding of each other.

It's been almost thirty years since I left our small Texas town. Recently, when I was in Costco, I found myself thinking back to this time. I was in line to buy a hot dog when I looked up at the big menu board overhead and noticed a new item—a salad topped with black beans and bánh mì ingredients.

A really strange combination for salad.

But *wow!*

Bánh mì had made it into Costco.

I thought of my parents and of Mr. and Mrs. Water. It occurred to me that appreciation of anything unfamiliar, of a neighbor, of a sandwich, requires time and an open mind.

* ✹ *

OANH NGO USADI was born in Saigon but grew up in an orchard in the Mekong Delta, where her family was exiled after the war. Her work has appeared in *The Wall Street Journal, The Washington Post, Forbes,* and elsewhere. Her award-winning memoir, *Of Monkey Bridges and Bánh Mì Sandwiches,* features more stories of her adventures between Saigon and Texas. The sequel, *Hawker Dreams: A Vietnamese American in Singapore,* follows Oanh's travels as an American expat in Singapore. You can follow Oanh on Facebook, Twitter, and the O&O Press website.

This story was told on December 12, 2019, at the Paramount Theatre in Austin. The theme of the evening was Holding On and Letting Go. Director: Meg Bowles.

THE BEST MEDICINE

MICHAEL FISCHER

About one week into my sentence, the guards put the whole prison on lockdown. I was in what's called reception, waiting to be classified and then sent to a different prison to serve out my two years. Rumor was that an inmate had convinced a civilian worker to smuggle in drugs, and so they'd shut everything down to look for the contraband. I still don't know if that's true, but we were on lockdown for weeks over *something*—in our cells all day, every day. No mess hall, no showers, no yard. Just guys yelling back and forth day and night.

I was in this big cell block—it was four tiers high on both sides and held four hundred other men—but I was alone. Every time the porter came by to drop a little bag meal on the shelf on my cell gate, I wanted to go for a handshake or a fist bump—anything, just to make contact with another person. But I worried the porter would only see some strange guy trying to grab him through the bars.

About ten days into lockdown, my cell buzzed open after morning count, and the tier officer sent me to medical.

I was born with a heart problem—I've been having surgeries for it since I was a kid—so apparently, I had to see a cardiologist before the state could decide which prison to send me to next. That meant leaving the lockdown behind for a day and going to a hospital in the free world.

To see a doctor on the outside, I had to be strip-searched and have my wrists and my ankles shackled. The handcuffs were connected to a chain around my waist, so I could only lift my hands a couple inches. Think of it like the choke collars some people use on dogs.

I wasn't used to ankle cuffs that early in my bid, and it was January in New York, so I waddled through the snow to the transport van with an officer on either side of me, and then sort of threw myself into the backseat because I couldn't use my hands.

How boring you think the waiting room at your doctor's office is depends a lot on where you're arriving from. I was so excited to sit on a real chair instead of a steel bench, to be in a quiet room that didn't smell like sweat or urine or disinfectant.

But when I shuffled through the front door of the doctor's office, one of the correctional officers with me said, "Come on, we're not stopping."

He led me down a hallway, and I stood against a wall while the other officer checked me in. Pretty naïve—to think I'd be allowed to sit and wait with the other patients. They would be afraid of me.

It occurred to me that this trip might not be the break I'd hoped for. I thought being in the free world for a day would be great: See mailboxes and streetlights again, look at people in their cars and wonder about their lives, and wish I was just on my way to work, like everybody else. I thought I would feel almost normal, not like some animal escaped from the zoo.

The staff clearly wanted me out the door as fast as possible, so pretty quickly the officers and I were shown into an exam room.

The cardiologist walked in with a nurse right behind him, and he looked at me and said, "Michael?"

He used my first name, as if I were any other patient on his schedule.

And I said, "Well, yeah, I'm Michael."

The cardiologist started a physical exam, and just the feeling of his stethoscope against my chest . . . I might as well have been at a spa. I started reciting my medical history, using the technical terms I've learned from dealing with heart disease my whole life.

When I'd finished, the nurse tapped my ankle cuffs twice with a finger and said, "You're too smart for these."

Which was supposed to be a compliment.

I wanted to tell her, *That's not how it works.*

The guys on my cell block weren't locked up for being stupid. But to be honest, a part of me felt flattered. This nurse and this doctor were treating me like I was a real person. They thought I was smart, and they weren't afraid to look me in the eyes and lay their hands on me.

After weeks of no human touch and no dignity, to suddenly have people do things as simple as speak to me kindly or listen to my heartbeat or feel for swelling in my legs . . . I decided I would pay any price for that. Just to feel a touch of another person for a minute, and to know that person is here to help me, and to hope that meant I still deserved help.

From the moment the officers put me back in the van, I had a new plan for my time in prison: Take as many medical trips as possible.

Even though it would mean getting woken up at four in the morning, and the cuffs and chains for twelve hours straight, and the looks from every person along the way, I needed that reward at the end. I needed contact with people who treated me as if I was still fully human, because I wasn't sure I even believed that anymore.

So, I started lying. I was transferred from maximum security reception to a different prison, and almost as soon as I got there, I started complaining to the medical staff about symptoms I didn't actually have. But because my heart problem really is serious, everything I said was believable. So, they started sending me out on more medical trips.

Sometimes more than once a month, I'd get to take these awesome long drives through the countryside into the city. Two officers and I would enter through a back door that was only used to take out the hospital's trash and bring inmates to appointments. It always took a while to reach the cardiology clinic because every time someone came walking toward me, the officers would have me turn to the wall, and I'd have to stare at my feet until the person passed. But I still caught sight of faces. I saw people pull their children close or dart down random hallways or pretend to forget something and just turn around.

Still, it was easier to mark time by my hospital trips than by what I was missing back home.

My sister got engaged and then married, but I had things to do too—I had an appointment to get a CT scan.

My grandma's dementia got worse until she forgot who I was, and it became hard for me to sleep through the night without having a panic attack. But at least my grandma couldn't remember to be ashamed of me anymore—and one time the doctors gave me what they called twilight drugs so they could put a scope down my throat, and that was almost as good as real sleep.

My aunt died of pancreatic cancer; because her funeral was out of state, I wasn't allowed to attend. But what I *could* do was stare out the windows of the transport van and pretend I was someone else.

I knew I was wasting people's time and the state's money, and scaring everyone I saw each time I left the prison, but I didn't care. I needed the connection, and I needed the escape. I remember lying fully conscious on an operating table, handcuffed to the side rails—during yet another procedure that I'd talked my way into but didn't really need—where the doctor was running a scope up through an incision in my groin. And I remember thinking, *This is so worth it.*

By the time my sentence was almost over, I'd taken more than a dozen medical trips. I should have been focused on my release, but I didn't want to think about life as a convict. I definitely wanted to get out, but there's a difference between getting out and truly going home. I was afraid home had changed so much for me that it wouldn't feel like I belonged anymore.

On my hospital trips, I could catch sight of freedom without having to really deal with freedom.

But as my release date approached, I started to wonder what good the trips were doing me. The officers would be taking me to some appointment, and I would think, *What if from now on, I only know how to navigate the free world as a tourist, like I am now? What's going to happen when I actually live there?*

On one trip toward the end of my bid, the CO parked the van by some dumpsters in the back, like always. But this particular doctor's office was special, because here I was allowed to sit in the waiting room—off in a corner, behind this big pillar. I didn't look at the other patients, even though I really wanted to—that seemed like the one nice thing I could do in public: Try not to bother people too much with the fact that, you know, I exist.

The nurse who called my name was around my age at the time— early twenties. Once we were in the exam room, she asked the officers to take off my handcuffs so that I could remove my shirt. They took off the cuffs, and I took off my shirt, and the nurse explained that she was going to stick some leads to my chest so that she could run a test.

So I lay back and closed my eyes, and when her hands touched me I had to grit my teeth to keep myself from crying.

In a different life, she could have been a friend of mine. But there in that room, I kept wondering if she was afraid of me.

She tried to run the test, but she wasn't getting a clean signal, so she started pulling off the sticky lead pads to rearrange them, and each one pulled out a little patch of my chest hair.

I remember she winced as she pulled off the last lead, and she said, "I'm sorry about this."

She apologized to me. And that—that broke the spell.

Suddenly I felt so embarrassed that I'd brought myself and these two big officers into this nurse's space, just so I could . . . what, deny reality? Feel better about myself for ten minutes?

She was just trying to do her job, and it was not her job to somehow make me fully human again.

It was my job to know that I'd never *stopped* being fully human. That I still deserved connection and compassion, whether anyone—in any courtroom or waiting room—agreed or not. Because the alternative was to keep feeling ashamed, and to keep thinking of myself as a loser, and to spend my life begging other people—like this nurse—to prove me wrong. To give me some small sign that maybe I'm not so bad after all.

That was my last medical trip. I told the prison doctors I was feeling just fine after that. And then, a few months later, I packed my stuff, signed my release papers, and they let me go.

Living in the real world again has been about as hard as I expected. But despite that, I have to make my way in the free world as a citizen, not just as a tourist. Because if I can't, I'll never belong anywhere.

MICHAEL FISCHER is a humanities instructor in the Odyssey Project, a free college credit program for income-eligible adults. He's a Luminarts Cultural Foundation fellow, Right of Return USA fellow, Illinois Humanities Envisioning Justice–commissioned humanist, and finalist for the PEN America Writing for Justice Fellowship and Education Trust Justice Fellows Policy Program. His nonfiction, which has been nominated multiple times for a Pushcart Prize and cited as notable in *Best American Essays*, appears in *The New York Times*, *Salon*, *The Sun*, *Literary Hub*, *Guernica*, *Orion*, and elsewhere. He holds an MFA in creative writing from the University of Nevada, Reno, and an MA in humanities from the University of Chicago.

This story was told on February 10, 2022, at the Anderson Theater, Memorial Hall in Cincinnati. The theme of the evening was Holding On and Letting Go. Director: Michelle Jalowski.

UNTIL THE LION LEARNS TO WRITE

WHEN THE TRUTH POPS OUT
LIN-MANUEL MIRANDA

It is January 16, 1997, eight P.M. Eastern Standard Time. My girl-friend, Meredith, has surprised me with tickets to see *Rent* for my seventeenth birthday.

This is the original cast, first-year *Rent,* and we go up to the last row of the mezzanine of the Nederlander Theatre. My mind is blown, and there's a moment in the second act where the truth just pops out.

Meredith and I are what you would call in high school "theater kids."

You know our kind. You've heard us warming up. You've seen our silly games:

Zip, zap, ZOP!
[recites rapidly] 10, 9, 8, 7, 6, 5, 4, 3, 2, 1!
10, 9, 8, 7, 6, 5, 4, 3, 2, 1!

You make fun of us, but we know something you don't know. We know that when we get to the auditorium, we are safe, and we are making something that is bigger than all of us. We know while you are in your separate grades—wondering who likes who, and who hates who, and whose life is *over,* and who is *thriving*—we know life is bigger than our grade, because we're making things with people of all other grades, to try to make the best thing possible.

Meredith and I met when I was cast as the pirate king, and she was the major general's daughter in *Pirates of Penzance*. And the romance is inevitable because the job of the pirate was to woo the major general's daughter.

We did show after show together. We did *Godspell* together; she directed *A Chorus Line*—I was her assistant on that. That year, she took me to see *Rent*.

There's a scene in the second act of *Rent,* where Mark and Roger—Anthony Rapp and Adam Pascal—are having this heated moment. Roger accuses Mark.

He says,

Mark has got his work.
They say Mark lives for his work,
and Mark's in love with his work.

I'm like, *Yeah, Mark!*
And he goes,

Mark hides in his work. From what?
From facing your failure, facing your loneliness,
facing the fact you live a lie.

What?

Yes, you live a lie. Tell you why,
you pretend to create and observe
when you really detach from feeling alive.

And that's when Jonathan Larson reached out and punched me straight in the heart. Because the moment that show started, I was like, *Oh, I'm Mark,* because I was the kid who carried the camcorder to school. When I wasn't in the auditorium, and I was hanging out with my friends, I was the kid who had a camera up instead of *actually* hanging out with my friends. While everyone else was getting to know each other, I held everyone at a remove and recorded the whole thing.

So, when Jonathan Larson's Roger says that to Mark, it felt like he was talking to me. I went from someone who likes musicals, and if he saves enough money, buys tickets on his birthday, to thinking, *Oh, the truth can come out in a musical. You're allowed to write musicals.*

That's when I went from being a fan of musicals, from being a theater kid, to trying to write a musical myself. I wrote my first musical that year.

It was called *Nightmare in D Major.* I wrote it in a feverish weekend over winter break. We had a student-written theater club at my high school. They would have five plays with student directors chosen from submissions from all over school. My musical got picked, and it was the first musical ever done because they're usually just twenty-minute one-act plays.

Fast-forward to opening night of *Nightmare in D Major,* April 1997. I should mention two things here:

One, my mother's a psychologist.

Two, *Nightmare in D Major* is *terrible.*

It concerns our young protagonist, who falls asleep and has a nightmare . . . in D major, and all of these Freudian concerns come to haunt him. Chiefly among them, the main villain of the piece is a fetal pig he dissected in AP Bio who is back for revenge.

Shakespeare, it ain't.

Rodgers and Hammerstein, it certainly ain't.

There are other characters that are all from the Freudian subconscious because, like I said, my mother's a psychologist. There's an alcoholic Uncle Steve and a scary clown from a child's birthday party, and they're all coming back to haunt the protagonist in D major.

The show is getting laughs. I'm sitting in the audience, and I'm thrilled that the students who are watching, and my parents who are watching, are enjoying it. There is a moment in the show where this little girl comes on stage. She was played by an eighth grader named Sarah Shweisky. She sings:

> *You probably do not remember me,*
> *but in fourth grade, you were in love with me.*
> *You don't know my name, but you know my face.*
> *Sometimes I get just a bit sad when I think that you have forgotten me.*
> *But I'll always be, in your dreams, in your dreams.*
> *And I'll stay right here, in your dreams, in your dreams.*

Several things happen at once. One, there is nothing funny or silly or student-like about this character. This character pops up. The main character tries to play with her and hang out with her, and he's cut off because he's told she passed away when he was young.

I suddenly remember that, when I was four years old, my best friend died. It's the nightmare scenario for any parent: Each of her parents thought she was with the other, and she drowned behind her home.

And this is what I remember: I remember my mother telling me in my room on a morning when I had nursery school. I remember crying. I remember getting in the car. My nursery school teacher ran a carpool of students to take us to Uptown Nursery on 179th Street.

I remember that teacher whispering "Lin's friend died" to every parent of the children she picked up along the way.

I remember about a year of gray; the memories are just gray. I remember that year more vividly than I remember her. And I realize if anyone laughs at this part of this student show, I'll die. Because I didn't remember her, but she showed up in my first musical.

I look over at my mother, who I'm sure has a lot to say about this. And the show goes on, and it's a very silly ending—the guy wakes up, and the play is over. But I get addicted to that feeling of the truth popping out in the show, and what are we all going to do when it's staring at us?

I remember when I was writing *Hamilton,* and the line "I imagine death so much, it feels more like a memory" popped up. That is not in Ron Chernow's book and is not in any history book. That's something coming out of me that makes me understand this person, and a lot of people think, *Oh, well, it's autobiographical. He's Hamilton,* but I felt the exact same way about death.

When Aaron Burr said, "If there's a reason I'm still alive when everyone who loves me has died, I'm willing to wait for it"—that's not in any biography of Burr you're going to find. That's the moment where you write and you write until the truth pops out.

There's a moment in *Hamilton* where the parents lose a child, and I have had countless parents come up to me in the years since and say, "How do you know what this feels like? And how did you find the words?"

One thing that is true is that it took me a day to write that song. It wrote pretty quick. Another thing that is true is that I have been writing that song since I was four years old—because I have imagined how that felt since I was four years old.

I remember poor Meredith, the girlfriend who got me tickets to *Rent,* coming home to six voicemail messages from me saying, "Call me when you get home. Call me when you get home. Call me when you get home."

Because I have imagined fifty ways she has died on the way home on the train from my house, because of that year of gray.

Jonathan Larson, one of my musical theater heroes, tragically passed away the day before his show *Rent* had its first public performance. I wonder how he felt writing the second act of that show, watching Mark and Roger talk to each other. As an artist in the midst of the plague of the AIDS crisis, as Jonathan watched friend after friend and a generation of artists die in this plague of this disease—how he felt when he got to those lines. And how sometimes as an artist, all you can do is hold up the camera and bear witness until the truth pops out.

* ✦ *

LIN-MANUEL MIRANDA is a Pulitzer Prize, Grammy, Emmy, and Tony award–winning songwriter, actor, director, and producer. He is the creator and original star of Broadway's Tony-winning *Hamilton* and *In the Heights*. His additional Broadway credits include *New York, New York* (additional lyrics, Tony nomination for Best Musical), *Freestyle Love Supreme* (co-founder, guest star, Special Tony Award recipient), *Bring It On: The Musical* (co-composer/co-lyricist, Tony nomination for Best Musical), and *West Side Story* (2009 revival, Spanish translations). Miranda is the recipient of the 2015 MacArthur Foundation Award, the 2018 Kennedy Center Honors, and the 2019 Portrait of a Nation Prize. He and the Miranda family are active supporters of initiatives that increase the representation of people of color throughout the arts and government, ensure access to women's reproductive health, and promote resilience in Puerto Rico. TV/film credits include *tick, tick . . . BOOM!,* Disney's live action *The Little Mermaid, Vivo, In the Heights, Hamilton* (2021 Emmy Award), *His Dark Materials, Fosse/Verdon, We the People, Sesame Street, Curb Your Enthusiasm* (2018 Emmy nomination, guest actor), *Saturday Night Live* (2017 Emmy nomination, guest actor), *Moana* (2017 Oscar nomination, Grammy Award for Best Original Song), *Mary Poppins Returns,* and *Encanto* (2022 Oscar nomination for Best Original Song, two Grammy Awards). He lives with his family in New York.

This story was told on June 30, 2021, at the United Palace in New York City. The theme of the evening was When You're Home. Director: Catherine Burns.

MY KNIGHT IN
SHINING SIDE CURLS
FRIMET GOLDBERGER

I was a Hasidic woman from one of the most pious Hasidic Jewish communities in upstate New York. Growing up, all forms of secular influences were strictly verboten: TVs, movies, the internet, newspapers.

We were expected to keep the highest standards of modesty. From the age of three, I wore shirts that covered my elbows and collarbone, skirts covering my knees, and thick stockings. This was the uniform of my childhood and my people. I knew nothing else, and I cared for nothing else. When I would catch a glimpse of someone in shorts and a tank top, I would think, *Ew, why would you want to expose your private parts?*

Tzniut, or modesty, was a concept so well ingrained in our minds and in our existence that we couldn't fathom why anyone would want to dress any differently.

I was a good girl, a wide-eyed Hasidic eidel maidel, but I didn't always want to be. I had a few transgressions under my belt, like the time a friend and I went to Walmart and filled our bins with trashy romance novels. I would hide them between my bedspring and mattress, and my friend and I would devour these titillating tales as if we were breaking the Yom Kippur fast.

Marriage was my ticket to freedom, away from the prying eyes of parents and matchmakers. I met my husband for the first time in my parents' dining room. I was seventeen and pining for a strapping man to fulfill my Nora Roberts–inspired dreams. He was twenty-one, and just trying to clear the way for his two younger siblings waiting in line. My mother thought it unsuitable for her young *good girl* to marry an older boy, but I begged and cajoled, and she finally relented and agreed to this shidduch, or arranged match.

I had heard through the grapevine of yentas that he wasn't in yeshiva full time, that he smoked, and he drove. I had also heard that he moonlighted as a theatergoer, and that to me was downright sexy.

So for the beshow, what we call the official meeting of the pro-spective bride and groom, we were ushered into my childhood play-room. I broke the ice by asking him about his family, the number of children and grandchildren, even though I knew them quite well.

His sister was my classmate.

His other sister is married to my first cousin.

My brother is married to his first cousin.

And two of my sisters are married to two of his other first cousins. It's a *doozy*.

So, after about twenty minutes, my mother poked her head in and said, "Nu? Did you make a decision?"

There were trays of cakes lined up on the kitchen counter—cakes that I had baked that day for a potential engagement party, and no one wanted to see them go to waste. And there was no good reason for either one of us to say no, but I desperately wanted con-firmation that he was indeed dabbling in secular matters. So when my mother left, I boldly asked him if he listened to the radio. He blushed, and something about his blushing confirmed it for me. I knew then and there that he was my knight in shining side curls.

We were not supposed to speak during our engagement, but he

further confirmed his renegade status when he sent his phone number, scribbled on a note, through a mutual acquaintance. And I would call him every Thursday evening, hiding behind the clothes in my closet so my mother wouldn't overhear.

We were married on a cold December evening, the first snow of the season blanketing the streets.

The next morning, my mother showed up to shave my head. All of it. Down to stubble, as is the custom in this particular Hasidic community. Everyone did it. All married women were required to shave their heads monthly for the duration of their marriage.

We settled into married life, or as best as you can *settle in* as two strangers.

After three days, I decided it was time my husband knew me better. I bedecked our little kitchen table in this dollhouse-sized apartment, and I whipped out a two-by-two-inch DVD screen. The next day, he one-upped me with a box of Yankees paraphernalia and a computer that he kept hidden in his parents' home. We were a match made in heaven, except we were practically strangers.

We watched movies and went to the library every Friday afternoon, and we would have to look right and left and back before making a beeline for the Blockbuster door, or the library door, because no one could see us heretics.

And after a while, about two to three months, we decided it was time to take our rebellion on the road. My husband suggested Florida and this place he had heard of called Wet 'n Wild waterpark. Now, I had never been to the beach. I had never been to a waterpark. I had never really traveled before, and certainly never flown on a plane. So, you can imagine, I was excited.

In preparation for this trip, we went shopping. I owned a bathing suit, and this bathing suit was called a shvim kleid. It's the kind of garment I imagine Mother Teresa would wear, when and if she allowed herself a dip in the water. This shvim kleid had sleeves, and it had a skirt reaching down to my knees, and I knew it was unsuitable for a waterpark.

So, we went shopping.

I can still feel my heart buckle when I think of the way we crisscrossed those bathing suit racks at Walmart and darted every time we saw a familiar Hasidic face. The suits all looked equally immodest to me. My husband picked out this backless one piece, and I was in this cramped women's dressing room, imagining a thousand eyes peering in from under the door slit.

I stripped out of my clothes, and I pulled on this bathing suit that simultaneously reminded me of hell and also of a delicious piece of babka.

I turn to the mirror, and I am seeing my bare arms and bare legs full length possibly for the first time. This backless bathing suit had a sun rising from the nether regions, which kind of sounds like a metaphor for my life. I look at myself in the mirror, and I imagine that this is what it must feel like to be on the cover of one of the magazines I peruse. I am young. I am perky in all the right places, and I know it.

We were giddy for days leading up to this trip. We told everyone about this trip, and we told no one *about* this trip. My mother called a few days prior to wish us farewell and asked if we packed the right clothes. Do we know that it's warm in Florida? I laughed. She had no idea what we were up to.

We landed in Orlando, and we visited Universal and Disney and missed *all* popular cultural references. I mean, I marveled at this thing that was part spider, part human. We were *so* sheltered. We felt like aliens walking around in those parks. Except, I can assure you, we did not know what aliens were back then.

And then came the big day, Wet 'n Wild waterpark. I'm wearing a bathing suit for the first time. We are fair-skinned newlyweds who had never used sunscreen before. I mean, bodies covered from head to toe literally have no use for sunscreen. And on my head, I am wearing a chin-length wig with a Yankees sun visor securing it. My husband was a fan, and of course that meant I was too, even though I'd never heard of baseball before our chuppah.

I'm wandering around on my husband's tail, ogling this bevy of bikini-clad shiksas in all their tan glory. I keep my arms on my chest, alternating between that and my thighs and knees and elbows, until I realize I am practically in the nude, and I just walk around in a self-conscious daze.

My discomfort was so palpable, a constant reminder of the grave sin I was committing. I felt like everyone around me could see right through my shame. I might as well have been curtsying in front of the Grand Rabbi. It felt so wrong to expose all these parts of my body that I was taught to keep hidden. And yet, it felt so right, and so darn liberating.

We make our way through the park and up to the tallest ride. It's a long, winding tube that shoots us down into a shallow pool. I am having the time of my life. And as I land in this shallow pool and bob my head out of the water, I feel a muggy breeze.

I turn around to the guy manning the pool, and he's holding up my wig, with a limping sun visor, and he's like, "Ma'am, ma'am, did you lose this?"

I was mortified.

But more than that, I was afraid.

I feared that someone would recognize me and report me back home to the authorities. And before you know it, my mother knows, and my neighbor's bubbe knows, and my mother's heart is broken, and my good girl status is stripped from me. And my future children won't be accepted into the only school in town.

I risked losing a lot.

I grabbed my wig and visor, and I started heading out of the pool, when I feel eyes on me. And I turn around, and they're pitiful eyes. Eyes that seem to say, *Poor woman. Poor, poor woman with cancer.*

I was relieved.

They didn't know me.

Cancer sounded plausible.

And I'd rather they believe I have cancer than know my shame. That way at least I can hide my shame behind their pity.

I head out of the pool both mortified but also accepting of the pity. But my husband is completely traumatized, and we leave the park soon after.

Thankfully, no one back home ever did find out.

We've been married for sixteen years, nearly half of our lives. We are no longer Hasidic. We moved out of the community a little over a decade ago with our two children. And what a decade it's been. It's been a decade of heartache, both for us and for our families. And it's been a decade of loss—loss of a community of people, a lifestyle. The only life we ever knew, and the only life we were taught was worth living.

We've made every effort along the way to be respectful of our families and their customs and traditions. And even though I know that my mother doesn't understand my choices, and she doesn't appreciate the life I live, and that I have veered from her beaten path, she has come a long way in learning to accept me. And for that, I love her dearly.

I no longer cover my hair with someone else's natural hair. I am not obligated to wear long sleeves or skirts reaching my knees. I am also no longer obligated to be a Yankees fan—my son stepped into those shoes. And we've returned to Orlando several times since, but I can never bring myself to go back to *that* park, where I imagine a thousand eyes are still staring at my bald head.

* ⊙ *

FRIMET GOLDBERGER is an award-winning writer interested in societal attitudes toward arranged and modern marriages, as well as the state of traditional Jewish communities in America. Her first book, *Matchmaker, Make Me a Match: Arranged Love in the 21st Century,* a deeply researched and reported cross-cultural portrait of contemporary arranged marriage, framed by personal experience and raising questions about secular romance, how we define love and happiness, and what we can learn from relationships that prioritize community and longevity over individual desires, will be published by Viking.

This story was told on February 6, 2020, at the Anderson Theater, Memorial Hall in Cincinnati. The theme of the evening was Between Worlds. Director: Meg Bowles.

STANDING AS 10,000
BRIGETTE JANEA JONES

In 2015, my then-boyfriend, now-fiancé, Sean, and I were living in Nashville, and one day on the way home, we passed a sign for the Belle Meade Plantation.

Clearly, my excitement was written all over my face, because before I could get the words out of my mouth, Sean was like, "Hell no. I am a Black man. It is 2015. What I'm not going to do is go to a plantation . . . for fun."

I said, "Why? It's our history."

And he said, "Because slavery is over."

So, I very audibly pouted for the rest of the ride home.

Later that day, about an hour into my attitude-induced nap, Sean comes to wake me up, and he says, "Get up, get dressed. We have somewhere to go."

So I get up, I get dressed, and I silently ride to our unknown destination, with an attitude, and lo and behold, we pull up to the Belle Meade Plantation.

Halfway through the tour, I'm feeling real confident because I have this brand-new, unused degree from the historically Black Tennessee State University, and my degree is in African American history with a focus in Southern race relations. I'm in my element, and I'm thinking to myself, *I can do this job, and I can do it better.*

So, I get all my Leo attitude together, and I go walking up to my tour guide, who, mind you, has on a full antebellum costume, and I say to her, "I can do this job."

Well, ten cold emails and an interview later, I landed the job.

Now, I immediately wanted to tell two people once I got the job: I wanted to tell my mama and my fiancé, Sean.

Sean was the easy one. He was just happy that I wasn't going to be calling him crying from the car because I got a rejection letter for another job.

But my mama was a different story. My mama was born in 1952 in Little Rock, Arkansas. So, to my mama, her baby girl going to work on a *plantation* in 2015, *chiiild,* she thought I was going to set *all* Black people back four hundred years.

But I'm the direct descendant of enslaved Tennesseans, and I have always been passionate about honoring their sacrifice, respecting their work, and acknowledging their tribulations.

My very Southern grandmother, May Roy Jones, was born in 1925 in Grand Junction, Tennessee, on the Ames Plantation. That very same plantation had enslaved her ancestors prior to Emancipation.

Now, I don't know about y'all's grandmama, but my grandmama loved pictures, and I can vividly remember being a kid staring up at what seemed to be hundreds of photos from the 1940s and '50s, '60s, '70s, and '80s that lined the walls of my grandmother's South Memphis home.

I can vividly remember eavesdropping on the grown folks' conversations as they talked about who was doing what with who, and what folks used to do back in the country. But what really piqued my interest were the conversations about a particular period in time where Black people specifically couldn't do this or that.

I honestly think it was those conversations and those photographs that sparked my initial love and interest in Black history and culture. Growing up knowing that I was only roughly an hour away from the very same plantation that had legally enslaved my ancestors made me look at the antebellum South and antebellum history in a way that fascinated me.

I can remember my very first day at work at Belle Meade. We did typical work stuff. I filled out paperwork and got an in-depth tour of the grounds. I was really excited to meet my new co-workers, but when I walked into the office, I noticed two things:

One, everybody had on antebellum attire.

And two, I had just become Belle Meade's only Black tour guide.

I remember clocking out that day with a binder, legit, y'all, the size of a Harry Potter book, and tons of other supplementary material that I was going to need to learn and memorize before I was cleared to give my own tour.

Eventually I was cleared. I had my own antebellum dress and everything, and honestly, I wish y'all could have been a fly on the wall the day that I, a then twenty-three-year-old Black woman with an afro, opened the front door to the plantation mansion in an antebellum dress for thirty white people.

Shocked was an understatement.

But I relished in that discomfort because I knew that their discomfort was rooted in their wondering about what side of history I was going to be interpreting.

In the early days of my work at Belle Meade, the interpretation of slavery was limited to two people. There was Bob Green, the head hostler, and there was Susanna Carter, the head of domestic staff. And I absolutely wanted to tell their stories, but I also wanted to tell what the institution of slavery had done to individuals like them—to a race of people like theirs, to a culture like theirs, and ultimately to a generation of their descendants.

But everybody didn't like my interpretation of history.

I can remember this one time in particular, there was this lady on my tour, and she was fly too, y'all, Gucci down, I ain't gonna lie.

And as I dug into the pain of slavery, I was getting deep, and she stood up in the middle of my tour and interrupted me by saying, "I don't need this. I have a *master's* degree."

And she left.

I remember looking over at her daughter, and her face was beet red with embarrassment.

Honestly, her embarrassment didn't have a thing on the anger that I felt. But I used that anger to push me deeper into the history.

Well, three years and by God almighty, a discontinuation of costumed tours later, I was named Belle Meade's very first Black director.

My title was director of African American studies, and I spearheaded the creation of the Journey to Jubilee Tour. This tour sought to stretch beyond the narratives of two people and tell a larger story of all 136 who had been enslaved on the property.

This tour was not just important, it was personal.

Now, my mama is a preacher, and we are Pentecostal. And in the Pentecostal church we speak in proverbs and quotes, and there's this one Maya Angelou quote that always stood out to me.

Maya Angelou said that "I come as one, but I stand as ten thousand."

I remember my very first day giving the Journey to Jubilee Tour. I got to work that day, and I had this yearning desire to sit with spirit, as I call it. I remember walking over to the clearing where the slave cabins once stood, and I just sat down, and I began to talk to the ancestors.

I told them that although my ancestors likely faced similar situations, the stories of the enslaved at Belle Meade were not mine. And I was going to need their help to tell this story. Essentially, I was going to need them to speak *to me* and *through me*.

I sat in that space for about thirty minutes, and I meditated in their presence. Then I wiped the tears from my eyes, and I got up, and I went back to my office to begin my day.

About an hour later, I was standing back in front of the slave cabins. This time I was in front of roughly twenty-five middle-aged white people, and I was nervous. I had all these thoughts and feelings, and I didn't know how they were going to come out.

The tour started smoothly, and eventually I told my guests that we were going to make our way from the slave cabin to the kitchen house. And on our short walk, I answered all of the usual questions:

"When was the house built?"

"Did the Civil War happen here?"

And my personal favorite, "Were they *good* slave owners?"

I can remember walking into the kitchen house and letting them look around for a moment, and then I told them to have a seat so that we could begin our discussion.

The weight of the room started to get a little heavier as I began to break down the myth of the lost cause and the supposed difference between enslaved field workers and house workers.

But what really broke the camel's back was when I told them that 11 percent of Belle Meade's population—11 percent of 136 people— were mulatto, half Black and half white.

Now I said, "We don't know where mulatto slaves came from, but what we do know is that mulatto people don't just fall out of the sky."

I pushed on and explained that there's this supposed idea that slavery only affected Black people. I wanted to take my guests on a journey and explore everybody who could have possibly had a role in this type of situation, and the first person I introduced them to was *master's wife*.

I began circling the room as I asked, "How does it *feel* to have to look into the face of your husband's mistress every . . . single . . . day?

"Now, what happens when that enslaved woman becomes pregnant, and now she has to look into the face of her husband's indiscretion's indiscretion every . . . single . . . day?"

As I'm asking these questions, I make sure to look each and every white woman on my tour directly in her eye. I made sure to acknowledge the lack of control that a white woman of that time period had over her husband and his actions. But I also made sure to detail the nature of revenge that many white women took out on these enslaved women and their illegitimate children: the threat of *sale* to alleviate her own emotional turmoil.

I pushed further and shifted my focus.

"How does the enslaved woman feel?

"How does it *feel* to have to bear the brunt of someone's anger and aggression and resentment for a situation that you did not ask for nor can you control?

"How does it *feel* to have to have a baby by a man—a man who only views that baby as property to be bought and sold at will? In actuality, that's not even really your baby.

"How does it *feel*?"

I saw a tear slide down the eye of a brunette woman in the group. Then I shifted my focus one last time.

"What if, just what if that enslaved woman had a husband too?"

This time, I'm looking at all the men in the group.

I ask, "How does it feel to have to go work six days a week, from sunup to sundown, and then come home to an eight-by-ten shack that you share with eight to ten other people and lie down on a cot next to your wife and know that she has been, and she is being, raped, but there's nothing that you can do about it?"

There were audible sobs in the room at this point.

I asked, "How does it *feel* to watch a baby come out of your wife? A baby whose shade of brown is going to be a whole lot lighter than your shade of brown and, even though you know who it belongs to, there's nothing that you can do about it. You can't help her, hell, you can't even help *you*. So you love it, and you love her, as best as you know how. But in the midst of loving them, *what did it do to you*—mentally, emotionally, physically, spiritually?"

In that moment there were tears streaming down my own face.

My hands were shaking.

I broke.

It was like I was there, but I wasn't there.

It was like I had emotionally transcended my present location and traveled back into my own family history of biracial babies on the 1870s, '80s, and '90s census records.

Time had merged, and I could feel the weight of 136 formerly enslaved men, women, and children hovering over that kitchen house.

And as I came to, out of my history-induced trance, I noticed that there was not one dry eye in the room.

I looked around and noticed the flood of emotions of fully grown white men and women, and I said to myself right then that *this is it.*

This is my Journey to Jubilee.

The feeling had shifted the room that day, like a spell had been cast. I had asked my visitors to come face-to-face with the ethos of Black people's plight. I asked them to *feel* it, and by God they felt it.

I showed them the pain that most Black people don't show white people.

I showed them just how deeply the legacy of slavery is still hurting on a personal level.

I took off my mask. I had no use for it.

I let them *see me.*

There's an African proverb that says, "Until the lion learns to write, the hunter will be glorified in every story."

I had become the lion that could write.

And although I was just one little Black girl from Memphis, I was standing in that room as ten thousand.

I now take the ancestors with me into every room I enter.

I walk with them instead of being led by them.

I have cried for them.

I have cried with them.

I have laughed at their ability to slight their oppressor without them ever even knowing.

I have *seen* them through the history books perform the alchemy of turning nothing into something for the last four hundred and some odd years.

I used to just know I was Black in color and culture, but *now,* NOW I stand in that Blackness, bold and proud of each and every person that has come before me.

BRIGETTE JANEA JONES is the assistant executive director for Arabia Mountain National Heritage Area in Lithonia, Georgia, and founder of Bridge Builders Historical Consulting, LLC. Her previous work has included the preservation and interpretation of the vast social histories of the many diverse cultures that inhabit the state of Tennessee as well as fostering the types of partnerships with community institutions that aid in the enhancement of their quality of life. Brigette is a Memphis native and holds a bachelor of arts degree from Tennessee State University, an HBCU in Nashville, Tennessee. In 2019, she gained certification through the National Association of Interpretation and the Smithsonian Institute: National Museum of African American History and Culture to become an official interpreter of the African American experience. Most recently, she served as director of equitable partnerships for Belle Meade Historic Site and Winery and curator of social history for the Tennessee State Museum, where her work blended the academic study of the lasting legacy of American chattel enslavement in Tennessee and surrounding areas and the need for reparative action as it relates to American descendants of enslavement.

This story was told on December 8, 2022, at St. Ann's Church in New York City. The theme of the evening was Now You See Me. Director: Meg Bowles.

DON'T CALL ME YOUNG LADY!

CAROLYN MEYER

The year I turn eighty, which was about eight years ago, I walk into my neighborhood bar, and the bartender says, "What can I get for you, young lady?"

He's *smiling*.

I tell him, "Well, I'll have a glass of red wine—pinot if you've got it—but *please don't call me young lady*."

Whether it's a bartender or a security guard at the airport, or even my doctor—they don't call a twenty-five-year-old "young lady," but they call me "young lady" because I'm obviously not young.

I haven't been a young lady since Richard Nixon was in the White House.

Now, maybe they think it's flattering or cute.

Well, it's not. It's condescending.

Because of my white hair they make assumptions about me. They have expectations. They deny the *wholeness* of who I am.

So, the bartender pours me a glass of pinot noir, and he says, "Oh, age is just a number."

Well, it isn't just *a* number. It is *the* number. Back in the day, it meant I was old enough to drive a car, to walk into a bar and order a drink, to *vote*. But the year that I turn eighty, age takes on a whole new meaning for me.

I've been a writer for fifty years. I've been divorced twice, widowed once—but I still think I have a whole lot of living left to do if I'm willing to step outside my comfort zone and take some risks.

So, I sign up for online dating.

I have a pretty good idea of the kind of guy I'd like to meet— a sapiosexual. A man who thinks the sexiest part of a woman is between her *ears*. I'm not looking for a husband—I've had three of those—but I definitely want a *lover*. Not just somebody to go to the movies with.

I decide not to lie about my age—low maintenance compensates for high mileage—and I write what I think is an intriguing profile.

I post some recent pictures—and the algorithms kick in. *You don't smoke. You both like dogs. You both lift weights.*

What more could anyone ask for?

So, I start meeting some of these guys for coffee dates, and they're nice. They're pleasant enough, but I always feel like I'm interviewing a man I don't want to *hire* for a job he doesn't want to *get*.

But then along comes Michael. Michael's an architect. There's a picture, a photograph of him—silver temples, a good-looking guy— and candid shots of him riding his Ducati motorcycle and strolling through a museum somewhere.

Now, Michael is ten years younger than I am. It doesn't seem to bother him, and it sure doesn't bother me. But there is an issue here. I live in Albuquerque, New Mexico, and his home is a thousand miles away, in Lincoln, Nebraska. But I think, *Let's see what happens.*

We exchange messages through the website and then on our personal email accounts. And then very quickly, we're talking on the phone. We have a lot to talk about. I'm talking about the book that I'm working on. He talks about his architectural projects. We talk about the personal stuff, our marriages and disappointments, our enthusiasms and our dreams.

Pretty soon we are talking every day. *Every day.*

He calls in the morning and says, "Talking with you is a ray of sunshine in my life."

And he calls in the evening and says, "You are my sweet addiction."

Oh my God. Yeah, I just love that. Who wouldn't?

One night—when we've been doing this for a while and I've really come to trust him and feel comfortable with him—I tell him about the double mastectomy that I had decades ago and how it still affects how I feel about myself as a woman.

We end the conversation and say goodnight, and Michael sends me a message: "My dear Carolyn, you're a strong woman. I'm growing fond of you. Thank you for sharing something so deeply personal with me."

Well, I am growing *very fond of Michael.*

Naturally, we begin making plans, talking about how we're going to meet.

Michael has an idea.

He has to go to Kuala Lumpur in Malaysia—he's the lead architect on the shopping center that's being built there. He'll be there for ten days, and on his way back, he will stop off in Albuquerque. We'll spend some time together and get to know each other and see where this is taking us.

I am so excited about this, but I am also apprehensive. When we actually meet and he sees me in the flesh, is he still going to be attracted to me? I mean, the wrinkles, the flab, the mastectomy scars. I worry about it.

But we proceed with this plan.

He flies to Malaysia, and we still continue to talk every day because we figured out this fourteen-hour time difference. He tells me about the delicious Malaysian food, and the translator he's hired, and the engineers he's working with. He has all sorts of funny stories to tell. It's almost like I'm on this journey with him.

Soon he will be coming to see me, and I begin to make plans

about what we're going to do. I get a haircut. I buy new underwear. I plan the meals that I'm going to cook for him and the trips I'm going to take him on around New Mexico. I am really, really excited about this.

The morning that he is to leave, he calls me, and he sounds terrible. He is so upset.

"Michael, what's wrong?"

He says, "I'm down at the port, at the customs house, and I'm waiting to sign off on some equipment—specialized equipment that we need for this project. And the customs people won't release it to me because the fees haven't been paid."

"Michael, that's terrible! What are you going to do?"

He says, "Carolyn, you know I'd never ask this of you if it weren't that my whole career is tied up in this. Could you possibly lend me some money to pay those fees? I promise I'll pay it back as soon as I get home to Nebraska."

"Well, of course, Michael. Of course I'll help! How much do you need?"

"Fifty thousand dollars," he says.

"Fifty *grand*? Michael, I don't have *fifty thousand dollars*."

My problem-solving kicks in. "Well, call the bank in Nebraska. Call your business partners. Call the shippers of the equipment."

He has a reason why none of this will work.

"Well," he says, "could you make it *thirty* thousand?"

As the dollar number drops, the red flag goes up.

There were probably red flags before, but I didn't see them—or maybe I didn't *want* to see them—but all of a sudden, everything is crystal clear.

His plan to come to visit, being his sweet addiction, who he says he is: *None of it is true.*

"No, Michael. No."

And I hang up. I end the call, and that's that.

Then I go to Google. Why, might you ask, did I not do this in the first place?

Nevertheless, I enter his name and add "fraud," and up pops his rap sheet. He's done this before, *more than once.*

I am not his first "sweet addiction," as it turns out.

The photograph of the good-looking guy with the silver temples? There's a Google thing for that too. The photo is Peter McAllum, an Australian movie star.

So, I report Michael to the dating site, and he is banished. Well, I'm beyond disappointed. I'm hurt. I'm embarrassed that I was fooled for as long as I was. I am also extremely pissed.

But I get over it. I move on.

I get back to writing again.

And then I think, maybe I should put myself out there and take another risk—decide to step outside the comfort zone, do something.

So, I sign up for an *improv comedy class.*

And a few months later, I'm back at that same bar doing stand-up.

I will confess to you that it's *pretty raunchy stuff.* The audience doesn't know what to make of it. Neither does the bartender.

Then I develop a one-woman show and perform that, and I do another one. I keep putting myself out there, all of me—taking the risk.

And you'd think that I would've learned to stay away from online dating, but I think, *What the hell? Give it another shot.*

So, I sign up again, and along comes Robert. Robert is a photographer. He lives in Albuquerque. Turns out we've met before. He came to see one of my performances.

I know over that first cup of coffee: Here is a man who really *looks* at me. He sees me the way I have always wanted to be seen. He sees the wholeness of who I am.

That cup of coffee was a couple of years ago.

Last June, the day before my eighty-seventh birthday, Robert and I were married.

I knew that this was the kind of man I was ready to take another leap with, and now the two of us are writing the next chapter of our lives—*together*.

* ✦ *

For more than fifty years, **CAROLYN MEYER** built a career as a writer for children and young adults. Then, with more than sixty books to her credit, Carolyn decided to take her storytelling in a different direction. Her first solo show, *Don't Call Me Young Lady!*, opened in Albuquerque, New Mexico, where she has lived for the past four decades, and proved that she could stand on a stage for over an hour and hardly ever forget her lines. Her next show, *The Old White Lady Tells It,* was a victim of Covid, but she continues to tell stories wherever she can to whoever will listen.

This story was told at the Silver Ball on May 26, 2022, at Spring Studios in New York City. Director: Sarah Austin Jenness.

LUCKY NUMBERS

BRIDGETT M. DAVIS

I was in my first-grade class one day, and I had just shown my teacher, Miss Miller, an assignment. We had to color paper petals, cut them out, and paste them onto a picture of a flower.

As I'm returning to my seat, Miss Miller stops me, and she says, "You sure do have a lot of shoes."

The week before she had asked me what my father did for a living, and I said, "He doesn't work."

And she said, "Well, what does your mother do?"

And I froze. I knew I could not tell her that my mom was in the numbers.

The numbers was a lot like today's lottery, except that it was underground, and it existed for decades before the state basically took it over.

My mom was a numbers runner. Every day, except Sunday, she would take people's bets on three-digit numbers, collect their money when they didn't win, pay out their winnings when they did, and profit from the difference. And the thing is, the numbers was wildly popular. It generated millions of dollars in every major city in the country. And so you can imagine, a lot of that money circulated through the Black community, and those dollars turned over many, many times.

Numbers money helped to provide services that Black folks desperately needed. It helped with launching small businesses and providing college scholarships. It helped folks get home loans, and it even helped a fledgling NAACP stay afloat for years.

My mom was high-ranking. She wasn't just a numbers runner, she was a banker, and so she didn't just have her own customers, other bookies turned their business in to her. She was the only woman in Detroit operating at that level for a long time. That's how she was able to give us a solid middle-class life—a *solid* middle-class life.

I was really, really, really proud of my mom. I thought it was incredible that she was able to give us this kind of life, but what I loved most of all was the sound of her voice on the phone taking her customers' bets.

She would say, "Okay, Miss Queenie, I'm ready to take your numbers. Six-nine-two straight for fifty cents, seven-eight-eight boxed for a dollar."

And folks had these really creative ways of coming up with the three digits they wanted to play. They would play their birth dates, or their anniversaries, or their addresses, or their license plates. Some people even liked to play their favorite Bible verse.

Hearing my mom reciting those numbers every morning was like a daytime lullaby because it meant that everything was right in the world. My mom was handling her business.

On the other hand, it is true that it was a livelihood based on a daily win-or-lose gamble. So yes, I also remember how we would all gather around and wait for the phone call every evening that would announce the day's winning numbers. They were based on race track results. This tense silence moved through our home like a nervous prayer.

When we actually heard the winning numbers, we took our cues from Mama. Either she looked relieved, or she looked worried. Either she'd been lucky that day, or one of her customers had been. And it wasn't that she ever resented her customers winning.

She would always say, "Folks play numbers to hit, so you cannot be mad when they do."

I was so proud of my mom. I knew she was not like any of my friends' mothers. I knew she was running things.

One day I decided I was going to organize all of her numbers-running materials. And so I went through the house gathering everything into this shallow cardboard box—her spiral notebooks, her white scratch pads, her black binders, and her red ink pens. Then I very carefully painted on the side of the box, *Mama's Numbers*. And I used bright pink nail polish. I was so impressed with myself because I remembered the possessive *s*.

I proudly show this to my mom, and she takes one look and says, "You cannot put my business out in the street like that."

And that's when it hit me that I had to keep my admiration for my mom private. She was never apologetic or embarrassed about what she did. There was no shame attached to it. My mom made it very clear that the numbers was a legitimate business that just *happened* to be illegal.

She had all of these ways to help mitigate the risk of exposure. My mom basically lived a low-key lifestyle. She never flaunted her wealth. Yes, she always drove a new car, but it was a Buick Riviera, not a Cadillac. We lived in a lovely home on a tree-lined street, but we did not live in one of the big houses in an exclusive enclave of Detroit. And we were well dressed. My mom was the best dressed of all, but her style was understated. She was classic and classy. No one would have ever described my mother as flashy.

My mom's edict was, keep your head up and your mouth shut. Be proud, but be private. And that's why, when my first-grade teacher asked me what my mom did for a living, I knew I could not tell her the truth.

I knew I could not reveal the family business.

We all knew to keep that secret.

The only problem was I hadn't been told what I *should* say.

So, I said to Miss Miller, "I'm not sure what my mom does."

And after Miss Miller said to me, "You sure do have a lot of shoes," she said. "Before you sit down, I want you to name every pair of shoes you have. Go ahead."

I was so nervous because it felt like a test, and I didn't want to get it wrong. I went through this mental inventory of all the shoes that lined my closet shelf, and I just started naming them—the black-and-white polka-dotted ones with the bow tie, the buckled ruby-red ones, the salmon-pink lace-ups. I managed to get through ten pairs of shoes.

And Miss Miller said to me, "Ten pairs is an awful lot."

And I could hear something bad in her voice as she ordered me to take my seat.

The next day in class, Miss Miller called me back to her desk, and she said, "You did not tell me you had white shoes."

I looked down at my feet, and I felt like I had been caught in a lie. I knew I had disappointed my teacher, and the rest of the day I was *so* worried that I was in trouble.

So, that evening, after my mother was finished taking her customers' bets and before the day's winning numbers came out—during that brief expectant pause in the day, when she was least distracted and still in a good mood—I told her what happened at school. I confessed that I forgot to tell Miss Miller about the eleventh pair of shoes.

I have never seen my mother get so angry. She was furious, and I thought, *I am about to get a spanking.*

But my mom said to me, "That is none of her damn business. Who does she think she is?"

And then my mom stood up and said, "Get your coat."

And I thought, *Oh my God, we are going back to school, and she's going to confront Miss Miller.*

But in fact, my mom took me to Saks Fifth Avenue, where we made our way to the children's shoe department.

She pointed to the most beautiful pair of yellow patent leather shoes.

And she said, "Those are pretty."

I still can remember when my mother pulled out a hundred-dollar bill and paid for those shoes, the saleswoman looked at her the way Miss Miller had looked at me.

On the way home, my mom said, "You're going to wear these to school tomorrow. And you better tell that damn teacher of yours that you actually have *a dozen* pair of shoes. You hear me?"

The next day I wore my new shoes with a matching yellow knit dress.

In class I was so nervous, but I did as I was told; I walked up to my teacher's desk, and I said, "Miss Miller, I have twelve pairs of shoes."

She looked down at my feet, and then she leveled her blue eyes at my face, and she said, "Sit down."

Miss Miller never said another word to me.

Sending me to school that day in those decidedly unsubtle bright yellow shoes, my mom really did risk raising Miss Miller's suspicions, but she did it to make a point. And it was one that I understood and heard loud and clear—no one can *ever* tell me what I'm entitled to.

My mom used material things as armor against a world designed to convince us, Black working-class children of migrants, that we didn't deserve a good life. And her mission was to make sure we knew otherwise.

So, yes, twelve pairs of shoes for a six-year-old girl who was going to outgrow them in a few months might seem excessive. But for my mom, it was an investment in how I walked into the future with my head up.

I did continue to keep my mouth shut for decades. I never told anyone what my mother did for a living, not even after Michigan's Daily Lottery became legal. And not even after my mother died, which means I never got to tell anyone how proud I was of her—until now.

BRIDGETT M. DAVIS is the author of the memoir *The World According to Fannie Davis: My Mother's Life in the Detroit Numbers,* a *New York Times* Editors' Choice, soon to be adapted to film by Searchlight Pictures. Her memoir *Love, Rita* will be published by Harper Books in spring 2025; she is also the author of two novels, *Into the Go-Slow,* named a Best Book by the *San Francisco Chronicle,* and *Shifting Through Neutral,* shortlisted for the Hurston/Wright Legacy Award. She is writer/director of the award-winning feature film *Naked Acts,* rereleased theatrically in 2023 to mark its twenty-fifth anniversary, and professor emerita at Baruch College (City University of New York), where she taught creative writing. Her essays have appeared in *The New York Times,* the *Los Angeles Times, The Washington Post, Real Simple,* and *O, The Oprah Magazine.* A graduate of Spelman College and Columbia University's Graduate School of Journalism, she lives in Brooklyn with her family. Visit her website at bridgettdavis.com.

This story was told on June 1, 2019, at the Ford Community & Performing Arts Center in Detroit. The theme of the evening was Out of Sight. Director: Meg Bowles.

LOVING GRACE

ROBIN UTZ

I was pretty sure about my husband right off the bat. When I met him, I loved how he talked about the things that he loved.

He would have me come over to his apartment, and we'd watch *Soul Train* YouTube clips until late in the evening, and he would look at me with these adoring eyes and say, "It's the happiest place on Earth."

And I was like, "It really is."

It took me no time to know I wanted to spend the rest of my life with him. And it took pretty much no time to realize I wanted to have a child with him.

The happily ever after has been easy—we're still as in love today as we've ever been. But the child part has not been so easy. It was after four years of trying, two rounds of in vitro, three frozen embryo transfers, and a miscarriage, that we finally got pregnant with our daughter, Grace Pearl.

We were just ecstatic.

The pregnancy went like a breeze. And before we knew it, we were at the anatomy scan, which happens a little over halfway through the pregnancy. I could not wait. I wanted that profile shot—the little side profile that everybody thinks about with an ultrasound. Jim wanted to see it too, so he came to the appointment with me.

We were having a nice time. We were chattering about where we were going to get lunch. And it took me a little bit to notice that the ultrasound technician, Nicole, was not seeing a lot.

She was kind of making concerned noises, and she goes, "There's not a lot of amniotic fluid. I want you to roll on your side, and I'm going to go talk to the doctor."

So I do that, hoping that it'll prompt Grace to move to a better position. The technician comes back and tries the scan again and no change. Grace has not moved.

And she says, "There's no amniotic fluid. I'm sorry, I know that's not what you want to hear."

And I'm like, "It's not? Okay. All right."

She leads us down the hallway to go talk to the doctor, and I google "second trimester, no amniotic fluid," and what stares me back in the face is "80 to 90 percent fatal."

I'm like, "Shit."

It does not improve when we get into the doctor's office. The office is full of pictures of newborns that my doctor has delivered—most of them featuring her, and they're all smiling.

She comes in, not smiling, and introduces herself to Jim, my husband, as Jen.

And I'm like, *Shit. Not Dr. Meyer. Jen. That's not a good sign.*

She then explains the following:

Our daughter's kidneys are huge.

They're full of fluid-filled cysts.

Basically, they're not working.

The way that babies work when they're in the womb is: Amniotic fluid travels through the kidneys and is urinated out, and it cycles, and without that cycling, their lungs will never develop.

They can't breathe.

She explains that the prognosis is not good, and we burst into tears.

To confirm this, she has scheduled an emergency second ultra-sound an hour later, also in this hospital. For now, she lets us leave out a side door, so we don't have to go through the waiting room full of expectant mothers with their full bellies, for all of our sakes.

I walk past a half-eaten birthday cake on the way out.

We get outside, and it is an unusually warm November day, and people are milling everywhere. And I cannot believe the Earth has not just stopped in place.

My parents knew that this ultrasound was happening right then. I can't not call them and tell them what's happened.

So I call, and my mom answers within a second, and she's like, "How was it?"

And I'm like, "Not good."

And she drops the phone. I can hear her sobbing.

My dad picks it up a few seconds later and asks what happened, and I do my best to tell him while Jim rubs my back and silently cries next to me.

My dad asks if he can be there with us for the second ultrasound, and we agree. We meet him, an hour later, in the waiting room.

He gives us each a huge hug and makes jokes about the reading material. I'm so grateful he's there, dad jokes and all.

We're soon taken back for the second ultrasound. It's about two hours of detailed pictures of our daughter. The technician shows us the kidneys and the little black dots on them, which are the fluid-filled cysts.

She shows us that there's no black background, which is what amniotic fluid is. So, there is not going to be that profile picture.

The doctor comes in and introduces herself as Dr. Grey.

And my dad goes, "Like *Grey's Anatomy*."

I don't think he's ever even seen that show, but I loved that he was trying to be humorous in that moment.

She asks what we know. We explained what we'd heard so far.

And she said, "That's right. There are two outcomes for your daughter. She'll either be stillborn, having been crushed to death by your body because there's no amniotic fluid, or she will be born, and the wheels will come off."

I remember that phrasing, "The wheels will come off."

Without working lungs, she'll never survive, and she'll die, within minutes, hopefully in my arms.

My dad thought to ask, "What are the odds for a baby like this?"

She looked at him and said, "None."

She looked at me and said, "Your baby would be the first if she made it."

She then starts to explain that if we choose to terminate, there are specific laws around abortion in the state of Missouri, where I live. She says that you have to first sign consents, which aren't always easy to schedule because only certain people can oversee the signing of them.

Then you have to wait seventy-two hours—I guess to consider what you're doing?

You also can't have an abortion after twenty-one weeks, six days. I'm twenty weeks and six days when this happens. And there's an upcoming weekend and the Thanksgiving holiday.

We have no time to think about it. We have to decide almost immediately if we want to be able to do this in time, if we choose to.

The doctor leaves the room to give us a moment, and we all just burst into tears. We're all hugging one another and just inconsolable.

And I think about it, and I'm just like, *What choice do we have? She's going to die 100 percent. And if we don't terminate this pregnancy, she will suffer 100 percent.*

I look at Jim, and I'm like, "We have to terminate, right?"

And he's like, "Of course we do."

Even my dad, who was raised Catholic, agrees it would be cruel to do anything else.

The doctor comes back in, and we tell her we've made our decision.

She says, "I didn't want to sway you, but your risk would go up seven times if you didn't do this now, and that's just the risk of being pregnant."

She explains that they will have somebody call us as soon as possible to get the signed consents scheduled because we're so short on time.

We're lucky to be able to get in the very next day, so Jim and I go to a facility where a doctor in scrubs meets us and takes us back to a conference room where there are papers laid out.

Before I can even look at them, she pauses us, and she says, "These are state-mandated forms. They're not medical. They contain judgmental language that is designed to make you feel bad. It is not how we feel about you."

I'm asked to sign something that confirms that I have been offered the opportunity to hear my daughter's heartbeat. I listened to my daughter's heartbeat on a home Doppler every other day. I have a recording on my phone.

We were asked if we had been offered the opportunity to see an ultrasound. I'd had three hours of ultrasounds just the day before. And I also had asked for extra ultrasounds because I wanted to see her anytime I could.

Then I open a packet, and on the very first page in bold, indented letters, it says,

"The life of each human being begins at conception.

Abortion will terminate the life of a separate, unique, living human being."

My grief was interrupted by outrage.

Nowhere in this documentation was how much Grace would suffer.

None of it talked about the increased risks to my health.

It was all just biased on one side.

I wanted to light the documents on fire, but I signed them.

I had to.

And that started the seventy-two-hour clock.

That was the longest time in my life. It was a slow march, where my friends seamlessly cleared their calendars to invite me over to do jigsaw puzzles and drink tea with them.

My parents came over and removed all the newborn supplies and every stitch of baby clothing from our home.

I took pregnancy-approved sleeping pills.

I hugged Jim harder than I thought possible and hoped we could just meld into one person.

I cried and cried and cried.

I thought about how sure I was about my decision. It was so definitive.

I knew other people might make a different choice than I did. And there was a part of me that wanted to give birth to her and hold her, but it felt selfish and cruel to do anything different.

I never thought I would have an abortion, but I'd never needed to think about it.

The night before the termination, I asked Jim how he wanted to say goodbye to Grace. He said he wanted to have a dance party for her. Our own little *Soul Train*. He made a playlist of songs he'd always wanted her to hear and always wanted to teach her about. And so, in our pajamas, late at night in our living room, lit by candles, we danced with Grace.

We played riot grrrl music and some Rolling Stones and laughed at "Let's Spend the Night Together" because we'd always thought it would have a different meaning with a newborn.

And when Mick Jagger sang "Baby," I patted my little baby bump, and we sang along.

We slow-danced to "Sitting on the Dock of the Bay," which Jim has always said is "a perfect song just the way that it is."

We had to be at the hospital at five o'clock in the morning the next day.

And in the operating room, as the pre-anesthesia cocktail hit me, I looked at my doctor and said, "I need you to know that I love my daughter. I'm doing this because I love my daughter."

The nurse rubbed my arms, and then I was gently turned and laid back on the operating table, and they put my headphones in. They told me I wouldn't be asleep. And so we played Grace's playlist. And that's how we said goodbye to her.

I'm pregnant again.

It's a girl again.

I'm so excited.

I can't wait to see what she's like and to teach her things.

I can't wait to hold her hands while she is learning to walk and to braid her hair.

I want to teach her about one of my favorite songs, "Harvest Moon."

And I really want her to grow up in a world where she is valued. Where her humanity and dignity, and her ability to make the best decisions for herself and her family, are respected.

* ✦ *

ROBIN UTZ is a storyteller and advocate for reproductive rights and health-care access. She has testified against numerous abortion bans and has been featured in *The Washington Post*, Al Jazeera, NPR's *All Things Considered* and *1A*, and *The New York Times*. She lives in Missouri with her husband and daughter. You can follow her story at DefendingGrace.com.

This story was told on October 18, 2018, at The Wilbur Theatre in Boston. The theme of the evening was Into the Deep. Director: Meg Bowles.

YOU KNOW WHO YOU ARE

MEETING TONY BLAIR

JEREMY JENNINGS

On my first shift as a guard on the mental health block at Camp Delta, Guantanamo Bay, there was a man locked in the rubber room, banging his head repeatedly on the window of the door, bleeding from his forehead, and rattling the door on its hinges. This went on for some time, until I started to worry that he was going to do some serious harm to himself.

And so, I alerted the sergeant of the guard and the medical staff, and they told me, "Fuck that guy. He's just trying to get your attention, and he's manipulating you. So, ignore him."

I followed my orders. But I thought to myself, *If my job here is not to keep the detainees safe, then what is my job?*

I joined the Army National Guard in 2000, after seeing a commercial on TV that summer. It had young guys my age doing the sorts of army stuff I had dreamed about doing since I was in Junior ROTC in high school. But I grew up in a military family, and I had an idea of what active duty and real war might be like. I didn't want to be a real soldier. I thought I could join the guard, I could train as a soldier, but I wouldn't have to be a real one.

And then 9/11 happened, and not long after, I found myself on guard duty at the Golden Gate Bridge.

As time went on, some of us were pulled off that mission and sent to Afghanistan. And then the war in Iraq started, and they pulled more of us off. And it wasn't long until my unit was activated, and we were assigned to detainee operations in Guantanamo Bay.

When we got there, the camp commander told us, "This is the front line of the war on terror. We're getting good information, and we're saving lives. But make no mistake, these guys are highly trained Taliban and al-Qaeda commandos. They know how to resist our interrogation. They know how to organize inside a prison. They know how to manipulate you, and if you give them the chance, they will try to kill you."

It made us all very nervous, because we were not a military police unit. This was not our job. We were field artillery. We were trained to shoot the enemy from long distances. But this was the mission we were given, so we were going to do it the best we could.

The first time I walked inside that prison, gate after gate locked behind me. I passed through row after row of concertina wire, until I felt like I was locked inside there, and it was terrifying.

Every time, it was terrifying.

The prison was constructed of steel shipping containers that had been chopped up and reassembled with steel plates and wire mesh to create open-air prison blocks that held about fifty detainees each. Every time we went inside that prison, we put tape over our name tags on our uniforms and a patch over our unit insignia that said "MP." And every time we interacted with the detainees, or any of their belongings, we wore rubber surgical gloves.

The number one rule was to not socialize with the detainees. You don't talk about the weather. You don't talk about sports. You only talk about camp business.

As time went on, some of those detainees did live up to what the camp commander had told us about them. But the vast majority did not, and this was troubling.

One night, in the barracks, I confided in my roommate, and I said, "This mission seems crazy, man. I don't feel like what we're doing here is right. In fact, I feel like what I'm doing is wrong."

And he said, "Yeah, man, I know. I feel the same way. But isn't that how it's supposed to feel when you get sent off to do war stuff?"

And we never talked about that again, because the last thing you want your fellow soldiers or your commanders to think is that you're a terrorist sympathizer.

Eventually, I was assigned to a special mission inside the camp, as a guard on the mental health block. And there, the rules were inverted. We were encouraged to socialize with the detainees and get to know them, establish a rapport, so that we could manipulate their behavior and keep everyone safe. And on that block, there were a number of permanent residents.

There was the man in the rubber room.

There was another man who saw ghosts of his dead family.

There was another man who just paced back and forth in his cell, all day long. And he never said a word to me until one day when he asked for a soccer magazine. And at night, when he lay down on his bunk to go to sleep, you could see the paint worn off on the floor where he had been walking all day long.

But down at the end of the block, near the entrance, there was a guy we called Tony Blair. Someone on a previous shift had given him that nickname as a cruel joke. But Tony Blair was a decent guy. Ninety percent of the time, he was no problem at all. He spoke pretty good English. He knew a bunch of rap songs. He knew a bunch of jokes. And he was good at imitating the guards. And if Tony Blair liked you, he would insist on giving you a fist bump through the wire mesh when he saw you, and he'd call you his homeboy.

But one day, Tony Blair came back from interrogation, and his behavior changed. He started acting out and he got very depressed.

I asked him, "What happened?" and he said the interrogators had told him crazy things, and he didn't think he was ever going home.

The staff and the other guards started to retaliate against his behavior, and there was nothing I could do to protect him. But at least I didn't have to join in and treat him like an asshole.

One night, when I was walking the block, I came to his cell. And he was twisting up his bedsheet into a rope, and he was threading it through the steel mesh and preparing to hang himself. I'd seen this before. I panicked because this was my worst nightmare—to have a detainee kill himself on my watch.

I thought maybe I could run down to the end of the block and grab the suicide kit and the keys to open his cell and the scissors to cut him down. But I didn't want to leave him there long enough to hurt himself. So, I just stood there.

I said, "Tony Blair, come talk to me. Just come to the door. Come talk to me."

Eventually, he did come to the door, and I said, "Tony Blair, what's going on? Why are you doing this?"

He just looked at me and said, "Because I'm never going home," and he went back to preparing a noose.

I just kept pleading with him, "Tony Blair, come back to the door and talk to me. Just talk to me."

Eventually, he did come back to the door, and he just looked at me. And he said, "I won't kill myself if we're real friends."

I said, "Of course we're real friends. You're my homeboy," and I offered him a fist bump.

But he refused it.

He said, "No. If we're real friends, then we should shake hands like brothers."

Now I thought to myself, *This is what the camp commander was talking about. Tony Blair has been manipulating me. And as soon as I open that bean hole, and I give him my hand, he's going to stab me with one of the steel welding rods that were left inside the prison when they built this place*—we had found them on cell searches.

But another part of me thought, *Tony Blair is not a killer. He's just given up.* And so, I opened the bean hole, and I gave him my hand, and he still refused it.

He said, "No, not with rubber gloves, but like real brothers."

So I took my gloves off, and I gave him my hand.

And he just held it with both of his hands very gently.

He didn't say a word. He just looked at me.

I don't know how long we stood there. But for the first time in that prison, I felt like I had done something right.

Then he quietly let go of my hand, and he turned around, took the sheet down, lay down on his bunk, and went to bed.

Not long after that, I did my last shift on that block.

And on the last day, I walked down past his cell like I usually did, and I gave him a fist bump, and I said, "See you tomorrow, Tony Blair."

I never saw him again.

I spent four more years in the army after that. The last year, they held me over my contract and sent me to Iraq.

When I got home in 2008, I had no obligation left to the military. I just walked away.

But I never forgot about those detainees. I was curious, so I obtained some Freedom of Information Act documents and searched through them until I found who I thought was Tony Blair. I discovered that they had never charged or convicted him of anything and that they had released him.

And I don't know when they released him, and I don't know where they sent him, I just hope he made it home.

* ☺ *

JEREMY JENNINGS was born in Northern California but grew up in a military family living in Japan, New York City, California, and Virginia. Jeremy enlisted in the California Army National Guard in 2000 and served eight years in the field artillery. He was ordered to active duty after September 11, 2001, and served on a security team at the Golden Gate Bridge in San Francisco, California, before deploying to Guantanamo Bay, Cuba, for detainee operations in 2004; New Orleans for Hurricane Katrina relief in 2005; the California-Mexico border for Operation Jump Start in 2006; and Camp Taji, Iraq, in 2007. Today, Jeremy is a fish ecologist working in the Pacific Northwest.

This story was told on May 7, 2022, at the Alabama Shakespeare Festival in Montgomery. The theme of the evening was Lost and Found. Director: Meg Bowles.

SO MUCH, AND ENOUGH

ANAÏS BORDIER

Growing up, I always felt that my birthday wasn't the day I was born, but rather the day I arrived in Paris. When I was three months old, my parents came to pick me up at Charles de Gaulle Airport, and this was the day we became a family.

I always knew I was adopted. My mom told me that I was always in her heart, but it was another woman who gave birth to me.

I grew up in the suburbs of Paris as an only child. I was a happy, balanced kid who could sometimes feel really lonely. It was a loneliness that couldn't be filled by friends.

In darker moments, I felt abandoned and wondered if my birth parents didn't love me. Maybe that was the reason they decided to put me up for adoption.

But whenever I had questions, my parents would sit me down, and they would take my adoption files out of the desk drawer, and they would read the story to me. Even when I was able to read my adoption records myself, it was always the same story.

My birth parents were from Busan, South Korea. They met when they were really young. They started dating, but my birth father had to leave Busan for a job. My birth mother had become pregnant with me. She wasn't married, she was still studying at university, and because of social stigma at the time, she and her family decided to put me up for adoption.

I never felt the need to reach out to them because I had my mom and my dad who loved me. They were my real parents, so it didn't matter.

One day, I had just turned twenty-five, and I was studying fashion at Central Saint Martins in London. My friend sent me a screenshot of a YouTube video featuring me, except I had never made such a video. So, I clicked on the link and discovered a short, humorous video entitled "High School Virgin."

It was made by a kid called KevJumba in Los Angeles. And it was starring a girl who looked very much like me, except she had an American accent.

I was startled. I was trying to look for her name or information about her, but there was nothing. So, I thought it was just a coincidence, and I dropped it.

Then, a few months later, my friend tells me that he saw that *look-alike girl* again in a trailer for the film *21 & Over*.

I found her credit in the cast list—she was listed as "Asian girl."

Her name was Samantha Futerman. She was an American actress who had been in films such as *Memoirs of a Geisha*. She was born in South Korea on the nineteenth of November, 1987. I stopped right there. I thought that I read it wrong, because it said she was born the same day as *me*.

We had the same birth date.

We looked *really* similar.

I knew my adoption records by heart, and I thought it must just be a coincidence.

I immediately called my parents. I really wanted to talk to them.

My mom got on the phone, and she said, "Do you think she could be your twin sister?"

All of a sudden, I was relieved, because that's what I was thinking and when she said that, I thought maybe I wasn't totally insane. It also allowed me to think that something that should be impossible . . . might be possible.

I got my dad on the phone right after and told him the same thing. He googled her and found another website with a different birth date. He told me that I must have got it wrong, but it was, indeed, quite a funny coincidence.

Except to me, it didn't feel like *just* a coincidence.

I couldn't really focus that day. I was just wandering around like a zombie. I decided I would spend the rest of the day just *casually* stalking her on social media.

I discovered that she was an American actress living in Los Angeles.

We were, indeed, born the same day.

She was also adopted from South Korea.

She recently discovered that she wasn't born in Seoul, but in Busan.

I was also born in Busan.

So, I decided that I should try and reach out to her.

But how do I do it?

I didn't have her email address.

I could tweet her? "Hi, seems we might be related, so private message me" didn't seem quite appropriate.

So, I decided to send her a friend request on Facebook, along with a message quickly introducing myself.

I told her about the video—about the common birth dates and birthplace. I made a joke about *The Parent Trap* film and asked her not to freak out.

I waited for her answer for three days. I started feeling really down and thought I was crazy. Then finally, I received a notification on my phone saying that she accepted my friend request.

My heart was beating. I was jumping all around in anticipation of what she might say. She wasn't typing anything to me; instead she sent a picture of her adoption records. Then she said she didn't have much time to talk to me, but we would chat more in the coming days.

I had made first contact.

I read through her file, and it confirmed that we were born the same day, and in the same year. We were both adopted from South Korea—both born in Busan. But apart from this, *none* of our background stories matched.

I started thinking that maybe my dad was right, and maybe it was all just a coincidence.

For the next week, I was looking at all of her pictures, trying to discover what her life might be like. As we chatted on Facebook and got to know each other a little more, we decided it was time to Skype.

It was the weirdest experience, when both our faces appeared on the screen.

I didn't know where to look. I was like, *Uh, no . . . that's her.*

We looked *identical.*

Where do you start? I wanted to ask, and I wanted to say, so many things at the same time. The call lasted about three hours. It was the middle of the night, and when it was time to hang up, I didn't really want to.

As we chatted more, she started to feel like a long-lost friend, or a friend that you haven't seen in a while and you dearly miss—except we'd never met.

We decided it was time to meet in person, but my dad, who was quite protective, said that we might want to take a DNA test before everyone got too emotionally involved.

Dr. Nancy Segal, who specialized in twins, helped us arrange the DNA test. She also warned us that there was a great chance we might just be doppelgangers.

It would take a few weeks to get the test results, but it was so intense that regardless of what the outcome might be, we really wanted to meet. So, we decided to meet in London and hear the test results together.

Samantha, her two older brothers, and her parents flew from America. My parents came from Paris. On the day we were going to meet, I woke up, I got dressed, and I remember looking up at the sky as I was walking toward the Airbnb in Shoreditch where the meeting would happen. I was thinking, *Oh my God, she might be in that plane right now. She's getting closer.*

My mom and I were in front of the flat, standing at the door, and I could hear loud voices behind it.

This was about to happen.

I stepped into the room, and it felt like two parallel universes suddenly merged together.

She was right in front of me.

It looked like I was seeing a mirror image of myself, except she wasn't moving as I was moving.

It took my brain a minute to readjust.

Then she started laughing hysterically—I did too.

We felt like two magnets that were attracted to each other, but also we had this very special force that would repel us from each other.

My mom, who was standing behind me the whole time, said, "Oh my God, I have another daughter."

My dad, who was, from the beginning, always warning that we might just be doppelgangers said, "Okay, I don't think you need a DNA test."

We went for lunch, and we were just observing each other.

We were staring at each other.

Everyone around us was just chatting.

We were amazed by our resemblance. We had a similar loud laugh, and our mannerisms were the same.

After lunch and experiencing all the emotions of our meeting, we suddenly both felt like we really needed to rest, so we decided to take a nap together, in the same bed.

That might seem quite strange, but at the time, it felt really natural. And it *was* really natural. We were chatting, and eventually, we fell asleep next to each other.

When I woke up, I felt this incredible sense of relief. It felt like we were being born again, but into the same world this time— together.

Later that evening, we sat down in front of our laptop, and we waited for Dr. Segal to call us on Skype. She was quite serious. She looked at us, and asked us to turn toward each other, and hug and kiss our identical twin sister.

She said, "DNA doesn't lie."

She gave us the *final* proof that this was all true.

We were really twins, separated at birth, both adopted on two different continents, who had found each other, through social media, at twenty-five years old.

Today, we still don't know what happened to our birth parents, or why we were given up separately, or which of our stories is true, but we remain open to the opportunities that life might bring us, including uncovering our past and having the chance to know our birth family. I'm no longer that young girl who felt abandoned. I went from being an only child to having a twin sister, two older brothers, and even more parents living in America.

Sam and I both have a big, extended family, and this is so much, and enough, to be happy about.

The fact that we met is a miracle. But the most important thing is that, from now on, we have so much life to live together, and now we know that our lives are intertwined forever.

* 🌀 *

ANAÏS BORDIER graduated from the fashion design program at Central Saint Martins in London and, after her MBA in luxury brand marketing and international management, she started working in France as a brand manager for her family-owned French luxury leather goods company, Manufacture Jean Rousseau.

This story was told on September 29, 2018, at the Union Chapel in London. The theme of the evening was Out of the Blue. Director: Meg Bowles.

ANGRY
AMBER ABUNDANCE

One time I woke up in the middle of the night, and my mom was praying over me. Just her in the dark sitting there having a little talk with Jesus over her badass daughter. See, when I was young, I had terrible anger issues.

One time at a family dinner, when I was about seven years old, I'm not sure what my uncle did besides breathe too hard in my direction. But I responded by calling him a "purple bastard."

When kids act like that, people think something's wrong at home. But honestly, my family was amazing. We laughed as much as we cried. We loved each other boldly and loudly. But we were living paycheck to paycheck, and I hated it.

My mom was a visionary, truly. She would turn the electricity being cut off until her paycheck came into these candlelit dinners. But as time went on, I could start to feel how much she worried and how hard she worked and how we never seemed to quite have everything we needed.

And it made me angry. It made me mad.

I was acting up at home, at school, even at church. So, my mom decided to take me to therapy. *Yes,* my Black mother took her Black child to therapy, okay?

And that was around the time I started getting nervous. Ten-year-old Amber was nervous because my mom had voluntarily taken me to white folks to talk about my issues.

I was sure this was the first step to ending up on *Maury,* where they yell in the kid's face and send them off to boot camp. Like I really wanted that for my life.

So, she takes me to this children's hospital, and as we're about to go in, she looks down at me, and she gives her speech: "Now, don't go in here and show your ass."

We walk into the building, and I sit with this perfectly fine white man for an hour telling him all about my life as this little Black girl growing up in Columbus, Ohio, with my two sisters. Raised by my mom and all of my family members who happen to live in a ten-mile radius of our home.

After I laid my little burdens down to this complete stranger— I'm sorry, my *therapist*—my mom came back into the room, and he gave her an update. And it had the perfect balance of respecting our new patient-doctor relationship, while also giving my mom the information she needed.

He said, "Amber shared a lot of feelings of fear and helplessness. Her hostility seems to be rooted in her feeling of lack of control because she doesn't have any money. So, I think that you should consider giving Amber an allowance."

I instantly felt betrayed. How did I explain this so wrong? If *I* don't have the money, it's *because my mom* doesn't have the money; we're broke *together;* we're *in this* together.

We leave, and she looks at me, and she says, "I will never make you go back there again."

So, at least we were on the same page. I think at this point my mom was really tired of her needs and the needs of her children not being met by these medical professionals.

And I was tired for her . . . but not tired enough to stop showing my ass.

You should also know that I grew up in a type of family that was always at church. So, if your grandparents weren't on the leadership of the deaconess and deacon board, you simply don't know my pain, baby—I was *always* in church. And around the height of my behavior problems, my mom became a secretary at our church. During that time, she became really good friends with a person I would grow to know and love as Aunt Gail.

Aunt Gail attended our church, and she was *amazing*. She was one of those people who knew the Lord *personally*. Her God was like that one auntie who would shake a twenty-dollar bill in your hand at the family dinner when you were on your last dime and unsure if your gas tank would even make it back home. Her God had seen her through some things.

And she sang. It was one of the things I loved about Aunt Gail. She could sing the Holy Spirit into any room. She was one of those "never shall a rock cry out in my name" praisers. She would bring her own instruments to church and would queue up her own solos from the pew even while the choir was singing—there was my Aunt Gail with the tambourine.

And I loved that about her. I couldn't wait to grow up and have that kind of audacity. But I was also afraid of Aunt Gail because Aunt Gail was one of those born-again Christians. Meaning, she was raised in the church—dipped out to have her little fun for a couple of years—and then made her return (a resubscribed Christian, if you will).

She was also the type of Christian who carried an *Our Daily Bread* devotional booklet in her purse next to her pack of Newports. And that told me that she was a *cussing* Christian. And so was I! But I was ten, and a kid, and shouldn't have been cussing.

So, another time I got a phone call home from school, this time for calling my teacher a "turtle-looking-ass bitch."

Creative.

That's when I woke up to my mom praying over me. And it

wasn't like she started by turning my mental health over to the Lord—she did seriously try other options. But now she was going to go with prayer and classic family shaming.

Black mothers are known for telling everybody your business (especially when you have shown your ass). And my mom told the last person on Earth I wanted to know, which was Aunt Gail.

Another thing you should know about Aunt Gail is when she wasn't singing and praising the Lord and catching the Holy Spirit on Sundays, she was known for crocheting during Bible study on Wednesdays. And I loved that about her too and wanted to learn.

So, after I got the call home from school, I come to church on Sunday, and I see her across the pews. And she looks at me and points and gives one of these "Come talk to me" looks. I drag my feet over, knowing she knew what I did.

She says, "I hear you want to learn how to crochet."

That was not what I was expecting.

And I look at her, and I say, "Yes."

And she says, "Yes what?"

I say, "Yes, ma'am."

The classic call and response between adults who are not your little friend and small Black children who are kind of trying their luck.

She tells me, "Tomorrow you're coming over to my house. I'm going to teach you how to crochet."

I was like, "Okay, good deal."

So, my mom picks me up from school, takes me over to Aunt Gail's house. And this time she let me hop out of the car without giving her "Now, don't go in here and show your ass" speech.

I think we both knew I was no match for Aunt Gail.

I go into Aunt Gail's house, and it has that incense smell. I like to call it "Auntiecore," where there's mail on the table, plastic on certain things that don't need plastic for that long.

She tells me her real story—the story underneath her testimony: "I don't look like what I've been through"—of when she *only* carried that pack of Newports.

And then she shows me how to crochet. She hands me a needle and ball of yarn, and she picks up *her* needle and ball of yarn. I watch her as she starts her first row. I copy everything she does. It looks like her hands are in a groove of her pattern as she's starting out her first knits. And I think I'm following, until it becomes clear to me that mine looks nothing like hers.

I say, "Mine doesn't look like that."

And she looks at me over her glasses, and she says, "And getting frustrated isn't going to help it look like that either."

Me, obviously frustrated: "I'm not frustrated. I just want it to be right, and this looks a mess."

She puts down her needle and yarn, and she says, "Look at your hands."

I stop right as these tears start to come into my eyes, because I'm getting angry, and I look at my cramping hands. My pattern was inflexible and rigid, whereas it seemed like she was just flowing with her work.

She says, "The number one rule of crocheting is *tension*. Tension determines what your pattern will look like. If your tension is too loose, your pattern will be loose and have holes in it. And if the tension is too tight, your pattern will be inflexible and rigid. Without controlling and maintaining your tension, you can't do shit. You can't make a potholder, let alone a blanket, without controlling and maintaining your tension. Do you understand?"

I say, "Yes."

She says, "Yes what?"

"Yes, ma'am, I understand."

In that moment, Aunt Gail *spoke* to my anger, where everyone up until that moment tried to *shrink* it.

Even if it meant shrinking me with it.

She taught me that you have to *use* that anger; you can't just get rid of it.

I'm grown now, and I still get *very* angry. I still feel the tension come into my body when I think about how this country treats poor Black people. It makes me *angry* that in life, George Floyd was assumed to not have twenty dollars, but in death, he was able to raise millions. It makes me *angry* that it took what felt like a literal crack in the universe for people to understand that *Black folks* are human beings who *of course* matter. And it makes me *angry* that I feel like I'm yelling into a void that Black *queer* people, Black *trans* people, Black *women,* Black *lesbians* are not only *worthy* to be *celebrated* but to be *fought for.*

So, I use tension, and I get to the root of my anger in systematic issues, instead of letting it control me.

And, *yes,* I still come into places and *show my ass*.

AMBER ABUNDANCE is a storyteller, filmmaker, and art director. She creates world-building narratives using warm visuals and vulnerable performances through her lens of being a Fat Black Queer femme Auntie from the Midwest. Amber recently released her first short film, *Abundance,* about the limitations and radical possibilities of identity. Amber is the producer, writer, and performer of *Abundance,* which was most recently a 2021 BlackStar Film Festival selection and won the audience award for Best Short Narrative. You can experience more of Amber's work on Instagram and Twitter @AmberAbundance and at AmberAbundance.com.

This story was recorded at a live performance at Alice Tully Hall at Lincoln Center for the Performing Arts in New York City on October 19, 2022. The theme of the evening was Great Expectations. Directors: Catherine Burns and Jodi Powell.

A THPOONFUL
OF THUGAR
PHIL WANG

I was eleven years old. I was living in Malaysian North Borneo. The year was 2001, and high off the adrenaline of surviving Y2K, my tiny primary school, in essentially a bit of seaside jungle, decides to put on a production of *Mary Poppins*. It will be its most ambitious play to date, and it had done . . . one.

Auditions were announced, and instantly the school was awash with gossip and conjecture.

When will rehearsals begin?

Who will win the eponymous role of Poppins?

What *is* a play?

Now, I want to be Burt *badly*. I loved the film *Mary Poppins,* and Dick Van Dyke's portrayal of the charming chimney sweep with his devil-may-care attitude toward social mores, and what constituted a Cockney accent, led me to believe that truly anything was possible.

The day of the audition arrived, and in that sweaty tropical classroom, I have to say, I bloody nailed it.

I was big and boisterous, fun and fabulous.

Burt was *mine*.

I strolled over to Pam, our Australian librarian and play director, to victoriously collect my chimney sweep brush and flat cap.

Pam asks me if there's a part in the play I'd want in particular.

"Ah, yeah, just a little bit, Pam. Burt, please."

At this point, Pam looks me up and down and goes, "Hmm. Okay. One question, Phil: Can you dance?"

Now, she says these words, "Can you dance?" in a way that I now know would be described as *pointedly.*

The problem Pam has noticed, and that I have not, is that the part of Burt requires quite a lot of athleticism and dancing. He twirls over rooftops and spins graciously into chalk drawings, and I was quite possibly the *fattest* boy in Borneo. Really huge. Very, very big.

I was an eleven-year-old boy in the body of a darts player on Boxing Day.

Pam suggests instead the part of Mr. Banks, the father.

I protest, but Pam assures me the role is more suited to my abilities. Mr. Banks is erudite and mature, and, most important, stationary.

I argue and argue but then graciously accept.

I'm a bit disappointed at first, but pretty soon I really get into the part of Mr. Banks and the process of rehearsing. I start practicing on my own at home, singing the songs and doing the lines.

One day my mother overhears me practicing, and she comes over, and she says, "Phil, congratulations on the part. Would you like to do something about your lisp?"

Now, I had never heard the word *lisp* before, so I was quite incredulous and a little bit angry, actually.

I said, "Lithp? What's a lithp?"

She says, "That is, dear. You can't say your *s*'s properly."

And I go, "Don't be ridiculoth. I'm fine."

And she says, "Are you sure?"

And I'm like, "Yeth!"

Now, I was cynical about my mother's claims because I knew my mother—I still do. She's a big worrier, my mother. She worries too much. And I was convinced that this lisp thing was just something she'd made up to satisfy her own sick addiction to panic.

It's just the way she is. My mother imbued in me two core values that have held on to this day—feminism and anxiety.

You might find it strange for me to describe anxiety as a value, but I assure you that your belief in the redistribution of wealth or cultural relativism does not enjoy the enthusiasm with which I still believe I've left the shower on.

Feminism and morbid anxiety. My mother has always wanted her children to know two things—that women are equal to men and that death is always around the corner.

So I ignore it. I let go of this lisping thing, and I move on. I continue going to rehearsals in *blithful* ignorance.

And the preparations for what must've been history's most humid production of *Mary Poppins* are going pretty well. We were not messing about.

We had a house—17 Cherry Tree Lane was *built*. One of the parents, Mr. Hei, was an engineer and built the house in two stories, with a living room, and a bedroom, and magical drawers that, through a system of pulleys and strings, would close with one of Poppins's twists of her wrist.

The rehearsals were not going quite as well. Teaching a bunch of Asian kids the full work of P. L. Travers and expecting them to memorize it is about as challenging as it sounds.

Malaysia is quite a culturally mixed place as well, and if Pam was not concerned with my lisp, it was only because she had about twenty different accents to deal with. Most notably, our Mary Poppins— a twelve-year-old Filipino girl, also by the name of Mary, with the voice of Whitney Houston but the accent of a twelve-year-old Filipino girl.

You've not seen the true beauty of multiculturalism until you've seen a little Southeast Asian child belt a world-class rendition of "A Spoonful of Sugar" before sternly telling Jane and Michael to brush their "teats."

But still, I'm enjoying the process. I'm getting ahold of my lines, I'm loving the songs, and all's going swimmingly in camp Phil.

Until the day of the cast recording.

We recorded a full cast album—we were not messing around.

A recording studio had just opened up in town, and its first signings were the children of Datuk Simon Fung Primary School.

We bowl into this recording studio, one by one. All the main cast, the singing roles and each of the soloists, go in to record their songs.

First, Jane and Michael:

If you want this choice position, have a cheery disposition.

Mary goes in:

Stay awake, don't brush your teats.

And then it's my turn.

I swagger in with all the gusto of a chubby eleven-year-old boy. And I sing Mr. Banks's song. I come back into the listening booth, and they play it back to me.

And that's when I hear it.

My lisp.

Clear as day. No ambiguity about it.

And I found my lisp out in the cruclcst of ways, with thc cruclcst of songs. Mr. Banks's big introductory solo starts:

I feel a thurge of deep thatithfaction,
Much ath a king athtride hith noble thteed.

Ath I returned from daily thtrife to hearth and wife,
How pleathant ith the life I lead.

They gave the kid with a lisp a song that was essentially a tongue twister for kids with lisps.

Now, I'm appalled. I'm so, so terribly upset. First of all, because my mother had been proved right, and that's always dreadful. But mostly because this was the first time I had been shown that how I saw myself was not always the same as how I was seen by others. It was a bitter pill to take.

I was just confused. Where did this lisp come from? Did I always have it? Had I just got so fat my cheeks had started growing inward and got in the way of my tongue? What I did know was I had to fix it.

Cue the Rocky montage.

At each of our many rehearsals, I'm sitting there doing my lines, pulling my tongue painfully back behind my teeth where it doesn't feel right. Hissing out this strange new sound with mixed results.

I feel a thurge of deep ssatith . . . sssatithfaction . . . satisfaction.

All the while, trying to keep this a secret from my friends, and the teachers.

I'm practicing at home. It takes diligence and practice and determination. I battle this daily war against myself—this war against my own speech impediment, strolling up and down the garden, practicing the lines out loud:

It's that Poppinth woman; it's Poppins that's done this.

But I feel I'm making progress.
Soon though, time is up.

The first night is fast approaching, and it's looking good. Preparations are coming together. The costumes are made. The cardboard hats are put on the heads of little prepubescent Chinese boys.

Mr. Hei has really outdone himself on a working carousel and flying chairs that are as incredible as they are terribly dangerous.

It really feels like the whole town has come together to make this thing happen. My mother also had her part to play. She was charged with the job of designing the front of a newspaper that I had to hold in one scene. And the Edwardian headlines she went for were:

Mrs. Pankhurst: Clapped in Irons Again

and

Titanic: Greatest Ship Ever Set Sail from Belfast

Because my mother wants children to know two things:

That women are equal to men.
And death is always around the corner.

Pretty soon, the curtains rise, and the play begins. As the overture starts, and I stand there, time is up. It's now or never.

Pretty soon my entrance comes on, and I strut onto the stage—bold, determined   round.

I get my first few lines out before the first volley of *s*'s hit. But hell, I go for them:

Money's sound, credit rates are moving up, up, up.
And the British pound is the admiration of the world.

I've done it!

I've cured my lisp.

I'm king of the *s*'s.

I'm on top of the world!

And then my song starts—my big introductory solo. And this is when I remember that we aren't singing the songs live. We can't be heard over the music.

We're lip syncing, like it's *RuPaul's Drag Race*—the underage and Asian special.

Lip syncing, of course, to the cast album.

And so, I have no choice but to go for it. And in front of three hundred people, I lip sync to,

I feel a thurge of deep thatithfaction,
Much ath a king athtride hith noble thteed.

But you know, it's okay. Because this serves as a reminder of what I had just overcome. This past self that I had fixed, corrected, with sheer determination and force of will.

And what's more, from the audience, a sound begins to ripple. A sound which I begin a long and vital addiction to.

Laughter.

A sound, which to this day, makes me feel a surge of deep satisfaction.

* ⚀ *

PHIL WANG is a British Malaysian stand-up comedian, writer, and actor. He released his first Netflix special, *Philly Philly Wang Wang,* in 2021 and has since performed stand-up on *Late Night with Seth Meyers* (NBC) and been interviewed by chat show royalty on *That's My Time with David Letterman* (Netflix). His first book, *Sidesplitter: How to Be from Two Worlds at Once,* was named a *Times* and *Sunday Times* Book of the Year.

Phil regularly performs stand-up to sold-out crowds around the world, and his other notable television credits include *Inside Amy Schumer* (Comedy Central), *Life & Beth* (Hulu), *The Comedy Line-Up* (Netflix), and *Taskmaster* (Channel 4).

This story was told on September 20, 2019, at the Union Chapel in London. The theme of the evening was Fish out of Water. Director: Meg Bowles.

BLUE GENES

CARMEN RITA WONG

I was born in uptown Manhattan in the 1970s to a Chinese father and a Dominican mother. Now, there was no mistaking that my mother was my mother. Guadalupe Altagracia a.k.a. Lupe—she was the constant in my life and very much my Latin mama.

When I was a toddler, though, she divorced my Chinese father, Papi Wong, as I call him, but my older brother and I still saw him on the weekends and here and there. And we loved it because he'd take us to Chinatown for shopping and to our favorite restaurants. I loved the ones that had the fancy chopsticks that went *click, click*. And even though he didn't live with us, I was raised as his daughter. I was raised as a Wong.

Now, my mother didn't stay single long. She remarried, and we picked up and moved from Harlem to New Hampshire. I've got to say, my stepfather, my new dad, Charlie, he was like a dad out of the Golden Books when you were kids, right? He was a white guy, wore a suit and tie, carried a briefcase to work every day, and came home at the same time Monday through Friday to dinner on the table.

Well, little Carmen thought she had hit the American daddy jackpot. But the best thing he gave me were my four little sisters, who I loved and adored. Pains in the butts, but I loved them so much, and I wanted to be a part of that family. I wanted him to be *my* daddy too.

But he wasn't.

And so, I grew up always feeling like an outsider, like an *other*.

And you better believe in 1980s New Hampshire, I *was* an other. I might as well have been an alien that landed there—an unwelcome alien—in a place that was supposed to be my home. The kids would make fun of me, pulling up their eyes or bucking their teeth or using all these new creative slurs that were thrown my way for being brown, and every once in a while even the grownups would get on that train.

When I was in fourth grade, at parent-teacher conferences, Sister Rachel said to my mother—my Latin mother, mind you—that the reason why I was getting all these straight A's was "because of Carmen's Chinese side."

Now, I may have been only nine years old, but I knew enough to be insulted and embarrassed for my mother and me. I liked Sister Rachel a lot less after that because here's the thing: Even though my mother wasn't the Asian parent, she was what some people would call a tiger mom, right? Lupe expected excellence from me at all times.

If I dared to bring home anything but an A, she would say, "Well, are you an A, or are you a B?"

Lupe saw education as a way of escaping her fate, working full time at fifteen years old to help support her family, married off by her father at nineteen, and there at that conference night in her thirties, pregnant with her fifth child. She wanted more for me.

In the car ride home from that parent-teacher conference, though, I was still pissed, and I just had to ask, "Mommy, Mommy, Sister Rachel said I'm smart because of Papi. Because I'm Chinese."

And my mother, the parent who was actually present, the one

who would kick my butt if I didn't do well in school, she kept her eyes straight on the road, but there was a little smile.

She shrugged, and she said, "That's okay," and in that smile, which was more of a smirk, I realized there were a lot of things my mother wasn't telling me.

See, Mommy came from a world of secrets. The 1950s, 1960s Dominican Republic, this was a place where speaking your mind or telling the truth could get you beaten or killed or kidnapped in the middle of the night. Like my grandfather who was tortured but then who later escaped the hospital dressed as a woman by his sisters. I mean, talk about *secrets*. This is cloak-and-dagger on a family level. This was my mother's normal. Wow.

But when I was in my thirties, my mother received a devastating cancer diagnosis, and for the first time in her life she was about to lose control of the narrative. My stepfather, Charlie, called me months after we found out that she was sick and said he needed to see me urgently and alone.

A couple of weeks later I'm sitting across the kitchen table from him, and he says to me, "Carmen, Papi Wong is not your father. I am."

Now, the first thing that came to my mind was, one, *I'm not Chinese anymore?*

And two, *Goddamn you two.*

All these years that I had so much wanted to be a part of that family, that picture-book American family—*his family*—and they both knew. It was painful.

I had to confirm this story, of course, with my mother, who I then told. And she confirmed it pretty much with a lot more dramatic flair. She was mostly just upset that he had gotten to me before she did.

"But, Mommy, you have stage four colon cancer. How long were you going to wait?"

So, there were many tears and questions and blame, but I made peace with my mother before she passed the following year. My relationship with Charlie, however, unfortunately has never been exactly the same. How could it be?

Well, years go by, and now we're living in a time when genetic testing is available to everybody, to the public, and affordable. And if there's one thing my family loves, it's a sale. So, last holiday season we all bought up a bunch of 23andMe kits and took the tests at the same time. I got my results back first, and I'm opening that app, and what I'm expecting to see is a confirmation of this family secret, right? I'm expecting to see that I'm half Charlie, which is Italian, and then half my mother, which would be African and Spanish.

Well, that's not what I saw: Portuguese. It says I'm *half Portuguese*.

I frantically texted my sister Nina.

She texted right back; she said, "Oh, don't worry about it, okay? Relax. Just wait until we all get our results back, and we connect, right? Because once we see our relationships, and we connect our data, then we'll know what's right, right?"

So I pick up the phone and call my brother.

He says pretty much the same thing; he says, "Don't worry about it. You know what? Maybe it's a mix-up. Once we connect and see our relationships, and we're all linked up, then you'll see. Plus, Italy and Portugal are kind of close to each other."

No, no, that's not what happened once we all connected. Now, remember my sister Nina, my baby sister, I'm supposed to be the same as her. I was supposed to be a *full sibling*. And there it was, in large, extra-large font: *half sister.*

There was a third father.

Six kids in my family, and I didn't share a father with any of them. I felt so alone.

But damn it, I was going to solve this mystery. So, I went digging in the past, and I dug up my godmother I hadn't spoken to in twenty years.

I tracked her down, and I called her up, and I said, "Pimpa . . ."—

this is her nickname, we called her Pimpa—"we all took this genetic test, and we found out that I have a different father from everybody."

And she was really surprised because Pimpa, she thought she knew all my mother's secrets. She was my mother's best friend. She lived down the hall from us growing up, and she was a scholar now: She was a dual PhD. She looked at historical records to find shipwrecks in the Caribbean.

My godmother was a treasure hunter. That's what I wanted right now. That's what I needed.

But she was surprised because even though she knew that Papi Wong was not my father—it seems like everybody knew that Papi Wong was not my father—she also thought that it had been Charlie.

I said, "No, Pimpa. It says I'm Portuguese."

"Oh. The optometrist on Delancey Street."

"What was his name?"

"Aye, *mija,* how can I remember his name? That was almost fifty years ago. Listen, your mother, don't judge your mother. She was lonely. Papi was already kicked out of the house, and so she was dating. And I was babysitting your brother on the days when the optometrist would come and pick her up. So yeah, there was Charlie and then the optometrist. She had a part-time job at an optician's shop on Delancey Street. But he's dead."

My heart could barely take it.

Have people thought about the fact that with genetic testing we're looking at the end of family secrets? You're looking at the members of probably the last generation whose parents could futz around about their futzing around. Here's the thing, my origin story, as I like to call it, or mystery, is still happening to this day. But here's what I do know:

I know that Lupe did everything she could, and came so far, and did so much to give me options.

I know that Charlie raised me as if I was one of his own: I used to talk with him about the stock market to bond, and I ended up hosting my own daily finance TV show on CNBC.

And Papi Wong, well, he taught me the street hustle that helped get me there.

I got a good deal, but I rail at my mother Lupe's ghost sometimes, for leaving out this incredibly important detail of my life, and I ask her to visit me in my dreams to drop a hint or a clue as to who it is I'm looking at when I look in the mirror.

The morning after I talked to Pimpa, I called my sister Nina.

I said, "Nina, what if I never find out who this man is?"

And Nina, who's super Zen, said, "You know, does it really matter, girl? Because you know who you are. You know who you are."

She's right.

* ☉ *

CARMEN RITA WONG is the author of *Why Didn't You Tell Me?: A Memoir.* She is a writer, producer, and nonprofit board leader, including the board of The Moth, and the former vice chair of the Planned Parenthood Federation of America. She is the former co-creator and television host of *On the Money* on CNBC and was a national advice columnist for *Glamour, Latina, Essence, Men's Health,* and *Good Housekeeping.* She has written for *The New York Times; O, The Oprah Magazine;* and *Oprah Daily.* A member of President Obama's "Business Forward" initiative to further African American, Latino, and Asian business owners, Carmen was also a faculty professor of behavior economics at New York University and is the author of two bestselling financial advice books. She also authored a novel series, created and hosts the podcast *The Carmen Show: Life, Money + No Apologies,* and invests in and advises female-led and -owned businesses, productions, and content. Carmen is always working on her next book and lives in Manhattan with her daughter and their two pups.

This story was told on October 18, 2019, at the Tarrytown Music Hall in Tarrytown. The theme of the evening was A More Perfect Union. Director: Catherine Burns.

DO WE KNOW HOW TO GRIEVE?

FRANCINE LOBIS WHEELER

It was Christmas morning, December 25, 2012, about eleven in the morning.

We had just opened presents, and I turned to my husband, David, and I said, "I can't sleep. I can't eat. I can't breathe."

And he said, "Honey, just try to relax. Go lay down."

I said, "No, I can't. I can't."

I was like that because eleven days before, on December 14, 2012, our son Ben was murdered in his first-grade classroom at Sandy Hook Elementary School.

So, that Christmas morning, I really couldn't do anything, but David convinced me to go lay down; so I did. I was so exhausted that I immediately fell asleep. As soon as I was asleep, I looked to the side of the bed, and there was Ben. He didn't say anything. He just opened the palm of my hand, he kissed it, and closed the palm of my hand, and I woke up.

I ran to David, and I said, "Oh my gosh, D. Ben came to me, and he kissed my hand, and I know why."

He said, "Why?"

I said, "Because of the book I used to read to him, *The Kissing Hand,* where the mother—the mother raccoon—she kisses her son

Chester's hand when he's scared to go to school. And she says, 'Just know that my love for you is always there.'"

And that's what Ben gave me that day.

After that, I was asking him to come back. *Please come back, show me another sign. Please come visit me, please, please, please. I miss you so much.*

And sure enough, a couple of weeks later, he did. He came back in another dream, and in this dream, I was standing in an elevator on the second floor, and I went to the first floor, and then I went to the basement, and the doors opened, and there was Ben.

He said, "Mommy, you made it. I'm so glad," and we hugged, and we kissed.

I said, "I love you."

And he said, "I love you."

And it was real.

He said, "Mama, I'm happy, but we're really worried about you. Don't let them trademark you."

Now, when Ben was alive, he wanted to be smart, like his big brother, Nate. He would often use these very long words to try and sound smart, but sometimes the words didn't always match the sentence.

So, in the dream, I said to him, "Are you sure you mean *trademark?*"

And he said it again, "Don't let them trademark you, Mama."

And then, I woke up.

I told everybody about the dream: "What do you think he meant by *trademark*? Do you think he meant the Sandy Hook shooting?"

When you lose somebody that traumatically, that violently, suddenly you go back, and you rethink things. And I kept thinking about the last day of his life over and over and over again in my head.

It was an interesting morning because I was getting Nate and

Ben ready for school, and I suddenly remembered that Nate had book club, and I said, "Oh my gosh, guys. I forgot. We've got to drop off Nate first. All right, get your stuff together. We've got to move."

I'm trying to clean up, and I'm stacking the dishwasher, and Benny comes over to me and he says, "Mama, what does forgiveness mean?"

And I was like, "Oh, Ben, why are you asking me this right now? Come on, we've got to go."

And he said again, "No, no, Mommy, what is forgiveness?"

And I said, "I don't know, Ben. It's like when you do something wrong, and the other person forgets about it. Now, come on, we've got to go."

So, I pack them up, we get in the car, we drop off Nate, and I say to Ben, "Okay, Ben, do you want to go back home and wait for the bus, or do you want to go to Starbucks for a treat?"

He said, "Starbucks."

So, we went to Starbucks, and he ordered a chocolate milk. (I used to tell the story and say hot chocolate, but then I found the receipt—it was chocolate milk.)

We sat down, and he said, "You know what, Mama? I'm going to be an architect when I grow up."

I said, "Wow, Ben, that's amazing."

And he said, "No, wait, wait. I'm going to be an architect *and* a paleontologist because Nate is going to be a paleontologist, and I have to do everything Nate does."

I said, "Well, you're your own person, Ben. You don't have to do whatever your brother does."

And he said, "Oh, no, no. No, I'm always going to be with Nate, I love Nate, and I love you, Mommy."

And I said, "I love you too. It's so nice to just be here, just the two of us. We never get the chance to do that."

And then, he said, "Mommy, can I have your iPhone?"

So, I gave him the iPhone, and a couple of minutes later, I took him to school, and a half hour later, he was dead.

I kept reliving that over and over and over. Did it happen? Was it that special? Did we really say "I love you" to one another? What was that? I kept asking him in my dreams if we really had that conversation. What did he mean about being trademarked?

And in the meantime, Newtown, where the school is, it just explodes like a bomb has gone off, and everybody is traumatized. And there are grief counselors and trauma specialists flying in from all over the country, trying to help us make some sense of any of it.

And while this is all going on, I just can't breathe. But I still have to raise my other child. So, I take my son Nate to Lego Camp one day in the middle of all of this craziness. I walk in the door, and I see these women.

They're talking, and they look at me, and they stop talking, and then I keep walking, and I could have sworn I heard one of them say [in a whisper], "She lost her son at Sandy Hook."

Another time I go to the grocery store, because I still have to get groceries, and I'm shopping, and I see this woman. She looks at me; she starts to cry. She goes in the other direction.

Most of the time I'd run into somebody I sort of knew in the grocery store, and they'd say, "Hi, Fran, how are you? Oh my God, I shouldn't have said that. Oh, I don't know what to say."

And I'd say, "I don't know what to say."

And then, they'd say, "I think about you all the time. If there's anything you ever need. We should get the boys together."

And I'd say, "I'd like that. That would be great."

But they wouldn't call, and I thought, *I just want people around me.*

One time, I am running a 5k for my son Ben's charity. I'm doing the run, and I meet this other runner.

He says, "Tell me about your son's charity."

I said, "Well, it's in honor of my son Ben who died at Sandy Hook School."

He said, "Oh my God, really?"

I said, "Yeah."

And he said, "Oh, I remember where I was that day, on December fourteenth."

And I thought to myself, *Please don't tell me where you were that day. I don't want to know.*

But he did.

He said, "Oh yeah, we were going to have a Christmas party for my company. We heard about all those kids and teachers getting shot. So, we canceled the party. We gave all that money to Sandy Hook. And I went home and hugged my kids. It was an awful day."

"Yeah."

I was so pissed at him. I couldn't understand why he would say that.

And I think Ben warned me because we *have* been trademarked. Every time the name *Sandy Hook* is mentioned, people will make assumptions about us, about Ben, and project onto us what *they* think about Sandy Hook.

But then one day, I was out, and this woman came up to me, and she said, "I don't know if you know me, but I'm from Sandy Hook."

I thought, *Oh God, please don't tell me. Don't tell me how this makes you feel. I don't want to know. I really don't want to know.*

And she said, "I happened to be at Starbucks on the morning of December fourteenth."

And I said, "Oh."

She said, "I'm not really in the habit of eavesdropping, but I happened to notice what a beautiful conversation you were having with your son that day. And I thought maybe you'd want to know."

I said, "Thank you," and I started to weep and weep.

And she said, "Oh my God, I'm so sorry. I didn't mean to upset you."

I said, "Oh, no, no, no, no. You have no idea what you did."

She gave me such a gift—verifying that this beautiful goodbye conversation with Ben really happened.

I've had almost nine years without Ben, and in that time I've often imagined what life would have been like if he had survived the shooting. And I bet I would have said something stupid or put my foot in my mouth or said too much or made it about me when I talked to a victim's family.

And I get it because we don't know how to grieve in this country. We don't know how to grieve in our culture. And I'm not mad at those people anymore. I forgive them.

What is forgiveness, Mommy? It's when somebody does something wrong and the other person forgets about it.

Don't let them trademark you. That's a little different. My husband, David, and I do not have the luxury of not being trademarked by the Sandy Hook shooting because our son Ben died that day. But nobody can trademark my kissing hand; my beautiful conversation at Starbucks; or the six years, three months, and two days that our son Ben lived. Nobody can trademark my love for him.

FRANCINE LOBIS WHEELER is an actor, singer, songwriter, teacher, wife, and mother to three boys. She has performed in regional theaters and sung with swing bands and recording artists.

Francine is the creative director of Ben's Lighthouse, a nonprofit promoting empathy and compassion for children, and she runs their summer camp based on her original programming, puppetry, and music from her children's program *The Isle of Skoo.*

Currently, Francine and her creative team are in preproduction on her teleplay *Just Five Minutes,* to be filmed and streamed. With music and book written by Francine, *Just Five Minutes* is her journey through grief, trauma, and survival after the murder of her son Ben at Sandy Hook Elementary School in 2012.

This story was told on November 10, 2021, at St. Ann's Church in New York City. The theme of the evening was Terra Firma. Director: Catherine Burns.

I WILL LIFT MY EYES TO THE HILLS

NOWHERE TO RUN

MONTE MONTEPARE

I'm in my truck, driving through the dark across Alaska. If you haven't been to Alaska, it's *big*. And I'm heading east toward McCarthy.

McCarthy is a redneck hippie town at the end of a sixty-mile dirt road in the middle of Wrangell–St. Elias National Park, the largest national park in the United States.

Don't feel bad, nobody's heard of the place.

The population of McCarthy is like two hundred people—and at least one hundred *dogs*. It's at the toe of a gigantic glacier, the confluence of two rivers, the base of some of the most spectacular mountains on the planet.

It might be the most beautiful place in the world . . . and I did not want to go back there.

The night before, I was on a couch in Anchorage, and I was excited to celebrate my second wedding anniversary with my wife. We'd been living apart that summer. I was living in McCarthy, taking people on adventures—I had been a wilderness guide for the last decade. And she was in Anchorage pursuing her own professional goals. She was living with friends, and we were sitting on their couch, which smelled like two kids and a dog.

And that's where she turned to me and said, "I cheated on you, two years ago, right before our wedding in McCarthy."

I crumpled, whimpering into the linoleum.

This was not what I was expecting to get for my second wedding anniversary.

I hear cotton is traditional.

The more I found out, the less I felt like I could deal with any of it.

When she revealed that it wasn't once, it was an *affair,* I told her I didn't feel safe there anymore. I gave her a hug, and I got in my truck and drove away.

I didn't know where to go. I called my parents in Colorado. I thought about going all the way home. And in all the years of exploratory river trips, twenty-one-day mountaineering expeditions, calling them with frostbite from some glacier that they can't even pronounce the name of, I had never heard my parents so concerned for my well-being. I was devastated.

But I had to go back to McCarthy because that's where my dogs were.

I remember the first day I stepped foot in McCarthy, Alaska. I was twenty years old, and I rolled into this town in my truck. The place was just waking up from being a ghost town. It felt like I found Colorado in 1970, as my parents had always described it. Dirt streets, sleeping dogs. The kind of place where you could go into the only bar and be sitting next to a mountain guide, a gold miner, and the mayor.

And the mayor was a dog.

I fell in love immediately. I tell people for the next ten years that I came for the mountains, but I stayed for the town. This place was a blank slate for me, and I knew how small towns work. Your actions accumulate over time, and eventually, your character is seen by all. The community was so small and tight-knit. And I worked hard. I kept my nose clean. I treated people with respect. I made my way from a first-year guide all the way up to a part owner of the guide service. And I shared the place with the woman that I loved.

I felt protected in McCarthy.

As long as I was respected, and my wife loved me, nothing else mattered.

But as I rolled back into town, I did not feel either of those things. I knew that people had known of this affair the whole time.

I was the last one to find out my own secret.

I felt I needed to hide. I didn't want to face anybody. I couldn't even face my cabin by myself.

So, I drove to my best friend Chris's house. Chris and I had moved to Alaska in that truck together when we were twenty years old. We'd known each other since preschool. And now he and his wife cared for me because I was incapable of caring for myself.

I've never felt an emotional pain that caused so much physical agony.

I had no appetite. It was hard to sleep, and when I did, I had nightmares. When I was awake, it hurt. Hours felt like forever, and the first couple of days felt like an eternity.

If this is what life was going to feel like, I wasn't sure I wanted to keep doing it.

After a couple of days of this, I wanted to give Chris and his wife a break—because living in a one-room cabin with your partner off the grid in remote Alaska is complicated enough without having your heartbroken buddy occupying your living room–slash–dining room–slash–*only room*.

So, when my other buddy Chester asked if I wanted to crash at his house for a night, I took him up on the offer.

I met Chester that first day that I got to McCarthy, ten years before, and we bonded over punk rock music. Our dogs are sisters.

Chris and Chester live in the same subdivision, but I feel that term is grossly misleading in this context. Think less suburbia and more a collection of cabins, shanties, trailers, and permanently parked school buses connected by a dirt road ripped through the forest.

I followed Chester through the woods—in the dark—to his cabin, and we proceeded to pull an all-night heart-to-heart. I told him that this whole thing felt like the last act of some bizarre Greek tragedy that's been custom-designed to wield my own inner demons as the means of my destruction.

I told him how I've always struggled with my masculinity and how I felt completely emasculated. I told him that I'd always struggled to control people's perceptions of me—and now the thing that I'd like to be the most private is the most public.

I told him I was angry—but I was afraid to let myself feel it because the feeling was so intense, I didn't know what to do with it.

I woke up in the morning with my eighty-pound husky lying on my chest, in her most demanding version yet of, *Maybe you'd feel a little bit better if you pet a big furry dog.*

Chester and I drank coffee, which I do, and smoked cigarettes, which I don't do, but that morning I felt like I should. And I smoked *the shit* out of some cigarettes.

As I'm leaving with my uncharged phone, I grab my sleeping bag, I put it over my shoulder, and Chester stops me.

He puts his hand on my chest and says, "You have an unlimited well of power inside of you."

Which, if you knew Chester, you'd know that's a very Chester thing to say.

It was just past peak foliage. The bright yellows and golds had faded to mottled leaves, dead but not yet fallen. I walked into the woods alone because my dogs had bailed on me and gone back to Chris's cabin for breakfast.

And I feel lost in the world.

I feel like my marriage was a lie. I feel my life was a lie. I feel like I died on that couch.

And then, I realize that I'm *actually lost*.

I am lost in the woods.

I'm a wilderness guide lost in my best friend's backyard because *I'm killing it*.

In my defense, it is bushy back there, and Chester is the kind of guy that meticulously doesn't walk the same way, just to *keep it wild*. But I am truly lost.

I'm disoriented, trying to get my bearings.

I take a step forward.

A twig snaps under my foot.

I look to my left . . . and I'm staring at a 750-pound grizzly bear.

Twenty-five yards away from me.

I've had a decent amount of bear encounters in my life, and I've even been mock-charged by a grizzly bear before, which is their form of pounding their chest, trying to assert dominance and scare you off. But I have never had any animal look at me the way that this bear looked at me.

It roared, and immediately charged.

This is the worst-case scenario.

I just scared a fall-time grizzly in the bushes.

This is not a mock situation.

I'm under attack, and I turn my head to run, *which you are not supposed to do*. But when you're presented with something that terrifying, it can be a difficult instinct to quell.

In that moment I knew exactly where my firearm was: five miles away in my cabin on my bedside table.

I had no bear spray or any other means of protection. I scanned the area looking for a tree to climb or somewhere to hide, which there wasn't—because there never is in Alaska.

Grizzly bears run forty miles an hour. So, I know if I try to run, this bear is going to be on top of me.

What you are *supposed* to do in the rare event that you are attacked by a grizzly bear is play dead. Lie facedown on the ground to protect your organs. Put your hands behind your neck to protect your spinal cord, and only if the attack persists—only then, do you fight for your life.

Well, what this bear didn't know is that I'd felt half dead for the past four days.

I felt like I'd been getting mauled by the world. I was being attacked from all angles, and it had persisted long enough.

I knew this bear wasn't going to stop. Nobody was going to save me.

I turned around, and I saw the bear barreling at me through the bushes.

I planted my feet, put my teal-and-lime-green sleeping bag over my head, and I took all of that confusion and pain and directionless anger, and unleashed it in a gut-wrenching, eye-bulging, vein-popping, primal scream.

And the bear stopped.

But now the bear was very close.

So close that this time when it roared, I could see spittle shooting off of its lips and feel its hot breath cut through the cold morning air.

But now, I was *committed*.

I wasn't going anywhere.

In fact, I just found out that I don't want to die.

So, I look the bear directly in the eyes—which you are *also* not supposed to do—and I dig down deep inside, past the burst bubble of McCarthy, past the shards of my broken heart, to a place that is *not* broken, a place that cannot be destroyed.

And from there, I roared.

And then, I *charged the bear.*

And I don't think that's what the bear was expecting. Because it looked at me, huffed, and ran into the bushes.

Many longtime Alaskans would tell you that the moral of this story is simple: "Carry your bear gun, you stupid hippie."

But to me, it felt much more profound.

I knew that this experience was going to summon my own personal demons in their most violent forms. And if I tried to run or hide, they were going to kill me.

If I was going to survive, I was going to need to be brave.

I was going to need to stand my ground and look them right in the eye.

* ☺ *

MONTE MONTEPARE is a mountain guide, comedian, and storyteller who grew up in Breckenridge, Colorado. At twenty years old, he and his best friend moved into a truck and drove to Alaska. He's spent two decades living in Wrangell–St. Elias National Park, taking people on the adventures of a lifetime as one of the owners of Kennicott Wilderness Guides. These days he splits time between Alaska and Los Angeles, where he lives with his partner, Jillian; their child, Rocky; and their chiweenie, Sage. Monte is a three-time Moth StorySLAM winner, a Moth GrandSLAM champion, and a regular on The Moth Mainstage.

This story was told on April 4, 2018, at the Lobero Theatre in Santa Barbara. The theme of the evening was Beneath the Armor. Director: Sarah Austin Jenness.

ABUELOS, APPLES, AND ME

LUNA AZCURRAIN

Thanksgiving at my house is not your typical Thanksgiving. Half of my family is from Spain, so we always add our little Spanish twist to it. We have tortilla de patata and gambas al ajillo instead of, what do you guys have? Your green bean casserole? I don't know.

My favorite part of Thanksgiving was actually this apple cake. And typically Thanksgiving was held at my aunt's house, so I just assumed that she was the mastermind behind it. But I actually found out that it was my grandfather, which completely surprised me because he's never in the kitchen. He's either reading a French newspaper or watching the Spanish news channel. So, when I found out it was him, I was like:

One, this is the perfect opportunity to get the recipe.

Two, I can actually have a time and place to connect with him, which I didn't really have before that.

Ever since then, I would go early on Thanksgiving morning, and we'd pull out this old recipe book that had all these food stains on it.

I would mix together the wet and the dry ingredients, and he would double-check my measurements, and then I would sit there mesmerized by the fact that he could peel an apple in one entire rind. And we'd combine everything and then go over and consult with my uncle about the placement of the cake in the oven because no one wanted to disrupt the turkey's cooking time (even though no one wanted to eat it anyway).

And then it almost felt like instantly the house would smell like cinnamon and apples.

At the end of the night when everyone got that thick slice, we'd get this big round of applause, and they would be like, "Oh my God, it's so amazing. It tastes so good."

And me and my grandfather would just look at each other from across the room and be like, "Yeah, we did that," and it became a tradition that I enjoyed and always looked forward to.

But as I got older, so did he.

One Thanksgiving morning he was sitting at the kitchen table, and I assumed that he was waiting to make the apple cake. I was unpacking the groceries, and I was putting the apples on the table.

He looks at me, and he goes, "Luna, what are you doing?"

And I'm shocked. I mean, I knew that he was beginning to forget things, but I didn't think that he would forget this. It was our tradition. It was our time of bonding. It was our time to connect. And he had forgotten.

I'm like, "We're making the apple cake. You know, the one that we always make."

And he goes, "Apple cake. Can you teach me?"

Now I'm terrified because he was my teacher, and now I have to be his teacher because I don't want this tradition to die.

And so I tell him, "I'll teach you."

As I'm telling him that, I'm putting the sugar and the eggs in the blender, and I'm putting the flour and the cinnamon in another bowl. And I hand him the apple, and he still peels it in one rind, and I'm like, *Okay, maybe he remembers a little bit.*

We put it in the oven. It comes out perfectly. But the entire time it just doesn't feel the same because even though he's there with me, he's not completely capable of being there like he used to be.

Fast-forward to this year, it's three years later, and I'm on my way to work, and I remember that it's going to be Thanksgiving. And so I call my mom, and I tell her that I need her to pick up the five freshest Granny Smith apples.

A few hours later she calls me, and she goes, "Luna, your grandfather was just admitted to the hospital. He needs to get minor surgery. He's going to be fine, but we're going to have Thanksgiving in the hospital this year."

My first reaction was, *Oh my God, is he going to be okay?*

But then my second reaction was, *What about the apple cake?* And I knew that everyone was really worried about him, and so I figured that I would just make the apple cake by myself this year, so that way I could bring a little bit of comfort to the family. I get home, and I'm looking at the apples, and I just *completely* forget everything. I don't remember if he does slivers for the apples or chunks, if they're big or if they're small. And I'm testing one with one apple, and I definitely can't peel it in one rind.

The entire time as I'm mixing everything together, I'm doubting myself. I'm like, *This is going to taste horrible. It's not going to look the same.* And as I'm putting it in the oven, I'm just like, *This doesn't have his touch.* He's not by my side. This cake will not be the same because what made it so special was him being there, was us being able to make it *together,* and he couldn't do that this time.

And so as soon as it comes out of the oven, I'm like, *We're not bringing it. This is not the cake. We're not bringing it.* But of course my mother insists. So, we pack it in the bag, and we're on our way to the hospital. As we enter, it's cold, and it smells like medicine. But as we get to my grandfather's room, everyone's surrounding him and creating some warmth.

I try to discreetly hide the bag behind my back, but my grandmother sees, and she goes, "What do you have there, Luna?"

I hand her the bag, and she pulls out the apple cake.

And then she tells my grandfather, "Look, Luna made apple cake."

He looks down at the cake, and then he looks back up at me, and he smiles. And I feel this rush of memories flowing back to him of every time we've made it together.

Even though he was in the hospital, it felt like we had made it together.

We had done it once again.

* ✦ *

LUNA AZCURRAIN was born and raised on the Lower East Side but loves to go all over the city to try new foods and restaurants. Like a true New Yorker, she loves taking the subway. It is the perfect place to listen to music while discreetly people-watching. Now she is a student at Binghamton University.

This story was told on January 28, 2020, at The Bell House in New York City. The theme of the evening was Hidden Treasure. Director: Jodi Powell.

THAT'S MY SHIRT

GEORGE SUMNER

I was drafted into the army in 1966 at the height of the Vietnam War.

I was a rural Utah farm kid, but my basic training drill sergeants stripped me down to the marrow and rebuilt me into this proud American fighting man with service and duty and honor at my core.

So later, when my jump school drill sergeant said, "Sumner, you should consider helicopter pilot training," what I heard was a call to duty, and I was willing, eager.

But he went on, "You can't do this as a two-year draftee. The army will expect you to voluntarily commit to a four-year reenlistment."

I made that commitment.

And after a year of training, I added pilot wings above the jump wings on my army shirt. Then I flew two one-year tours in Vietnam.

The first morning of my first tour I got pulled out early from an orientation class and was given a cursory briefing and a five-minute check flight and sent off to fly. Logistics, they said—not combat. For those first three days, from dawn to dusk, I repeated the same four-hour round-trip mission hauling supplies out to a big battle—and back hauling the reeking bagged bodies of American soldiers.

At the time I thought my whole tour was going to be like that, but it wasn't.

There was combat. Hostile fire was always possible, it was often expected, and it was sometimes guaranteed. There was a lot more logistics flying, because everything went everywhere by helicopter, but there was also downtime for beach volleyball, late-night poker.

And all of that, especially the combat, was in fulfillment of that commitment I pledged back in jump school. At the end of my second tour, I was honorably discharged right from Vietnam.

I wore my uniform for the long flight across the Pacific to Fort Lewis, Washington. But there the officer who processed my paperwork told me I should lose the uniform and wear civvies—civilian clothes—to avoid conflict with antiwar protesters. I felt insulted, but I joined the crowd picking civvies off the racks at the PX.

In the PX dressing room mirror, I looked like a soldier in brand-new civvies.

I *felt* like a phony.

I tossed my uniforms angrily onto the pile of discarded uniforms overflowing out of the garbage can that the PX had put right there in the dressing room for that very purpose. And then I thought, *Wait a minute. They can disrespect my service*—I had no idea who *they* were—*but they can't make* me *disrespect it*. And I took back one army shirt with my wings and my name on it, and I stuffed that into the bottom of my brand-new civilian rollie bag.

As my departing taxi drove through the gaggle of protesters chanting outside the gates, I thought how unfair it was that I should shamefully hide my uniform while they proudly display their standard get-ups of denim and paisley and beads and hair.

When I got home, I reclaimed my little two-seater convertible sports car, and I put the top down, and I hit the road with the sun on my face to see America. To breathe free.

Only ten days later I was speeding through Minnesota cropland when Simon and Garfunkel's "Cecilia," blasting up out of my radio, was interrupted by a news bulletin: *National Guard troops sent to maintain order had fired into a crowd of student antiwar protesters at Kent State University in Ohio, killing four and wounding nine.*

I was on the road. I was curious. I drove to Kent State. I *walked* that ground, and I imagined an unruly crowd of antiwar protesters advancing toward that outnumbered, thinly dispersed, probably frightened line of part-time citizen soldiers. Men like me. And I thought the soldiers showed extraordinary restraint, only killing four.

But public opinion and news media condemned those guardsmen for the senseless, brutal murder of American children.

If Walter Cronkite was right, if *that's the way it was,* then I was wrong. But if I was wrong, I thought it meant my commitment, honorably, no, *nobly* fulfilled was wrong.

I had to be right.

And I set off to find people who agreed with me, and I probed for opinions in casual conversations in back-road county-line beer joints and freeway truck stop cafés and national park scenic overlooks.

But everywhere on that road trip, and even after I got home, although I found a lot of people who did not condemn the war, I couldn't find anybody who didn't condemn Kent State.

And that was a problem because I still had to be right—but I couldn't honestly believe everyone else was wrong.

That problem was so great it dragged me into a profound and lasting spiritual emptiness.

That fall I returned to college, where I brushed aside the students handing out antiwar literature on the quad, and I pointedly ignored the booths and tables set up in building lobbies. I let the protest rallies be background noise.

Until the day I heard a protest leader tell his crowd that because the war was wrong, the soldiers were war criminals.

That *pissed me off,* and I liked the feeling—because angry was better than empty.

I vowed right then, I wasn't going to hide who I was behind long hair and civvies anymore. I would proudly, *defiantly* wear my uniform on campus.

And I went home, and I walked out back to my garden shed, and I dug my rollie bag out from under a pile of camping gear. I unzipped it, and I rummaged through those musty PX civvies—and there it was. My army shirt with my wings and my name on it.

When I wore that shirt on campus, other students eyed me warily and gave me a noticeable amount of extra room—except other soldiers.

One day in the cafeteria I felt a clap on my shoulder, and a friendly voice said, "Come join us at the veterans' table."

I had avoided these informal affinity groups that form cafeteria tables. You know: The nerd table is over here, and the stoners' table is over there, and way over there, isolated in the corner, is the veterans' table.

This time I stood up, and I offered my hand.

I said, "I'm George."

He shook my hand and said, "I'm Mike. Welcome home."

"Welcome home" was, and still is, a common greeting between Vietnam veterans. It was a fake welcome home. An ironic nod to that greeting we never heard, except from each other. It was so certain if you heard it, that another veteran was saying it, that it was like this warrior secret password.

I joined the veterans' table. I came back a lot because I enjoyed the mess hall banter. There was friendship in that banter, but there was challenge as well, and wisdom. There, Mike, who was an antiwar veteran, could acknowledge that he felt honor and glory in battle, yet still oppose the war. And a prowar veteran could admit he saw senseless brutality and death in battle, yet still support the war. And I found that opposing the war didn't mean opposing the soldiers but rather *supporting* them, so that no other pilot would ever have to transport that cargo of reeking body bags.

One spring day, Mike told me, "There's a Veterans Against the War march Saturday morning. I'm picking you up."

I told him, "I'm going as your friend, not as a protester."

But that Saturday when I saw those veterans, chests out, shoulders back, chins up, marching with intense purpose, I saw unity, and I saw courage, and I saw honor. And I thought, *A nation that sends men like this to fight, to kill, to die, only to condemn them when they come back, shouldn't be sending them in the first place.* And I stepped forward, and I walked toward their formation.

Now, I don't change easily or quickly, and I didn't then. But eventually I marched, and I chanted, protesting the war with the same commitment I had fought it with.

My army shirt had turned into my Veterans Against the War shirt.

I started wearing it everywhere. Protests, of course, and on campus, but also for projects around the house, exercising, backyard barbecues, keggers, camping.

In 1982—this is years after the end of the Vietnam War, and a decade after my first protest march—Mike and I wore our faded, tattered, now sleeveless army shirts hiking Zion Narrows in southern Utah. On the drive home, Mike plucked at my shirt.

He said, "We got to get rid of these rags."

I told him, "I know. I thought of burning mine like a flag disposal, but I couldn't even do that. I rescued this shirt from a garbage bin."

Mike had an idea.

He said, "I'm leaving mine at the dedication of the Vietnam Memorial in Washington, D.C., this fall. You should come too."

I told him, "I can't. Work. School. You take mine too."

He shook his head.

"No, man, that's going to be a moment. You got to do that yourself."

Eventually I did. I cleaned the shirt up. I ironed it. I folded it neatly. I took it to Washington, D.C., and I placed it reverently at the base of the wall.

And Mike had been right. That was a moment.

Ten years later, it's 1992; I'm married now. My wife, Tina, and I are walking through the Smithsonian Museum of American History, and we round a corner into an exhibit . . .

And there's my shirt.

It's behind glass, under lights.

It's in the Smithsonian.

I had to gasp for breath just to say it: *"That's my shirt."*

Tina had already turned to check out a rack of Purple Heart medals in this exhibit of artifacts left at the wall. When she heard me, she turned back, and she took my hand, and I stared at my shirt.

I was weeping, and Tina stared at me. She was concerned.

She squeezed my hand, and she asked, "Is that a lot like the kinds of shirts that you used to wear?"

And I pointed out the wings and the faded Sumner name tag, and I confirmed it was indeed *my* shirt.

Tina leaned in.

"That's your shirt!"

She was laughing and crying at the same time.

"I thought you were using metaphors, that it was this symbol of every Vietnam vet's shirt."

And I found myself hoping she was right, that it was every veteran's shirt—so that every veteran that saw it might gasp, "That's my shirt."

And maybe weep a little, but especially feel what I felt right then for the first time.

A thank-you from a grateful nation.

Welcome home.

* ⦿ *

GEORGE SUMNER lives in Salt Lake City with his wife, Tina Hose. One of six siblings, George was raised in rural Utah but says he grew up in Vietnam, where he served as a helicopter pilot. George started his firefighter career in Salt Lake City in 1971 and advanced through the ranks to deputy chief. He retired from Salt Lake City after twenty-eight years to accept the position as fire chief of neighboring Bountiful City, where he worked for seven more years. George took job-related college classes all during his career, completing associate's degrees in fire science and paramedic, a bachelor's in social studies, and a master's in public administration. In retirement, George and Tina are active in community and political affairs, serving on community councils and nonprofit boards. They enjoy traveling, especially visiting their friends and family scattered throughout America.

This story was told on March 19, 2022, at The Music Hall in Portsmouth, New Hampshire. The theme of the evening was Between Worlds. Director: Sarah Austin Jenness.

A BRATZ LIFE

TALAYA MOORE

My obsession with Bratz began when I was eight years old, and I was gifted one for my birthday—Bratz are dolls, kind of like Barbies, but better. They didn't have unrealistic dimensions. Instead, they stood about ten inches tall with these full lips, curvy physique, and they had the coolest makeup. They also had these glittery punk-rock boots that I loved.

I knew I was hooked, and I wanted more, but I could not ask my mom for more, because we were homeless. We had been homeless for over a year, and she had bigger worries, like if she had enough money for train fare or food, what borough we would end up sleeping in, and if I had a clean uniform for school. I knew that if I wanted these dolls, I would have to get them myself.

In the shelter, I started selling paper fans that I made and decorated to the guards for seventy-five cents, and they would give me more money because they saw I was hustling. And I would take that money and buy pens, pencils, loose-leaf paper, and candy and sell it to the kids at school for a markup price, which I was good at. I also braided hair in the shelter. And when I saved up enough money, my mom took me to the big toy store in Times Square.

When I arrived, I ran straight to the Bratz section, and I searched the shelves for Sasha. Sasha was the Bratz doll that I really wanted. I had read about her in a pamphlet from the previous doll I had.

She was this aspiring businesswoman; she just seemed the coolest.

After searching and scanning the shelves and not seeing her, I asked the sales rep if he had any more in the back, and he said, "Sorry, kid. She's popular, high in demand, all sold out."

And that day, I left with Jade. I was disappointed, but I was still happy to leave with a Bratz doll.

It had been over a year of living in the EAU, which was short for the Emergency Assistance Unit, and me and my mother had been waiting for overnight placement. It was Christmas Eve, and I was sitting there, and there were children screaming and making noise, and I was tired, I was hungry. I had been there since eight A.M., and it was now going on eight P.M. And just as I was about to turn to complain, they called us to the triage window for our placement. As we approached the window—this thick glass in between my mother and me and the worker—it kind of reminded me of a check-cashing place or quarantine, like we were kept away from all things clean. Once we received our overnight placement, we went back to sit down.

Then I heard an uproar, this cheering and chanting from the kids in the rooms next door. I peeked my head out the doorway to see what was going on, what was the fuss about, and I saw the guards dragging these clear plastic bags down the hall. And I remembered that we were going to get donated toys; it was Christmas Eve. I almost forgot. See, I had been here last Christmas, and I knew how things went. We would all be in one room, called one by one to receive a toy. As the guards are dragging the bags, I notice, as clear as day, untouched, unwrapped . . . a Bratz doll. And I knew I just had to have it. I honestly felt like I deserved it. I had all A's and B's in school. I stayed out of trouble. I even helped my mom fold clothes at the laundromat. So, I knew I had to be first in line.

When the guards came to my room, I jumped up, and they said, "Step right up," and I dived, digging through those bags.

You weren't even allowed to do that. You were supposed to just step up, get one toy, and keep it pushing. But these were the same guards that would buy my paper fans, and they were cool enough to let me search. And as I'm going through the third bag, I'm digging, I feel the outline of that Bratz doll, that box. I pick it up, and there she was:

Sasha.

I held her up like they did Simba in *The Lion King,* and tears of joy ran down my cheeks. Sasha was wearing this ice-blue princess gown with a tiara to match. She looked magical, like Brandy when she starred in that *Cinderella* movie featuring Whitney Houston. I felt like I had met a celebrity. I was starstruck, like I met Tyra Banks or Raven-Symoné.

Sasha was beautiful. She was Black, and I was Black. She was gorgeous. She had long, dark brown hair, and her clothes were the best out of all the Bratz. And in the pamphlet that she came with, they told me things about her: how she wanted her own urban clothing line, how she wanted to be a music producer, how she had two parents and her own room. She seemed like she had it all, and I wanted that.

I had this carry case that I could keep only one Bratz doll in; I always chose to put Sasha in it. It was blue velvet, and had a spot just for Sasha, and a wardrobe where I kept all her clothes neatly stacked. It was like her room—sometimes I would pretend that it was my room. For a second, I felt like the other third graders in my class. I had a room and a closet full of clothes. It was me and Sasha's world.

It had been nearly two years of staying in the EAU, two years of waiting, two years of being denied permanent housing, and I was tired. Finally, we were moving to a semipermanent placement called the Ellington. Inside the Ellington, we had one room, and it had a bunk bed, a half-top stove, a mini fridge, a dresser, and a bathroom. A lot of the time, I sat in the hallway, and I would play with other kids. But most of the time, I played alone with my dolls. Next door lived this girl, and she always wanted to play with me and my Bratz dolls, but I didn't let her because I saw how she treated her toys— I didn't need her messing up my girls.

One day, I came home after school, and I immediately ran to the dresser where I keep my dolls.

And as I'm approaching the dresser, I notice that they were all gone.

My Bratz were gone.

Sasha was gone.

I began to panic.

I felt like someone had stabbed me in the chest, like pins and needles all throughout my body. And me and my mom searched the room, looking for the dolls. I didn't know what to do, so I grabbed her phone, and I dialed 911.

I said, "Hurry, come quick! We've been robbed! They took everything. 110th and Morningside."

After I hung up, my mom's looking at me in disbelief.

"Did you just call the cops?"

In my head, I'm like, *These are my girls. They're missing. Where's the AMBER Alert?!*

When the officers arrived, I was standing there, eyes bloodshot red, T-shirt soaking wet, nose dripping, and I said, "It was her. It was the girl next door."

I knew she took my Bratz dolls. So, they started the investigation. They knocked on the door, and they questioned her, and she said no, that she didn't have my dolls. But I *knew* she had my dolls. They said they couldn't help me any further, because they didn't have a warrant to search.

And one of the officers bent over and said, "I'm sure they'll turn up. They're just dolls."

Just dolls? They were more than just dolls to me. They were my family, especially Sasha. She was my row dog, my ride-or-die, my best friend. She was the first to know about my crush on Adolphus in the third grade and how he looked like milk chocolate. She also was there with me that night when I slept in my coat and my shoes in this nasty, bloodstained motel, and I held her tight the whole night. She was also there when I wanted to jump in the bed with my mom, but there wasn't enough space—I would hold on to her.

That night, before bed, I was on the top bunk, and I just kept looking at the dresser—it was empty. I felt empty. I went to bed with my pillow wet, and I woke up with my pillow wet. My mom asked me what I wanted for breakfast, but I didn't have an appetite. Instead, I sat in the hallway almost all day, in between my door and the girl next door, waiting for her to come out, waiting to just see if she had my girls in there.

Later that night, I got a knock on the door, and there she was, the girl next door, standing there with an attitude, with a plastic bag full of my Bratz dolls. I didn't even have the energy to say anything. I grabbed the bag, slammed the door, and spilled them out on the bed to examine them. They looked like they had been through something awful. They were all undressed, and they smelled like chicken grease. I dressed them, clothed them, and put them back on that dresser.

As I was doing so, I was holding Sasha. I realized that when they were gone, that was the first time I actually really felt homeless. And having them back, I felt whole again. Sasha was . . . she was there for me. These dolls were there for me.

Everyone has someone or something that may get them through the day or even a year, and for me, for nine-year-old me, it was

Sasha. It was this Black plastic professional businesswoman who doubled as a superstar in my eyes. She was a constant reminder that, in a world filled with uncertainty, there could be a happily ever after.

* ☉ *

TALAYA MOORE is a musical performing artist, influencer, producer, and overall creative. She received her BS from SUNY Oneonta in mass communication in 2017 and went on to study improv at UCB (Upright Citizens Brigade).

This story was told on February 4, 2019, at Aaron Davis Hall in New York City. The theme of the evening was Out of Sight. Director: Jodi Powell.

SWIMMING THROUGH IT

PARVATHY ANANTNARAYAN ✳

"Are you okay, miss?" the flight attendant asks, looking concerned.

I can understand why he is concerned. We were six hours into a fourteen-hour plane ride. And throughout the six hours, I hadn't stopped crying—great big gulping sobs, like I was trying to catch a breath. In fact, I hadn't stopped crying since my sister's phone call the evening before, when she asked me to get on that plane.

A few months earlier, my fifteen-year-old son had left the United States to go to India to visit my sister—his aunt—and his grandparents. A few weeks ago, he had started to feel unwell. A few doctors' visits and tests later, it was confirmed that my son had lymphoma.

He had cancer.

After my sister's call, I immediately got on the next available flight, bidding goodbye to my daughter and husband, not sure when I would see them again. When I landed, my sister met me at the airport. Together, we headed to the hospital to see my son. In the week that followed, there were several more doctors' visits and consultations.

We were told at the end of that week that it would not be possible for my son to come back to the United States at that point in time. The doctors said that his heart had two liters of fluid surrounding it, and it would be too dangerous for him to fly, that he would need surgery and chemotherapy right away. They also asked me if we could consider moving nearer to the hospital, so that his treatments wouldn't be so difficult with the commute.

And so, my son and I went apartment hunting.

Next to the hospital was a building, and on the seventh floor of this building was an apartment that we went to look at. As we walked into the apartment, I observed the white tiled floors and the kitchen that seemed to me a little too small, while my son eagerly opened doors and closets, checking out which would be his bedroom. And I stood there and closed my eyes and thought to myself, *Please, please, God, let this be a place of healing for us.*

I watched him as he slid open the balcony door and stepped out. He called out to me, "Ma, come see!"

I walked over to see what it was he was pointing at. Below, on the ground floor, was a great big blue pool.

He said, "It's a swimming pool, Ma! You can finally learn how to swim!"

A little background here: I never fully learned how to swim growing up. As a teenager, I tried, and I made it through two days of lessons. On the first day, it wasn't so bad. The instructor said we would learn how to float.

"Now, remember," he said, "floating is not the same thing as swimming. You don't go anywhere; you don't move."

But I learned how to lie back and keep my head above the water. I could breathe, and I could look around, and it was okay. The next day when we went back, he asked us to go to the end of the pool to start our first real swimming lesson. And, in this lesson, we would need to put our faces under the water.

I remember lowering my face into the water. As the water started to rise up, I felt it entering my nose and ears. I couldn't see two feet in front of me. My feet started to lift up off the floor as my head went in. Panic started to rise up within me.

I was losing control, and I said—

"*Hell* no!"

—and clambered out of that pool, and I never went back. So, I never got to the swimming part, really.

And now here we were in this apartment.

My son said, "Ma, promise me that if we rent this apartment, you will go into that pool every single day and practice until you learn how to swim."

I felt the old rush of fear of a loss of control come over me.

But I looked at him, and I said, "Okay. All right. I'll do that. But you have to promise me that when I go down into that pool, I can look up to that balcony and see you sitting here, so I'm keeping my eyes on you while I'm down at the pool."

"It's a deal," he said.

A week later, we moved in. For a few days after that, this was the routine:

My son would say, "Ma, it's your swimming time."

I'd grab my towel and head downstairs to the pool.

I'd lie back in the water and keep my back straight like I remembered how to.

I'd look up over at the balcony, where I would see my son sitting.

He waved down at me, and I would wave back up at him.

And in this way, we spent five or six days.

Right after that, it was time for my son to go into the hospital for surgery and chemotherapy. The week in the hospital was a blur. I don't remember much of it, except that I sat by my son's side, and the nurses would sometimes come in and fuss and tell me I needed to go down to the cafeteria to get something to eat or drink. I kind of resented them for this because the only real control I had over the situation was being able to sit there, by my son's side, while he lay in the hospital bed with tubes coming out of his arms.

I do remember going into the cafeteria, and I would get these tiny cups of milky tea that were scaldingly hot. I got them down in a rush to get back to his side again.

A few days later, he was discharged, and we came back into our apartment. He was exhausted. He climbed into bed, and I drew the blinds in his bedroom and pulled the covers over him.

He tiredly looked up at me, and he said, "Ma, remember, we're back at the apartment; it's your pool time."

"Yes. Yes, I remember. I'll go."

I took my towel and headed back downstairs. I stepped into the pool, lay back, and by habit, I turned to look at that balcony on the seventh floor. But of course, it was empty. My son wasn't there. He was still in bed.

And, at that moment, I could feel fear, like a wave washing over me. *What if?* I thought. *What if I look for my boy one day, and I never see him again?*

I was floating, and tears were running down from the corners of my eyes into the water. And even though I was floating, it felt as if the tremendous panic and loss of control I was feeling would drown me.

I got out of the pool, and went back up to my son. The days that followed began to blur together between treatments, and a few months passed by. Finally, my son was well enough to come back home to the United States to resume treatment here.

We were back home, and, in between chemo treatments, we could be at a poolside together again.

It was a beautiful day. The sky was blue, and the sun was shining, and I watched my son sitting over by the pool, scrolling on his phone.

I hesitantly, gingerly, placed my feet into the cold, cold water. I waded into the pool and, as the water rose, I plunged my head under its surface. Water rushed up my nose and into my ears. I couldn't see two feet in front of me. My feet started to lift up, and I felt the panic, the loss of control—all of it.

But this time, I kicked.

I kicked fiercely, and I raised my arms out of the water, and I propelled myself forward.

After a few strokes I came up, gasping for air. And I heard my son laughing, laughing so hard over on the side. I looked up at him, and his eyes were shining.

He said, "You're doing it, Ma; you're swimming."

* ☺ *

PARVATHY ANANTNARAYAN is a mom, an educator, and a collector of stacks of unused notebooks. She came to The Moth through a teacher professional development workshop in NOLA and as a participant in the Moth Teacher Institute in New York City. She loves stories—reading them, listening to them, telling them, and most of all, wondering about all the stories that will never be told.

This story was told on October 21, 2020, over Zoom at a virtual Education Program Showcase. The theme of the evening was Rise and Shine. Director: Chloe Salmon.

BEING A FOOT SOLDIER
DR. SYBIL JORDAN HAMPTON

In 1982, I was living and working in New Rochelle, New York, and I received a letter inviting me to the twentieth reunion of the Little Rock Central High School class of 1962.

It was quite a surprise because in the twenty years since graduation, I had never heard anything about *any* class activities. More importantly, I had no desire to do anything with any of its members and even less desire to put my foot in that school ever again.

It made me feel like I was being invited to return to the scene of the crime.

In 1957, nine brave Black young people attempted to desegregate Little Rock Central High School, and they will forever be known and revered as the Little Rock Nine.

The world knew the terrible things that happened to them because we saw the coverage of events on ABC, CBS, and NBC. There were articles in national news magazines, and even the local newspaper carried the story of the way they were taunted, the physical violence they experienced, the threats they received, and finally the fact that President Dwight David Eisenhower had to send the 101st Airborne to Little Rock to escort them to school.

Arkansas's governor, at the end of the 1957–58 school year, closed all high schools in Little Rock in an effort to prevent the desegregation of schools from going forward. The NAACP Legal Defense Fund immediately filed suits, and eventually, the federal courts ordered the schools to be reopened so that the desegregation process might move forward.

As a result, in September 1959, I was the youngest of five Black students attempting to desegregate Little Rock Central High School again.

I was fifteen years old and the only Black tenth grader.

I remember my first day of high school. My father stayed home and had breakfast with us. After breakfast, he prayed.

He prayed for me to be brave, to be calm, and most of all, to remember that the Lord was my shepherd, and he would watch over me.

In the past, my brother and our friends and neighbors and I would walk right past Little Rock Central High School on the way to our junior high school. We'd be laughing and talking. But on that day, we drove the six blocks from my home to Little Rock Central High. We were all very quiet. I wondered what was going to happen and what it would be like to be the only Black student in the tenth grade.

When we arrived at the school, I was relieved to see that there were no crowds and no media outside.

I thought, *Well, at least we're not going to have to fight our way into the school today like the Little Rock Nine did.*

We began to walk along the sidewalk to the steep, stately stairs leading to the high school's front doors. And as we did, there were Arkansas National Guardsmen standing top to bottom on either side of the steps.

I wondered, *Are they going to have to come into the school to protect us, and* will they?

I was so frazzled as we walked past those National Guardsmen.

We were met at the front door by the principal, Jess Matthews, and the assistant principal, Mrs. Elizabeth Huckaby. She welcomed us very warmly and took us into her office. She gave us directions for how to make our way through the building, gave us our class schedules, and then walked us to our homerooms.

My homeroom was on the first floor. As we walked, there was no one in the hallways because everybody else had already gone into their classes. We got near the door of my homeroom, and I saw out of the corner of my eye a door to the outside. I was relieved and made note of it in case I needed to make a quick exit—I would know where to go and how to do it.

My homeroom teacher pointed me to my seat—the middle seat in the middle row.

I was not introduced to anyone in the class.

No one spoke to me.

One guy continuously muttered things under his breath. Everybody else looked away.

It was clear to me that my homeroom teacher was not going to be my ally.

When the bell rang to go to the first-period class, I cannot tell you how apprehensive I felt. It would be the first time for me to walk in the hallways with other students—alone.

My parents had said, "Stand up straight, hold your head up high, and remember to be very aware of what's going on around you and keep your eyes always focused forward."

As I began to walk, I heard voices saying, "There's a nigger coming. The nigger is coming."

The students moved to the side against the walls of the hallway, and a pathway opened up in the middle so that I could walk alone.

That went on for a few weeks, and then it stopped. After that, no one spoke to me.

No one looked me in the eye.

No one smiled at me.

No one positively regarded me.

During the three years of my homeroom, the only time the other students in the class ever heard my voice was when it was my turn to read the Bible after the Pledge of Allegiance to the flag.

I always read Psalm 121: "I will lift my eyes to the hills, from whence comes my strength. My strength comes from the Lord who made heaven and Earth."

When graduation time rolled around in May 1962, I was truly ecstatic.

I had done what I came to do, and that was to be a successful student, to stay in school and not get kicked out, but most of all, to be a foot soldier who stood proudly on the shoulders of the warrior Little Rock Nine.

The three years that went by were all the same—I was shunned. I had been so alone. I was treated as if I was a ghost. I was invisible, but mostly I was treated as if I didn't matter.

But I was done, and I was thrilled.

My class had 544 students who graduated, and I remained the only Black student in that class all three years.

Our graduation took place in Quigley Stadium, a place I had never been. By law, the Black students could not attend any activities, including athletic activities, or participate in any clubs or organizations. Police ringed the stadium inside and out, and only our parents could attend because there was a fear of violence.

As I walked across the stage, I held my head up high, and I smiled because I felt tremendously relieved. As Mr. Matthews handed me my diploma, there was no applauding or cheering, only the silence I was used to.

But all of a sudden, some wise-acre yelled, "There goes Black Beauty."

I thought, *Insults from beginning to end.*

As we were seated, people in the class were busy talking about who they were going to miss.

I listened and thought, *Not one soul. I am not going to miss anyone. I do not expect to see any of these people ever again in life, and I'm not planning to put my foot in the building ever again.*

Then in 1982, this letter arrives, inviting me to come to the twentieth reunion.

After I reflected on it for a while, I thought, *I really do want to go back to see what, if anything, has changed with my classmates.*

So, I called my parents, and I said, "I'm going to fly home because I don't know what this invitation means, but I think I want to go to the banquet only. I need you to go with me because during my three years at Central, you could never come into the building. I want you to see the cast of characters that I lived with, but I also just want you to be there with me."

And so we went to the banquet, and we were met at the door by this guy named Ron from my homeroom who had never spoken to me. I don't think he'd ever looked at me. He said that he was responsible for me being invited. He also wanted us to know that nobody else in the class felt comfortable with our being there, and so we would have to sit alone, but he was going to sit with us.

I was so outraged.

I wanted to run away, but my parents gave me the eye, and I understood what that meant.

We went in, and we sat with Ron. And during the course of dinner, students came over to speak to me for the first time. Some students said they regretted not being kind to me. Other students said they thought I was rather brave, and they congratulated me on coming to a twentieth reunion with people who had been unkind to me. And I thought, *That was an understatement.*

Awards were given, and I received the award for being most educated.

Unbeknownst to me, at the end of the evening, they had planned a sock hop. Some of these new *friends* were very eager for me to stay. My jaws locked, and I was trying to prevent my eyes from rolling.

And then I thought, *I am here because I am claiming my space, and I am taking my place with this class of students.* I also thought, *I know what to do; I know how to do it. I probably can do it better than they can.*

And so I stayed for a while, but we left early because, as you can imagine, I was so fatigued.

As we were driving home, I talked with my parents about how clear it was that you can pass laws to legislate social change, you can pass laws to improve racial and social justice, but laws don't change hearts.

What we had experienced and witnessed that evening was how difficult it is for hearts to change.

I said to my parents, "I now recognize that this work is hard, but even so, I am more convinced than ever that I have to continue on this journey."

Some days it feels like trying to grow roses in concrete. But that's where the real work—my real work—lies.

DR. SYBIL JORDAN HAMPTON, EdD, grew up in Little Rock, Arkansas, and was a member of the second class of African American students entering Little Rock Central High School in 1959. Dr. Hampton has participated in numerous professional and civic organizations over the years, including the Japanese American National Museum and the Eastern Association of College Deans and Advisors of Students. Some of Dr. Hampton's awards include the 2019 Alumni Diversity Leadership Award, University of Chicago;

the 2018 Distinguished Alumni Award, Teachers College, Columbia University; and the 2017 Award of Excellence, Little Rock Central High School Tiger Foundation. Her latest professional pursuits center on consulting with foundations, nonprofits, and colleges and universities; public speaking; and volunteering in her home community.

This story was told on December 13, 2022, at the Paramount Theatre in Austin. The theme of the evening was Great Expectations. Director: Meg Bowles.

IT WAS
BRUTAL. AND
IT WAS
BEAUTIFUL.

EL CONQUISTADOR

SHAUN LEONARDO

In 2010, I'm standing in this grimy little gym in Oaxaca, Mexico, finally watching la Lucha Libre.

For those of you who don't know what that is, la lucha is the art of Mexican wrestling. The pageantry and acrobatics are second to none. The storylines and narratives of good versus evil might feel familiar to you, but there's a special magic to la lucha because, in Mexican culture, it is sacred.

I've had a fascination with la lucha ever since watching it on TV with my dad. It always felt spectacular, but those warriors were so foreign to me, in their masks and regalia, flipping every which way. I would learn later that those same warriors were your everyday teachers, taxi drivers, office workers—but in the ring, when that mask went on, they were *gods*.

As a scrawny kid from an insignificant neighborhood in Queens, New York City, I wanted to feel that.

I wanted to know what it meant to be a hero.

And so now, standing there, I was in complete awe. So much so that I waited three hours after the event just to approach a promoter and ask if I might start training with the local luchadores.

Two important things to know. I'm not Mexican. Yes, I'm Latino, but I'm from Queens.

Maybe more importantly, at the time, I had zero wrestling experience. I may, however, have fibbed just a little bit and told the promoter that I was a wrestler back home in the United States.

Whatever it was worked—the promoter goes backstage, comes back with a little piece of paper with an address scribbled on it, and says, "Show up here Friday."

He didn't say what time, just, *Show up here Friday.*

So, I did . . . but five hours too early.

But I waited, and I waited, and then, after a while, in comes the trainer.

It was the legendary Rigo Cisneros from *Nacho Libre* fame.

I lost it.

He comes up to me, silently sizes me up, and in the quietest voice goes, "Hop in the ring."

And the ring! It's an iron frame with plywood on top and some sprinklings of rubber with an old vinyl billboard securing it down. Not the bouncy thing you might imagine.

The wrestlers were amateurs *twice* my size. Everything I attempted was clumsy and tense. The luchadores saw that and decided to deliver the punishment, just to see if I would come back the next day.

The slaps to the chest started stinging more.

The body slams were a little more vicious.

And the blows, the falls, or *bumps* as we call them in wrestling, were that much more aggressive for me than anyone else in the ring.

But I came back, and I kept coming back, because where I'm from, giving up is not in the cards.

After three months of training, I'm finally granted my first match. And because of my hard work, and likely the novelty of an American luchador, I am slated as the sub-main event. Now, to be clear, that is not the *main* event. I'm still the warm-up act.

The night comes, and it's the same rickety ring in some makeshift arena with folding chairs, but the lights and the mariachi music are blaring, and it feels glorious.

When they call out my name, all the blood rushes right out of my body.

It all becomes a blur.

But I pull myself together, I get pumped, and I step out in all white and gold. The knight in shining armor, with a fourteen-foot velvet cape!

I hit that ring, and I'm looking *good*.

And then I get my *ass* kicked.

I lose that match, *bad*.

I go backstage, beaten and battered, but at least it's all over.

But then Rigo Cisneros, the trainer, comes over and says, "Go back in the ring. Get the crowd pumping and go save the good guys."

I said, "What the hell are you talking about?"

I panic. I run out there. I do what I'm told, only to get annihilated *again*. By the end of the event, there are three bad guys, or rudos, as we call them. One is pinning my shoulders down onto the mat, the other is kicking me repeatedly, and the third *unmasks* me.

The *ultimate* embarrassment in Mexican wrestling.

I leave with a mixture of emotions. I'm embarrassed. I'm defeated. But despite the beating, I feel I achieved something amazing. I had become a Mexican wrestler, for Christ's sake! I had lived out a childhood fantasy.

But I decided, enough is enough, the adventure was over, it was time to go home.

A month later, I'm back in my little apartment in Queens when I get a phone call from a promoter asking me if I would consider wrestling the welterweight champion of the world. It seems I, this American luchador, had caused quite a stir, and audiences were still talking about it. He told me it would be planned as a special event for the seventy-fifth anniversary of the largest Mexican wrestling promotion in the world and would be staged at the National Museum of Mexico City, which is literally a palace.

How could I say no?

Of course I'm terrified, but I had to see how far I could take this thing. So, I accept.

My opponent, the welterweight champion of the world, was Sangre Azteca, Aztecan Blood. I failed to mention that *my* wrestling name was El Conquistador, The Conqueror. For anyone here that recalls their colonial history, the conquistadors didn't do such nice things in Mexico.

It was a match made in heaven.

The storyline was set. But when I touch down in Mexico, I'm explicitly told there's no way I'm winning this match. And then, I'm told that Sangre Azteca refuses to choreograph the match.

If you know anything about wrestling, you know that the outcomes are predetermined, but the matches are also more or less scripted. So now, not only am I being forced to lose the match, I could get *really* hurt.

This has all gone too far.

Ironically, I'm billed as the good guy, or tecnico, as we call it in Mexican wrestling.

But when the announcer finally calls out, "El Conquistador de Nueva York," the entire audience turns on me.

Mexican wrestling is a familial affair, so everyone from the abuelas, the grandmothers, down to the kids, start cursing at me.

I feel like the entire arena wants to see me massacred.

In front of over a thousand audience members, Sangre Azteca and I go mano a mano, one on one, two out of three falls, for more than forty-five minutes.

And we go at it!

We're going blow for blow, putting each other into submission moves.

We're fighting outside of the ring.

We're kicking each other, and we're going hard!

At one point in the match, revved up by the insults of the audience, I looked down at my opponent, who I just body slammed, and I smacked him.

This was a *terrible* mistake.

All of a sudden, the chops started stinging that much more. The punches and kicks are a little heavier, and the bumps are more vicious. Things are going a little too far. But we go *at it,* and I stay in there.

For the climax of the match, I climb up to the top rope to finish him off with a high-flying maneuver, and it's just like I imagined as a kid.

It's magical.

I'm soaring through the air, only to get caught midair with a drop kick to the chest.

He pins me for the one, two, three.

I lose again.

I leave the ring confused and beaten, when a swarm of kids surround me. They're embracing me, asking me for autographs, and taking photos, and it's all so bizarre.

I bend down to greet a few kids, and I feel this little pat on my shoulder.

A little boy says in my ear, "Sí, se puede."

Yes, you can.

I'm beaten, and this kid still wants to *believe*.

He wants to believe that this character should keep fighting.

And so, I do. I take that childhood fantasy, and I turn it into an eight-year career as El Conquistador.

It's been almost ten years since the last time I stepped in the ring. Of course, I think about my adventures as a luchador all the time. But more than anything, I think about that little boy's words. Because when times get difficult, and these last two years have been some of the most challenging and tragic years of my life, El Conquistador reminds me that it's not always about winning.

It's not about being the hero all the time.

It's about moving through the failures and getting up after the losses. Because as that little kid said—that kid that just wanted to believe, "Sí, se puede," "Yes, you can."

Yes, we can.

* ⊙ *

SHAUN LEONARDO is a Brooklyn-based artist from Queens, New York City, recently profiled in *The New York Times* and on CNN. His work has been featured at the Guggenheim Museum, the High Line, the New Museum, MASS MoCA, and the Bronx Museum, with his first major public art commission staged recently at FDR Four Freedoms State Park. For his early performances, Shaun investigated the popular icons and role models that impacted his sense of manhood. He strived to transform his body and psyche into that of the hypermasculine figures he was fascinated with as a child—exploring wrestling, mixed martial arts, boxing, and bullfighting. Shaun now has a much gentler arts practice, working and living in Brooklyn with his wife and two daughters.

This story was told on October 14, 2021, at The Wilbur Theatre in Boston. The theme of the evening was Who Do You Think You Are? Director: Meg Bowles.

THE ALPHA WOLF

ELIZABETH GILBERT

Last summer I was walking down the street in New York City, in the East Village. It was a glorious day, and the sun was bright, and I had the love of my life on my arm—and she was dying. Really dying.

She had advanced pancreatic and liver cancer, and the tumors had grown, and they had spread, and she had recently discontinued all chemo and medical treatment because it was hopeless. All she wanted at this point in her life was to try to find small ways to enjoy whatever was remaining to her. And what that meant on this day was that she wanted to try to mobilize to get herself out of the house and walk to Tompkins Square Park and get a soft serve ice cream cone.

Now, Tompkins Square Park was four blocks from where we lived, but it truly might as well have been Kilimanjaro for the amount of effort that it took her to do it on this day. She is on her cane, she's leaning her full weight against me—what's left of her full weight because she's gotten so thin. I've got my arm around her, and I can feel her little bones through her sweater, and my heart is breaking because this day signifies a turning point in her illness that I had known was coming and I had dreaded was coming, and now it is here.

It is the day where she has gotten so frail and so weak that we can officially say that this once formidable person is now completely dependent on me.

And the reason that's so particularly heartbreaking—it would be heartbreaking for anybody—but the reason it was so painful in this case is this: What you've got to know about my girl is that for the seventeen years that I knew Rayya Elias, I never once saw that woman walk into a room where she was not the most powerful person in that space.

Never once; didn't matter what.

She was so tough, so strong, so *hot*. She was a Syrian-born, Detroit-raised, glamour butch lesbian, punk rock, ex-heroin addict, ex-felon, rock and roll music star, artist, filmmaker, hairdresser, writer, *phenomenon* of a human being.

And in the circles that we rolled in, Rayya was a *legend,* not just because she was so tough and so street-smart but also because she had this enormous, capacious, generous heart, and she was ferociously protective of anybody she cared about.

If you were lucky enough to be one of the people who Rayya loved, she would just tuck you under her arm and name you as one of her little cubbies, like we were all the little wolf cubs and she was the mama wolf. And she would take you through the world, and you were never in danger when Rayya was there. I have never experienced a feeling like it, and it's exactly why I fell in love with her and why I blew up my entire life to be with her—it was precisely and expressly because of that power.

But now she's powerless.

And as we're inching along the sidewalk on Avenue A I'm feeling that for the first time, and I'm feeling how the tables have turned because now I've got her tucked under *my* arm, and now it's *my* job to protect *her* from a world that she used to dominate effortlessly.

I don't know if you've ever taken care of somebody who's sick and dying, but when somebody who you love is very fragile, one of the things that happens is the entire world starts to feel incredibly perilous. You know, every crack on the sidewalk is something that could trip her, and she could hurt herself; every kid on a skateboard, every big dog could knock her over. So, it's my job to keep her safe, and I've got her bundled up, and I'm navigating her down this road.

And it's so terrible to watch her decline that the one consoling thought that I'm having in that moment is, *Thank God she has me. Like, thank God, or what would we do, who would protect her if I wasn't here?*

And at that moment, this sketchy guy on a bicycle comes tear-assing up the sidewalk superfast. He's this gross, meth-head-looking, crusty-bearded, nasty guy. He's got a furious face, and he's tearing so fast up the sidewalk, careening into pedestrians, and he's coming right at us. He almost plows us over, and I manage just at the last minute to grab Rayya and pull her out of the way for safety—but he clips her; he hits her on the arm with his bike handlebar as he goes by.

And I'm like, "Oh my God, my baby!"

At which point Rayya turns on her heels and says, "Get the FUCK off the FUCKING sidewalk, motherFUCKER!"

And the guy screeches to a halt, drops his bike, grabs his crotch, and goes, "Suck my dick, bitch!"

And Rayya goes, "If you had a DICK you'd be driving a car, not a bicycle, ya fucking LOSER!"

And I'm like, "Whoa. Kids. I'm from Connecticut. Gonna need everybody to just take it down a notch."

But I'm also looking at her, and I'm thinking, *What are you literally backing this up with?* She weighs eighty-seven and a half pounds at this point, and I'm thinking, *What are you going to do, Rayya, if this guy comes at you?*

And then I see it: He's not going to come at her because she's locked eyes with him, and she has communicated to him very clearly that *she* is the alpha, and he is the mutt, and everybody can see it, him most of all.

He drops his eyes, grabs his bike, and scuttles off, and Rayya keeps on inching down the sidewalk with her cane, gets her soft serve, finds herself a nice little sunny spot in the park, smiles up at me, and says, "Today's a good day, babe."

So yeah, this story that I had in my head when Rayya got sick about how helpless and dependent she was going to become, that never actually happened, because somehow, despite the advances of the disease, Rayya managed to remain the apex predator in every situation that she came into. And every plan that I had made—because you know I made plans to take care of her—every plan I made based on my perceived idea of her helplessness, that all blew up too. My whole planning had been based on this idea that I was powerless to stop her from dying, but by God, I was going to make sure that she had the gentlest, the safest, the most Zen, the most enlightened, the most cushioned death that a human being could possibly have.

But she didn't want any of what I was providing, as it turned out, because Rayya didn't want gentle; that's not how she rolled. So, she didn't want to talk to the bereavement counselor that I brought to our house; she wanted to watch football that afternoon with her nephews.

And I made her all this beautiful organic food to keep her as healthy as we could keep her, and she didn't want it; she wanted to live on Oreos and cigarettes, and *did* live almost exclusively on Oreos and cigarettes for a solid year past her original expiration date (as she called it).

And of course, I got her signed up with hospice because I wanted to make sure that she had the best and safest quality home care, and then Rayya got kicked out of hospice because she wouldn't let the nurses in when they came to check on her. They'd come for their weekly check-ins, and she'd send them away. She didn't want to look at their faces, didn't want to deal.

So, hospice threw her out, which causes me to beg of you and of the universe, *Who the hell gets kicked out of hospice? How is that a thing?* But that's what happened.

I went through all this trouble to rent and create this beautiful apartment for her to spend her last months in with everything that I could imagine that she could possibly need: a doorman building and an elevator and wide hallways for the inevitable wheelchair that would be coming. An extra room for a caregiver if we needed a night nurse toward the end—everything that I could possibly imagine, this beautiful, soft, sunny space. And then two months before she died, Rayya decided that she didn't want to be in New York, that she wanted to move to Detroit. She wanted to go back home to be with her family and to party with her friends from thirty years ago.

So she moved: My fragile, terminal cancer patient moved to another city. And what did I do? I did what I've always done with Rayya: I followed. I scampered after her like the little cub that I had always been and blew up my life once again just to try to keep up with the she-wolf.

But not even Rayya, tough as she is, of course, was tough enough to withstand pancreatic cancer, and the disease continued to eat at her.

By November the doctors said, "It's anytime now. She's on borrowed time already, but it could be at any moment."

Knowing that she was so close to the end, Rayya called in her ex-wife, Gigi, who she had been married to ten years earlier, and asked her to come and help take care of her. She had also already called in her ex-girlfriend Stacey from twenty years ago. And she had me. So, now what Rayya's got is a hot blonde from every decade of her life waiting on her hand and foot with devotional love, which is Rayya Elias's version, of course, of hospice. And that totally worked for her, the *Charlie's Angels* way of being taken care of. And we did it—we did it because we were crazy about her, because she had been that mack daddy, and she still was.

She managed to live till Christmas; I don't know how, but she pulled it off. It was important to her. And on Christmas Eve and Christmas Day she couldn't get off the couch, and she was in and out of awareness. But she knew that we were there, and she knew that we were loving on her, and she was happy.

At midnight on Christmas night we put her to sleep, and at four o'clock in the morning I had to wake her up to give her her pain medication, and I couldn't rouse her. This was the first time that had ever happened. So, I just lay with her and waited for another hour, and I tried again, and I couldn't get any response from her. Another hour and no response.

By the time that the light of dawn was breaking through the snowstorm outside, I could hear that her breathing was ragged, and her lips and her hands were turning blue, and I knew—this is it.

So, I went, and I got Stacey and Gigi, and I said, "It's now. Come."

What happened next was so exquisite; it was so beautiful. It was like the three of us, these three women who had loved her so passionately for her whole life, we just knew what to do, like it had been scripted or we were born to it. We came into the bedroom, and Gigi put on sacred music, and Stacey lit a candle, and then the three of us as one got on the bed, and we wrapped our bodies around her body, and we took turns telling her all the last things that she needed to know if she could still hear us.

That we loved her; that she was incredible; what a grand, stellar life that she had lived; that we would never be the same for having loved her and been loved by her. That she had forged our hearts in the furnace of her power, that we would always love her, and that we would never stop telling the world her name.

And then it was like this silence descended, and a portal opened from some distant, uncharted part of the universe, and this river of the infinite entered into that space, and we could feel it, that it was taking her very gently from us.

And that's when Rayya opened her eyes and said, "What the FUCK are you guys doing?"

And we're like, "Nothing. Nothing."

She's like, "What's going on?"

I'm like, "Definitely not a bedside death watch, no, that's not . . ." (We're wiping sheets of tears from our eyes.)

She goes, "Babe, why are Stacey and Gigi in our bed?"

I'm like, "They're not, they're just . . . dropping off some mail."

You know, I'm kicking them out of bed; Gigi's running to turn off the music.

Rayya's like, "Why does it smell like a fucking candle in here?"

Stacey's like, "It doesn't, we're just, it's my shampoo . . ."

And Rayya's like, "You guys are weird."

She sits up in bed, lights a cigarette, looks at me, and goes, "Babe, what's today's date?"

I said, "It's December twenty-sixth, my love."

She said, "Cool. I want to hit that 60 percent off sale today at lululemon."

So, that's what we did. A couple hours later we're all at lululemon; there's Rayya in the dressing room, surrounded by her attendants, trying on athleisure wear for some future that she's still very much intending to have.

Somebody once told me, and I wish to God that I had got it sooner, that there is no such thing as a dying person; there are living people and there are dead people. And as long as somebody is alive—as long as they have any sentience or sense about them—you have to expect and allow them to be who they have always been. Never more important than at the end of somebody's life that they get to be who they are and who they always were.

And I think that goes a long way toward explaining why Rayya was so resistant, why she was so stubbornly oppositional to every story that I had in my mind about what her death might be or should be; she just wasn't having it.

From the beginning of the diagnosis till the end of her life, she was like, "I'm not your story whore; you don't get to script this. I'm Rayya fucking Elias. My life, my death. I'm doing it my way. You don't write this one; I'm doing this one."

So, it was just a handful of days after Christmas when she did die, and hers was not a gentle death, I'm sure you'll be shocked to hear. She went down fighting, and it was rough.

Even there, at the end, I still had stories in my head about what I wanted it to be and how I wanted it to go.

I had this very airy, dreamy, romantic idea about what Rayya's last words would be to me, that she would gaze up at me from a soft pillow and say, "I love you," or "Thank you for everything you did for me."

You're getting the idea.

Rayya Elias's last words to me were "No, baby, no" as I was trying to walk her from the bathroom to what would be her deathbed.

"No, baby, no."

It was the last steps that she was ever going to take in her remarkable life.

"No, baby, no."

Her legs didn't even work anymore.

"No, baby, no. I got this."

And what I got, but I only got it at the very end, was that Rayya didn't want my help; she didn't want my pity; she didn't want my planning; she certainly didn't want my story. The only thing that Rayya wanted from me was that thing that I had always so effortlessly and naturally given her, which was my devotion and my awe. She just wanted me there in the room, in love with her, and bearing witness as she took that last ride.

She just wanted me standing back in amazement (and horror, but mostly amazement), watching as she went down, as she came out of this Earth, not gently but like a ship going down in a storm at sea, like the force of nature that she was. And in the end, the only thing that I could do for her in those last harrowing hours was . . . nothing.

Was nothing.

Except to surrender to my powerlessness, and to have to let her go, and to have to watch her go. And she went down swinging and battling to the last awful breath.

And it was brutal.

And it was beautiful.

And she was brave.

And I howled like a wolf when she was gone.

And I will never stop telling the world her name.

ELIZABETH GILBERT was born in Waterbury, Connecticut, in 1969, and grew up on a small family Christmas tree farm. Elizabeth is best known for her 2006 memoir, *Eat, Pray, Love,* which chronicled her journey alone around the world, looking for solace after a difficult divorce. The book was an international bestseller, translated into over thirty languages, with over 12 million copies sold worldwide. In 2010, *Eat, Pray, Love* was made into a film starring Julia Roberts. The book became so popular that *Time* magazine named Elizabeth as one of the one hundred most influential people in the world.

In 2010, Elizabeth published a follow-up to *Eat, Pray, Love* called *Committed*—a memoir that explored her ambivalent feelings about the institution of marriage. The book immediately became a #1 *New York Times* bestseller and was also received with warm critical praise. Her 2013 novel *The Signature of All Things* is a sprawling tale of nineteenth-century botanical exploration. *O, The Oprah Magazine* named it "the novel of a lifetime," and *The Wall Street Journal* called it "the most ambitious and purely imagined work of [Gilbert's] twenty-year career." Janet Maslin called it "engrossing . . . vibrant and hot-blooded."

In 2015, she published *Big Magic: Creative Living Beyond Fear*—a book that encapsulates the joyful spirit of adventure and permission that Elizabeth has always brought to her work and to her life. Her latest novel is *City of Girls*—a rollicking, sexy tale of the New York City theater world during the 1940s.

This story was told on November 8, 2018, at St. Ann's Church in New York City. The theme of the evening was First Light. Director: Catherine Burns.

IF THE SUIT FITS

PHILL BRANCH

My senior year in high school, I am your average all-American teenage boy, interested in average all-American teenage boy things, like having a cool car and taking a hot date to the prom . . . and designing my date's prom dress.

I'm five foot six, 129 pounds, and this might be surprising, but I could not catch and/or dribble a ball of any sort. So, the fact that I had a date at all was a miracle. My girlfriend's name was Dana, and she was the most beautiful girl that I had ever seen. We were together most of senior year, and as we got closer to senior prom, we began planning.

When I say *we* began planning, what I really mean is that I began to sketch what we were going to wear to the prom.

Prom was a big deal in my family. My parents went to the prom together, and several of my aunts and uncles went to the prom together. All those pictures were up on the family wall. I knew it was my turn, and nothing could go wrong.

One day, I was at home watching music videos, and there's this artist named Christopher Williams who was really popular at the time. He was this tall, gorgeous man with great curly hair. It was a music video called "Promises, Promises." He was wearing this white Nehru-collar suit. He just looked so regal and strong.

I looked up at him with my 129-pound self and said, "I'm going to look like *that* for prom."

I began sketching the suit.

Now, I'm not going to completely rip off Christopher's style because you can't steal another artist's work. I'm going to design a suit that looks like his but has my flair. It's all white, but the sleeves have this satin material that has a sort of paisley design to it. I use that same material for the trim that's going to go down the pant leg *and* to cover the buttons that are going to go all the way down from my neck. (You're judging!)

Just something simple.

For my date, I comb through all the hottest fashion publications of the time to decide what Dana's look would be. I'm in the Sears catalog and the Spiegel, JCPenney. I finally decide that she's going to wear a mermaid dress, and it's going to have some of the material from my suit because my suit was the base. She would have this pink lace overlay at the top and it would be great.

I couldn't actually draw or sew, so, I took my scribbled sketches to my seamstress-slash-friend's-mother and said, "Do you think you can make this?"

She said, "Sure, give me about a week or so, and I can put it together once you give me all the fabric."

I said, "Great."

The plan was in motion.

I had no idea that asking my date to accept my design for her senior prom dress was going to be problematic, and Dana was not into it *at all*.

So, she broke up with me.

Now, I wasn't necessarily in the closet at sixteen because I wasn't conscious, per se, that I was gay. But apparently, I was *so* gay that I wasn't aware that designing my date's prom dress in white silk with a pink shimmer when it hit the light was essentially my coming-out quinceañera.

For that whole school year where Dana was my girlfriend, it felt great to just be one of the guys, and to feel like I had the things that other guys had. To believe I could have this future and maybe I could get married and have this life. It was a really powerful feeling I hadn't had before. When she left, it was equally powerful. It affirmed all the feelings that were starting to brew up in me that I was indeed broken.

And I was hurting.

But I had about fifty yards of satin and *somebody* had to wear it. So, I asked a freshman who I knew would go, and things just moved along.

The day before the prom, I go pick up my suit from my friend's-mother-slash-seamstress, and I take it home, and I put it on.

For the first time, I realized that you might need to be able to draw if you are going to design a suit. It didn't quite work, all the colors and the materials. Then, one sleeve was shorter than the other. The pant legs weren't even, and the trim was crooked.

My mom is waiting for me to come down so she can see this suit. I go downstairs in the suit, and she does her best not to laugh in my face. After a few moments, she runs off in her room and just lies down in the bed and cries real tears.

So, the suit didn't work.

The next morning, I say, "Well, maybe if I get the curly hair, it'll balance it out."

Now, at the time I had what was called a Gumby cut, it was sort of like Bobby Brown–ish. It was up and to the side, and I was really proud of it. I rip out a picture of Christopher Williams from a teen magazine, and I take it down to a salon in my neighborhood that I had never been in before (because I wasn't a lady).

I take it inside, and I say to the stylist, "Can you make me look like this?"

Now, anyone with eyes that functioned should have said, "Absolutely not," but she said, "Sure."

I sit down. She begins to work her magic. She puts the cream in, and she's doing all this stuff. I'm just sitting there. At first, I'm really excited, but then I start to feel like someone's poured acid on my head.

I'm confused why everyone is still singing along to music on the radio and reading *Ebony* magazines when I'm clearly dying in this salon chair. And just before I scream, the stylist runs over and rinses my scalp. It feels so good! She turns me around to the mirror.

I don't look like Christopher Williams.

I look like Sade.

My hair is bone straight, and I am freaking out.

She goes, "Calm down. We're not done."

I said, "Okay."

She turns me back around, and she starts putting more things in my hair and trying to do something, and then she turns me back to the mirror.

And she was right. I didn't look like Sade anymore.

I look like Salt-N-Pepa.

I had this curly bob, and it was awful. I was about to cry. She tried a few more things, and nothing was working.

Then, she looks at me and says, "This one's on the house."

Do you know how bad your hair has to be for a stylist not to take your money?

I get up and go to the barbershop where I should have been in the first place, and he does a little something, makes me presentable enough.

I go home and put on my crooked suit. I take the freshman to the prom, and we have a good enough time.

A few weeks later, the prom proofs come back—the pictures. My date looks great, props to me, but I look *insane.*

The pictures weren't ordered. They weren't given out to family like we normally would do for people at prom time. And worse, I did not make it to my family's photo wall. I had failed at being normal again, and it was disappointing.

Years later, I'm in college, it's my senior year. I hear from Dana again, and we hadn't talked since high school really. We start to reconnect, and it feels good to hear her voice. I start to wonder if maybe we could still have something. But by this point, I knew I was gay because there had been clues.

I still invite her down to Virginia to visit with me and go to my senior ball in college, and she agrees. She comes down, and we get all dolled up in clothes that I did not design. We go to the ball and have an amazing time. For a fleeting moment, I wonder, like, *Could this be my life?* But I'm not sixteen anymore, and I know that I don't love her in that way.

I knew that I had to let her go and let that life go or that idea go, and that was really rough.

On the upside, the pictures were *amazing.*

I had the right hair, the right suit, and the right date. That picture made it up to the family wall with my parents, my aunts and uncles. I am smiling in that picture, but the truth is, I am terrified because it was the first time that I had told myself the truth.

I was scared to death.

We often talk about coming out to other people, but the truth is, you have to come out to yourself first.

After all this goes down, I accepted that it was okay for me to be me. I ended up with all the things that I thought that I wasn't going to have when I became my true self. I have a wonderful husband and a home and two amazing kids that I love. It's a beautiful life.

As it turns out, the picture of my life now hasn't made it to the family wall, but that's okay, because I have my own walls now, and I can hang any damn thing that I want.

* ◉ *

PHILL BRANCH is a storyteller working in film, creative nonfiction, and the-ater. He is a 2023 recipient of the Maryland State Arts Council's Creativity Grant and a 2019 Rubys Artist Award grantee for storytelling and perfor-mance. He was the 2018 GrandSLAM champion of The Moth in D.C. An alumnus of the American Film Institute, Branch directed *Hampton Univer-sity: One of the Wonders of the World,* about the history of HBCUs. His previous film, *Searching for Shaniqua,* a documentary about the impact names have on our lives, won the HBO Best Documentary award at the 2016 Martha's Vineyard African American Film Festival.

This story was told on October 17, 2019, at The Wilbur Theatre in Boston. The theme of the evening was Holding On and Letting Go. Director: Jenifer Hixson.

SURVIVOR'S GUILT

DAVID GASKIN

It was September 10, 2009, and I was located in Gouverneur Correctional Facility. Gouverneur Correctional Facility is a medium classified correctional facility, and I was at the tail end after serving nine years and eight months of an eleven-year bid. *Bid* is a terminology that we use to describe the length of a sentence. I was standing inside my cube, looking around, and I had a thought: *Dave, you need to get rid of some of this crap.*

The crap that I thought about getting rid of was my personal belongings that I had accumulated over the years. I was scheduled to be released the very next day. Upon having this thought, I looked around the dorm, and I caught the eyes of my comrades, and I motioned them over to my cube with a nod of my head like, "Come over here."

They came over, and once they got to the cube, I just told them, "Go in there and take whatever you want."

My comrade June walked in first, and he decided to take some of the clothes. He took some sweatsuits and some shirts that we call "visiting room shirts" that allowed us to look cool while we were out in the visiting room.

Animal was the next one inside the cube. He went straight for my books, about two or three reading books, and my collections of

BBW and *Black Tail* (which are smut magazines). And Eyes, who's the greedy one out of the whole crew, went directly for my locker. He went right in; he started digging into nonperishable items—the snacks, the canned goods, even the little packets of sugar he decided to take.

Right there, I was feeling great.

I'm about to be released the next day, and I'm doing something great for my guys. And then I feel it snatched away.

I began to feel a pain in my chest. It happened so fast—it was sharp. And just as fast as it happened, it left just as fast.

So, I continued on with my day, and I did something that usually young Black men would do when they encountered a feeling that they do not know: I disregarded it.

I went about my day as a gym worker, to my mandatory program, and when that was over, I returned back to the dorm. When I walked in, I noticed the usual: some people standing around talking; some sitting down watching TV; others playing card games, chess, or checkers. But then, I noticed the *un*usual. I noticed Eyes, June, and Animal in the far back of the TV room standing around in a circle. To the untrained eye, they might have just been standing there, but to *my* eye, they were having a meeting, and this meeting was pretty intense.

I immediately had two thoughts.

The first, *The fuck is going on over there?*

And the second, *Why wasn't I invited?*

I decided to make my way over to this circle to be fake nosy (that's being nosy, but first you have to fake it). So, I slide over, and I start moseying around.

As I get closer, I say to June, "What's going on over here?"

And he turns around really fast and says, "We're trying to figure out what to make you for your last meal today."

As he goes to turn back around, he snaps back real fast again, and he says, "And I don't know why we're thinking about making you anything because your ass is going home tomorrow."

Shocked, I step back. I look at Eyes and Animal; they begin to chuckle.

I turn back, and I look at June, and I say, "Sounds like you hatin', bro."

Me and June stare at each other for a second, and we both break into our own little laugh mixed with a handshake and a bro hug.

They decided to make some of my favorite items that night: honey barbecue chicken, baked macaroni and cheese, some yams, and coconut rice.

Now, Animal, who is from a Caribbean family, actually Jamaican, made this coconut rice, and this coconut rice was everything. I mean, ten plus years, I've been out here in the world, and I have yet to find anybody, any place, any restaurant who can make coconut rice like Animal. I mean, it was *fire*. So, after we made the food, we all sat down to begin to break bread, share some stories, reminisce on the time that we have spent together.

And I remember feeling very appreciative, very grateful, like, *Look at my guys. They communicated, took their time out, put together this meal for me.*

Those feelings and emotions were ripped away once again by that pain in my chest. But this time, it was much more intense. I felt like I had to coach myself to breathe.

As we were sitting there having conversations, I was hoping nobody noticed. And then, the count was called, and the feeling went away.

I returned back to my cube and lay on my bed. I put my hands behind my head with my fingers interlocked, I crossed my legs, and I began to look out the window and zone out. I noticed that the feet shuffling and lockers opening and closing began to die down. Staring out the window, I began to have these thoughts.

Like, *I wonder how many people slept in this bed that I'm sleeping in right now. I wonder how many people slept in this bed who were supposed to be scheduled for release the next day.*

And, of course, I thought about those that will never be released. Staring out of the window, I noticed that the sky went from being dark black to a dark gray. And that dark gray turned into a light gray, and those feet shuffling and locker doors opening and closing that had died down, they began to pick back up.

Those thoughts were broken by the sound of a telephone ringing, *ring ring, ring ring.*

The corrections officer snatched up the phone, but didn't say anything. Only thing I could hear was a loud bang when it slammed. *BOOM.*

And then, I heard something I'd been waiting to hear for a long time: "GASKIN," which is my last name.

My moment had come, and I was about to be released, y'all.

As I began to walk through the small corridor, who else is there waiting for me? June, Eyes, and Animal. Soon as I walked through the door, here goes June throwing his best combination of air punches—some jabs mixed with some body shots.

Eyes is standing behind him; he's screaming, "Yeah! Yeah!"

And Animal, who is about six foot four, 230-plus pounds, casually walked up to me, put his arm around my neck, his big arm. And what I thought was just going to be a humble hug began to get tighter and tighter and tighter around my neck.

I found myself hitting him with a little jab, like, "Come on, bro. Loosen that up some." And right there, I was attacked again by the same underlying feelings and emotions that I was having before, but this time it was very intense. I felt like somebody was squeezing on my esophagus and my heart at the same time. I had to coach myself to breathe again. I felt like I was getting a little bit dizzy. I didn't know if I was bugging out, or Animal's arm was just that tight around my neck. So, I hit him again with a little elbow, like, "Nah, bro, you got to get up off me." We said our goodbyes, and I began to make my way.

The next steps through that jail were like a blur. I remember going down to outtake, which is the opposite of intake. They gave me forty dollars and a bus ticket. I was waiting with about thirty guys for the facility bus to take us to the nearest city, where we could catch a Greyhound or Peter Pan to get down to our city. Mine happened to be New York City.

I remember getting off the bus and looking at the people walking around so freely—men, women, and children. Because I was so used to walking in a straight single-file line, I was like, *Wow.* Some were on cellphones, and that blew my mind.

I remember the smell. It was the McDonald's and the Burger King mixed with the pollution in the air. I was like, *Yeah, I'm almost there.*

And I remember the guys talking about what they were going to do when they got home, some of the food that they were going to eat, their loved ones they couldn't wait to see, the things that they wanted to do with their girlfriends.

But I could think about none of that.

The only thing I could think about was the guys that I left back in the facility—my comrades. I wondered what they were doing at this moment.

What were they having for lunch?

Were they still working out our regular scheduled workouts? You know that guy, June, that I spoke to you about? Well, he'll utilize any excuse to miss a workout. So, I was pretty concerned about him.

And then, I thought to myself, *What is wrong with me? Why am I not having the thoughts that these guys that have been released are having?*

It wasn't until I got my first job, facilitating a group full of young men, and I shared this story, and a young man inside that group said, "That's survivor's guilt."

I turned around like, "Facts."

But the fact is, I didn't even know what survivor's guilt was. Thank God that Google is our friend. So, I learned that survivor's guilt is commonly associated with PTSD. Post-traumatic stress disorder is when an individual or people survive an incident that most people did not survive.

And it was then that I began to understand those attacks that I was having.

When I was giving away my stuff to my comrades, that was cool. *But what I really wanted to do was be able to give them their freedom.*

When they took their time out to make me that meal, I was grateful. *But what I really wanted to do was something like what June said, for all of us to be on the outside, eating whatever that we wanted to eat.*

And then, in those last final moments when we were saying our goodbyes, *what I really wanted was for them to be able to embark on our journey with me.*

I still get those attacks to this day. But instead of disregarding them, I use them to fuel the work that I do.

When I work with men and women who are formerly incarcerated, and I help them navigate the barriers to successful reentry, I like to say, "Yes, that's what I do."

When I work with young men and women who are closely associated to gang and gun violence, helping them change their mindset, which will ultimately help them change their behaviors, I like to say, "Yeah, that's what I'm doing."

What I'm doing is helping other survivors.

* ☻ *

DAVID GASKIN was born and raised in Bedford-Stuyvesant, Brooklyn—the old Bed-Stuy, not the new Bed-Stuy! He recently discovered his interest in storytelling by assisting and encouraging formerly incarcerated men and women to share their stories. David is a community leader around anti-gang and gun violence. He is also one-fourth of the consulting team at Conspiring for Good, which provides capacity building, staff training and development, and conflict de-escalation.

This story was told at the Silver Ball on May 26, 2022, at Spring Studios in New York City. Director: Larry Rosen.

EXPECTING
TRYSTAN REESE

It's a bright spring morning in the middle of the backwoods of Oregon, and I am volunteering to cut trail with my partner, Biff. He is just ahead of me on the path, and suddenly I know that it's time for me to ask the question that's been building up between us for months.

"Hey, Biff, do you want to have a baby?"

Silence.

He turns around, and I see that he is laughing at me.

"This is the stupidest idea you have ever had. No, I don't want to have a baby."

In his defense, we had our hands full. We were actually *already* parents. One year into our relationship, his sister couldn't take care of her kids, and they came to stay with us for a little while. Well, "a little while" became a long while, and then it became forever. Our adoption of Hailey and Riley had just become final. They were ages five and seven, and we were just starting to get that taste of freedom that comes when you have older kids.

The second reason that he said no is because he knew that when I asked if we could have a baby, I was actually asking if I could get pregnant and give birth to a baby. This isn't some kind of feat of modern science—I'm just transgender. For me, that means that I was assigned female at birth. I was raised as a girl. When I was a teenager, I thought the best way of explaining what was going on with me was to joke that I was a gay man trapped in a woman's body.

As I got older, the feeling of being trapped in the wrong body got more and more pervasive and painful until it became unbearable, and I wasn't sure I could keep going.

And then I met a transgender person, and I realized that it wasn't a joke at all; I actually *was* a gay man trapped in a woman's body. And this was great news because it meant that there was a solution to this problem, and there was a name for it, and there was a community of people that I could go to. But most importantly, it meant that I could stay alive, and I could transition, and I could be happy.

I started taking testosterone, and that made me look like I do now: like every other gay man in Portland. And it turns out that I'm the kind of transgender person who is fine with just taking hormones. I didn't have any gender-affirming surgeries, which means that I have a fully functioning uterus and totally healthy eggs. And Biff is not trans . . . he's just a normal gay dude. (He's not normal—he's special—but you know what I mean!) So, between the two of us, even though we are two men, we have everything we need to make our own baby.

We've known dozens of other transgender men like me, with beards and everything, who have given birth to happy, beautiful children. We knew it was possible. But it had been hard for pretty much all of them, and Biff was really worried about my safety navigating the world as a pregnant man. But I live in a world of rainbows and unicorns, and I just hoped that it was going to be okay, and *also* . . . I am not good at taking no for an answer.

So eventually, Biff did say yes, and I went to a doctor, and my anatomy was in good working order. I stopped my hormones, and we started trying. A few months went by, and nothing happened, and I started to think maybe parenthood in this way wasn't going to happen for us after all. And just when I started to feel peaceful about that, I woke up one morning, and I felt *really gross.*

I had read all of the pregnancy books. I knew everything about pregnancy, and I had been tracking everything on the app, so I knew it wasn't the right time in my cycle for me to be pregnant. I didn't want to take the pregnancy test and be disappointed, but Biff insisted.

I took it, and there were two lines, and I was pregnant.

And there was going to be a baby!

I was so excited, but also super scared because you have to do a lot of things to get ready for a baby, like pick a name and buy diapers and learn how to take care of a baby. Hailey and Riley had been toddlers when they came to live with us, so I didn't know what to do with a baby.

And then, my body started to change really quickly. And all of those markers of femininity—everything just got bigger, everywhere, and I had anticipated this: that it would be the worst part of being pregnant. But it actually ended up being okay, and I think it's because really early on in my transition, I just had to accept the fact that my body is going to be different. I can't go back in time and be born with a body that's more like Biff's or my dad's, and I could spend the rest of my life obsessing over all of the things my body cannot do . . . or, I could get excited about the thing that it *can* do that their body *can't,* which is to create life.

And that's what I did. I just leaned into that, and let the rest go.

And right around this time, we had a chance to tell our story publicly. And I don't know about you all, but basically every story I've ever heard about a transgender person has been "something terrible has happened to us." I think that was why it had been so scary for me to come out as trans, because the media reports that our lives are misery. I thought maybe we could tell a different kind of story. Because, yes, there is hardship in being transgender, especially for transgender women and trans people of color, who have to grapple with sexism *and* racism *and* transphobia. But for all of us, there's also joy and love and resilience and family! And I wanted to tell *that* story, and I hoped the world was ready.

We didn't think it was a big deal for me to be a pregnant man— but everybody else did. And I don't know if they still say "go viral," but that is what happened to our story. Basically, overnight, the Pregnant Man was everywhere, like Yahoo News (if anyone still reads that), CNN, *The Washington Post, People* magazine.

"Pregnant Man!"

And I thought, *Maybe this is good. Maybe people are ready for this next evolution of what it could mean to be transgender.*

I live in Portland, and let me tell you, people were *ready* for my story in Portland. In Portland, if you see a pregnant man at Starbucks, maybe that's not the weirdest thing you've seen that day. They were into it, you know? And trans kids would come up to me with their parents, like in the grocery store, and thank me for helping them understand that there's more than one way to be a man and more than one way to be trans.

One lady told me she thought it was marvelous that my body could give me the life I deserve while also bringing new life into the world.

But outside of the Portland bubble, not everyone was ready for this story. I became really good friends with the puking emoji because I would just get hundreds of messages on Facebook that was just that. People would tell me that I'm not a man at all, I am just a really ugly, hairy woman, and that I was going to give birth to a monster.

And then, one woman sent me a message that said, "As a Christian, I hope that you give birth to a dead baby because that baby would be better off than a baby that has to be born to someone like you."

I was six months pregnant when I read that message.

Now, I have been trans for a long time: fifteen years. Actually, at age thirty-five, I am past the point of average life expectancy for a trans person in America today. I like to think that I am resilient and strong and powerful, but the truth is, I started to lose hope for our country and for trans people—that we would ever be loved in the way we deserve. All of the stories and negativity started to seep in.

One night, I had a really horrible nightmare where I was giving birth, not to a baby but to a monster with two heads and a forked tongue and a tail, and I woke up crying and shaking, and Biff was like, "What's wrong?" and I couldn't tell him.

All I could say was, "They hate us."

I didn't really know that before, that people hate us.

That fear that I was going to give birth to a monster came with me into every doctor visit.

I would look at the ultrasound and ask the technician, "On a scale of one to ten, what are the chances that I'm going to give birth to a monster?"

I carried that fear with me until I had to call the hospital to let them know I was coming in to give birth.

I talked to the head nurse on the phone, and I said, "Listen, I'm a man, and I'm coming in to give birth in your hospital, and it is my expectation that you will make sure that I am treated with integrity by every single person that comes into my room. Doctors, nurses, midwives, the person who comes to change my trash; I want them all to understand what they're walking into because I can't deal with that on top of dealing with this."

And she said, "I got it!"

And she did. Every single person that I worked with at that hospital was amazing, and Biff was there, along with my mother-in-law and my dad, who came down from Canada.

It was two days of labor, and I learned why it's called *labor* . . . because it's hard work!

But then, before I knew it, they're putting the stirrups up and telling me, "It's going to be time to push soon."

That's when it hits me that I had learned everything about pregnancy but *nothing* about actual childbirth. My brain flashes to a book sitting unopened on my bedside table. It's called, *Prepare to Push*. I had not read it. I was not prepared to push! I start hyperventilating, panicking.

I turn to Biff, and I say, "I'm so sorry, but I can't do this. I'm not strong enough."

I turn to the midwife, and I say, "I'm going to die."

She is not fazed by this; she had heard it before.

She bends down and gets nose to nose with me, and she says, "You are doing a good job, the best job. No one on Earth is doing as good a job as you are right now."

And this is like a magic spell. I know I can do this, and I hold Biff's hand, and I hold my dad's hand, and I push. I push as hard as I can, and at one point, I look down, and there's just goosebumps all over my arms and all over my legs, and then I don't know what's going on, but I start puking all over everyone. And because I'm Canadian, I start apologizing to everyone for throwing up on them while I'm in labor. But eventually, they start screaming at me to slow down and stop pushing, to just push in teeny tiny bits. And everyone is yelling and there's all this noise and then everything stops—and there's this wet slurping sound.

And then, he's out.

And they hold my baby up in the light, and he's glistening, like all those movies you ever saw. And he opens his mouth, and he lets out his first cry. His voice echoes through me, and all of that hope that I thought I lost, it all comes rushing back, because a baby means hope. It means you believe there will be a tomorrow, that the world is good enough for your child.

They put him on my chest, and he feels like a baby bird. And before Hailey and Riley run in to meet their baby brother, I look down at him, and he has ten fingers and ten toes, and a full head of black curly hair, just like me. And I think, *He could have been a monster. He could have had two heads, and a forked tongue and a tail—and I would have loved him just the same.*

To me, he would have been perfect.

TRYSTAN REESE has been organizing with the trans community for nearly two decades and has been on the front lines of this generation's biggest fights for LGBTQ+ justice. His unique parenting journey launched him onto the global stage in 2017, offering an opportunity to bring his message of resilience and resistance to mainstream audiences everywhere. Trystan is the author of *How We Do Family,* and he lives in Portland, Oregon, with his partner, Biff, and their three children. They are very happy.

This story was told on April 19, 2018, at the KiMo Theatre in Albuquerque. The theme of the evening was Unbridled. Director: Catherine McCarthy.

A LIGHT
SHINING
THROUGH

OPERATION: BRUIN ESCAPE AND RESCUE (BEAR)

ELANA DUFFY

So, no shit, there I was—twenty-five thousand feet in the air on my way to a vacation, with friends I hadn't seen in ages, in Ecuador and the Galapagos Islands. Trip of a lifetime.

They pass out the customs forms. I reach into my bag, searching for a pen. And as I'm searching, I'm going deeper and deeper into my bag.

I found the pen—but what I didn't realize until that very moment was that I had forgotten a critical piece of my standard operating equipment.

Paddington D. Bear was purchased on a business trip to London that my father had taken while my mother was pregnant with me. He had been to every state my family went to on vacation. He went with me to space camp (because, yes, I went to space camp—twice).

He went with me to college. He went to six continents. He went to the top of four mountains. He has been through every friendship, every breakup that I have endured.

Even when I joined the army, he went with me. He just had to stay locked in a duffel bag in the back room with all of the other civilian accoutrements that you're not exactly allowed to have with you.

And when I deployed, he went with me to Afghanistan and to

Iraq and rode on every convoy that I went on, right in my pocket. He survived a roadside bomb explosion and dozens of mortar attacks with me. He went with me to the surgeries I had to have afterward. He was just always there. He was my comfort. He was what was going to get me through whatever I had to get through.

Except right now. Right now he was sitting next to my door because I had to get up for a zero dark thirty flight. And I had just walked right by him.

I had forgotten him.

And so now I am thirty-two years old, with a decade of decorated military service and two engineering degrees, crying my eyes out in public over a teddy bear.

Paddington is not a pretty bear by any means. He has lost all of his fuzz. He is on ear set three, foot set two and a half. His beans are scattered all over the world. But every stitch and scar on him was a result of his constant companionship, a reminder of our survival through the decades.

I was not going to sit here and cry over my bear and not come up with something to do. Oh no. When I landed, I had a plan.

The first thing I did when we touched down was I called home and said, "Look, you take that bear, you go to FedEx, you put that bear in a box, and you tell them very specifically if he can get here in a week, you send it to location one. If he gets here a couple days after, send him to location two," and so on down the line.

I then visited each and every hotel that we were going to be going to and said, "If a box arrives for me, please hang on to it in case I'm not here. I will come back and get this. It is critical."

Our schedule was very tight. I needed to make this whole thing foolproof.

The next week I spent climbing mountains, wandering around, exploring the cities. We went on a zip line. We did some weird thing with some tires that they said was whitewater rafting. Definitely not safe. And as much fun as we were having, every single night, I still went back to the hotel and checked. *Where was the box?*

By the time we left the Galapagos, I saw the box had made its way to Ecuador. It was sitting in customs. Paddington was in the country. I could finally relax.

As soon as we got back from the islands for our last day in Quito, I checked on Paddington. We hadn't even gotten to the hotel yet. I'm burning up data minutes to look and see where he is. When we saw he was at one of the hotels we'd checked out of, we diverted the cab. My friends had piled in with me. They were super jazzed about this reunion we were about to have.

I get out, I go in to the front desk of the hotel where the tracker said the box was, and the hotel clerk is like, "Oh no, we don't have a box for you."

"Can you check again?"

He checks again—"No, there's no box."

There's no box at the desk. There's no box in the storeroom. No one has a clue where the box might be. Now, I'm thirty-two years and two more weeks older and crying again. And I get back into the cab, and call FedEx.

"What have you done with my bear?"

The FedEx agent explains: Ecuador has a major drug problem. As it turns out, you can't accept a package on behalf of someone else, regardless if you are a hotel clerk or anything else, unless the person is there to take it off your hands.

No one really knows about this law because I guess not a whole lot of people are emergency shipping teddy bears internationally.

So I am desperate.

I'm talking to the agent, and she's like, "Look, there's nothing that we can do here. There's only one storage facility for this type of package in the entire country of Ecuador."

"Where is it?"

"Oh, it's in Guayaquil. Are you near Guayaquil?"

"No, I'm in Quito—Quito is several hundred miles away. I have twenty-four hours left on land here, and I've got to report back to my army unit back home."

"Well, they said that you have to come in person to pick up the package."

"Okay, great. I guess I'm going home, and I'll figure it out from there."

And so, I had to go home empty-handed and completely devastated. And the army, of course, didn't care as long as I returned to work the next day.

See, I was the lead noncommissioned officer for my section at an elite military unit of investigators and interrogators, all with long and storied careers that they couldn't tell you a thing about if you asked them. They were also mostly men, almost all of them ten or more years my senior, and all of them extremely well-trained operatives of some sort.

So here, essentially, I was alone. At least in Ecuador I had had my friends with me, supporting my drive to get my teddy bear home. I had their shoulders to cry on for those two weeks.

Here, I'm not crying on any of these guys' shoulders, that's for sure.

In the military, women are already looked at as a little too emotional, a little *too much,* a little weaker, and so you have to prove every single day that you are going to make it through and that you are tough. You are even tougher than the guy sitting next to you or sharing your foxhole (as if we did that anymore).

But you know what? I steeled my resolve. As far as I saw it, this was a hostage crisis. And wouldn't you know it, I had done a stint in hostage rescue a couple years back. I knew exactly what I needed to do.

So, for the next month, from a desk in a more secluded office, away from the prying eyes of the gentlemen, I contacted FedEx every single day. I befriended this FedEx agent, who I now saw as my sole ally. She too became emotionally invested in getting Paddington back—including activating her entire chain, all the way through the chief of the international shipping division at FedEx, who were now concerned about the whereabouts of this bear.

The only people who didn't seem to care that much were the ones in the customs office. They simply could not be convinced that someone would go through all this trouble for a beaten-up little bear—unless, of course, there's some contraband shoved inside his beans.

No matter what anyone did, I had to go in person to pick up this bear. Back down to Ecuador.

And by the way, packages can only be held in this facility for forty-five days.

I was sitting at my desk when the email arrived.

"*Come to Guayaquil in the next week or the box and its contents will be incinerated.*"

Looks like Ecuador had issued their ransom note.

I am out of options. I have no more leave; I just burned it. I had no way to get down there. I had nothing.

My friend, my comfort, my companion was about to be destroyed, and there was absolutely nothing that I could do about it.

At that exact moment, a co-worker walked in. She happened to be the only other female operator in my section and just wanted to know where I was on one of our other projects. There was no quick wiping of my face and slapping a smile on.

Instead, I'm staring at her, as if my life is over.

She asked me, "Okay, what's wrong?"

I look at her, and in a rush, the whole story just tumbles out—that my teddy bear is in Ecuador and is about to be thrown into an incinerator, and there's absolutely nothing I can do, and I'm at a total loss.

And then I shut my mouth super quick and wait for her to laugh at me.

She considers me for a moment, nods, and says, "Okay, come follow me."

We go to the other section where she works. We're weaving through all of the other desks. And as we're going, she's handpicking people one by one until there's about five people in our little entourage following behind.

We get back to her desk, and she looks at me, and I mumble my story and stare at the floor.

Well, the room has gone completely silent. Everyone has heard.

And then, all of a sudden, it was the biggest hive of activity. Everyone had a suggestion. Everyone had someone to call. The people that she had picked all had experience in South America. Someone knew someone who knew somebody else who owed them a favor at the last government office that they had been to.

We were taking this hostage crisis, and we were turning it into an international incident.

So, after some calls between three embassies and five customs control officers in two different countries and a personal visit in South America from one old friend to another, Paddington was finally released from Ecuadorian customs—less than twenty-four hours before he was scheduled to be incinerated.

When the box arrived, it was battered and travel-stained and looked like it had been through way more than anything that I had seen in my deployments. I tore it open. I pulled Paddington into daylight for the first time in two months, and my fingers fell into this long slit that someone had cut in his back to check for contraband.

But someone at U.S. Customs had lovingly put his spilled beans back into him and made a little diaper out of Customs tape so that he could retain them for the rest of his journey.

I snapped a little proof-of-life photo of him popping out of the box so that I could send it back to my co-workers. And they, of course, forwarded it on to all of the other people at all of these embassies and so forth.

I sent it to FedEx, and I was getting emails from the FedEx agents.

And when I went back to the office, the little proof-of-life photo had been printed out and put up on the wall next to this *Free Paddington* poster that we had had made as we were waiting for him to be shipped home.

It seemed impossible to me, throughout this whole thing, that I was just a sad army NCO with a careworn teddy bear—and yet all of these people had jumped at the chance to help rescue him.

And then one co-worker walked up to me and showed me a picture that he had carried with him in his wallet since high school. And another one pointed to a little trinket that was on his desk that had been on every military mission he'd been on. One of the embassy agents had sent along a picture of his own teddy bear, which sat on a shelf behind him in a place of honor at the embassy where he now worked.

And I realized, as tough and independent and strong as we all make ourselves out to be, everyone has a Paddington.

ELANA DUFFY is an engineer, a decorated U.S. Army veteran, and—whenever possible—an explorer. Despite sustaining combat injuries that required neurosurgery and, later, the loss of her leg, she has visited all seven continents and reached the summit of multiple mountains. Since leaving the service, she has become a fierce advocate for the military and veteran communities and other underserved populations, using her skills and training to offer assistance to those who need it while inspiring individuals to push personal boundaries and do more for themselves and others. She spends her free time writing, rock climbing, and providing a lap for her cats to sit on while watching (and rewatching) science fiction shows.

This story was told on July 30, 2021, at the Green-Wood Cemetery in New York City. The theme of the evening was All That Remains. Director: Larry Rosen.

KNOCKOFFS

EDGAR RUIZ JR.

Back in the summer of 1993, I was twelve years old, living with my mom in the Bronx, and she decided that she was going to send me back to Puerto Rico to live with my dad for the entire summer.

When wealthy kids act up, they probably get sent to boarding schools. When Nuyoricans act up, we get sent back to the island. I wasn't a delinquent or anything like that, but let's just say puberty was hitting me really hard, and my mama wasn't feeling me.

She divorced my dad when I was two, and we left Puerto Rico shortly after for New York, leaving him behind. As a child, I barely remember my pops. Like the earliest memories I have of him are long-distance phone calls for my birthday and sometimes on Christmas.

You can say that the summer of 1992 started off on the wrong foot, literally. The only pair of sneakers I took with me to Puerto Rico were stolen out of my suitcase at the airport. So, I had to wear flip-flops in the mountains for a few days until my mom, who was still in New York, called and forced my dad to get me some sneakers.

Now, this is probably a good time to let you know that at the age of twelve, I was already six feet, one inch tall, 230-something pounds, and I wore a size twelve sneaker.

Not a lot of size twelves in the small town of Cabo Rojo, Puerto Rico, where my family is from.

After walking out of three discount shoe stores empty-handed, my dad was heated. He knew he was going to have to take me to the mall and actually spend some money on me. He was mad.

Not me though, I was excited. I'm a true city kid. We *love* sneakers in the hood. On my block, what you wore on your feet represented where you were in the food chain. You wore some busted-looking kicks, the kids were going to have jokes and eat you alive.

So, when we got to the mall, I went straight to the Nike section, picked out some Air Force Ones, and brought them back to my pops. My dad had a serious face on.

He looked at the sneakers, he looked at the price, then he looked at me and, in Spanish, he said, "*No.*"

(Y'all speak Spanish?)

He told me to get something cheaper. So, my next logical step was to get some Reeboks for like $29.99. But before I could even walk back to him, he was shaking his head emphatically, as if I was juggling grenades or something. I could see the frustration on his face, and I barely knew this guy, so it was kind of intimidating. I gave up quickly and let him pick out whatever sneaker he wanted.

I don't really remember the name brand he chose, because I think I repressed it, but I'll never forget how *ugly* these sneakers were. They were like a taupe-ish, gray-ish color. And they were complete knockoffs of the Reebok Pumps. Y'all remember the Pumps? They had a little ball on the tongue, and you could fill them up with air. Those sneakers were so dope.

These knockoffs were *not.*

They cost him $13.99.

I was so disappointed he didn't buy me those Nikes!

I was twelve years old. So to me, him not getting me those sneakers obviously meant he had no love for me.

Gossiping with my mom on the phone that night, I remember telling her, "My dad is *so* cheap. Mom, I promise you when I have my own kids, I'm going to buy them the most expensive sneakers I can afford to show them that I love them."

(Those are lies now. If my two- and five-year-old want some sneakers, they better get a job.)

Here's the crazy part—even though I felt my dad didn't have love for me, I definitely had love for my father. So much so that I actually fell in love with those ugly sneakers, just because he bought them for me. And when I got back to New York, I literally wore those things till they ripped apart. People made fun of me for wearing them— I didn't care. My dad gave me those sneakers, and my dad never really gave me anything. Those ugly things hugging my feet were the closest I was going to get to a hug from my dad, and I held on to them as long as I could.

After that trip, I took a long hiatus from Puerto Rico. I didn't go back till I was nineteen years old. By then, I was a high school graduate—college sophomore, actually. I was working, and I had a little bit of money in my pockets. So, I went back to Puerto Rico wearing name-brand *everything*. It was the early 2000s, so I was rocking them shiny Sean John shirts, super baggy Pelle Pelle jeans.

But most importantly, I was rocking *Jordans*. Not just any Jordans, either; we talking about the shiny patent leather *Air Jordan 11s*.

If you don't know anything about sneakers, just know that the Air Jordan 11s are on top of the food chain.

I was showing off. I was trying to show my dad the man that I was becoming without his help. But I learned a few things on that trip.

I was completely wrong about my father. My dad wasn't cheap;

he was just struggling. He lived most of his life living paycheck to paycheck, trying to support his family, my younger siblings. I looked it up: Minimum wage back in '92 was like $5.25, *if* he was lucky enough to be making that in the factory. So that $13.99 that he spent on them ugly sneakers must have been like half a day's work for the dude.

I was embarrassed. And I was humbled.

It was on that trip at nineteen that I finally laid the foundation for the relationship that I always wanted with my dad. And the more I got to know about him, the more I got to know about myself. Ironically, several weeks prior to that trip, I wrote this psychology paper on nature versus nurture.

Nature versus nurture is a theory in psychology that tries to de-bate what are the most important factors in the development of a human: their genetics or their environment? And when I wrote that paper, I was on the side of nurture because I thought I was a product of my mama, a product of the streets of New York.

But then I got to know my dad, and I realized I had a lot more of Cabo Rojo, Puerto Rico, coursing through my veins. And it was scary. I wasn't raised with this guy, but there we were, liking the same types of music and movies, sharing personal philosophies. Little things from the way we signed our names the same to even the type of girls we liked. (All of them. We liked them all.)

It was scary. It was like looking into a mirror for the first time and seeing your reflection. Dude is one of the nicest people you'll ever meet, but he's also one of the most sarcastic, *just like me*. He is extremely charismatic, the life of the party, but loves to be alone, *just like me*. Extremely artistic; really good with his hands; loves to draw, paint, and build, *just like me*. And his skills with the ladies? Impec-cable. (Nothing like me. I didn't get none of those genetics!)

I love my dad. I always knew who he was, but during that sum-mer, I finally allowed him to be my father.

Now, I want to tell you things have gotten better for the guy, but you've probably seen some of the news coming out of Puerto Rico: political unrest, earthquakes, Hurricane Maria—and that was *before* the pandemic. But my dad is a survivor, and he does what he has to do to make ends meet. And I try to do as much as I can for him, but he's one of these prideful Puerto Ricans that would rather live in a house with half a roof and no power than take a handout.

But I do what I can. I have to. He's a part of me.

Not too long ago, while on vacation, we were hanging out, playing pool, and I noticed that his sneakers were looking run down. Like, I've seen better sneakers hanging off power lines in the hood.

So, I tricked him, took him to the mall, the same exact mall he took me to when I was twelve.

We went to the Foot Locker, and I told him to pick out whatever sneaker he wanted.

And after a twenty-minute argument, because he's hardheaded, *just like me,* he finally picked out a twenty-dollar pair of no-name-brand sneakers.

And I turned to him, and in Spanish, I said, "*No!*"

Hell no.

That day, my dad walked out of the mall with a fresh pair of Nikes. They looked really good on his feet. And I know he loved them, but not as much as I loved those ugly knockoffs he got me.

EDGAR RUIZ JR. is a proud Nuyorican born in Cabo Rojo, Puerto Rico, and raised in the Bronx. After graduating from the distinguished DeWitt Clinton High School, he received a BA in sociology and English literature from Lehman College at the City University of New York. Having worked for over twenty years in the nonprofit sector, he has long been devoted to underserved communities in New York. Edgar first came to The Moth as a storyteller in 2018 and slowly climbed up The Moth ladder, taking jobs as a

StorySLAM host and as an instructor. Currently, he is the manager of The Moth Community Engagement program, where he inspires confidence through storytelling and deepens relationships with communities throughout the country. This stand-up philosopher enjoys healing people with laughter and bringing positive vibes wherever he goes. If you catch him daydreaming, he's probably on a beach with his wife and two young children.

This story was told on October 23, 2021, at the Music Hall Center for the Performing Arts in Detroit. The theme of the evening was Lost and Found. Director: Jenifer Hixson.

SURVIVE, THEN LIVE
PATIENCE MURRAY

I heard gunshots.

They were firing off over the music, and it sounded like they were coming from another room in the club.

People were screaming, ducking, and scrambling for cover.

I was twenty years old.

It was my first time going to Florida. My first trip alone with friends—Tiara and her cousin Akyra. The trip was the only thing we talked about for weeks.

It was my first time getting on a plane.

And it was my first time being at Pulse nightclub in Orlando.

It was an eighteen-and-up club, and we had so much fun that night, dancing and being silly. The club was closing soon. My feet were aching, my armpits were drenched, and the sleek ponytail I had in the car had turned into a bushy mess. We embodied the phrase "Leave everything on the dance floor." And we did . . . until we heard the first shots of the machine gun.

I dropped to the ground. Things started moving quickly. It was like the room was spinning. I could hear other people, but I couldn't hear myself. I couldn't hear my thoughts. I couldn't think.

I was on the floor scooting backwards away from all the chaos, and I kept moving and moving until I felt the cool ground underneath my palms. Somehow, I'd miraculously scooted my way through an exit and made it outside.

When I looked up, I saw Akyra coming toward me. She said Tiara was still inside.

I lifted myself up from the ground and, without any hesitation, we rushed back in for her. It was the first time I felt that kind of determination, but leaving Tiara behind wasn't an option.

The gunfire was still blasting, and it sounded like it was getting closer. Tiara was squatting by the bar, paralyzed with fear. Her eyes were lost. We didn't have any time to think. The exit seemed way too far, and the gunfire seemed way too close.

We saw people rushing into the bathrooms, and we really needed to hide, so we decided to follow them. The bathroom only had four stalls, so we jammed ourselves into the handicapped one with twenty other people.

We could still hear the gunshots, the screams, but by this point, the music had stopped. There was a brief moment of silence. Then everyone started talking again. Some people were on their phones, and others were begging people to remain quiet. I saw a girl bleeding on the floor, holding her arm.

Then the gunfire started again, but this time it was inside our bathroom.

We were screaming and scrambling around on the floor as the shooter fired endless rounds of bullets at us. Then the shooter's gun jammed. The gunfire stopped.

When I looked down at my leg, I saw a hole the size of a penny, red streams of blood. I tried to wiggle my way into a space on the floor, but the pressure surrounding the bullet wound was so heavy, it felt like a boulder had just dropped on my leg, crushing it. It stunned my entire body. I could barely move an inch. I could barely breathe straight.

Underneath the stall, I could see the shooter's feet and his machine gun. It was nothing like I had ever seen.

It was the first time I ever saw a machine gun in real life.

I lifted my head from the floor, and Akyra had her phone raised to her ear while she was bracing her bleeding arm.

I heard her say, "Please come get us, please. I've been shot."

I desperately hoped that her calls would save us all.

Then out of nowhere the man said, "Get off your phones."

Not in a yelling voice, not an angry voice. It was a calm voice, which was terrifying.

I didn't dare pick up my phone, and besides, the only people I could call lived a thousand miles away. I was on vacation, and it was the first time I'd left the state without telling my father.

I started crying. I felt a hand rubbing my arm, trying to console me, and I don't know whose hand it was, but I appreciated that hand so much.

I tried to slide forward, but my right leg was bent and pinned under the man lying next to me.

I asked him, "Please get off my leg. It's been shot," but he was shot too and couldn't move either.

We needed someone to come save us because there was absolutely nothing that we could do to save ourselves.

It was going on three A.M. We'd been lying in each other's blood for hours. Phones were ringing. They were making the shooter agitated, and I found it harder to keep my eyes open. I wasn't sure if I was falling asleep or if I was dying.

Then a phone rang, and rang, and kept ringing.

And then the shooter started making his own calls to 911.

He warned the police to stay away, claiming that if they didn't, he'd detonate the explosives he had in his car. At first all I had to worry about was him shooting me again. But now I feared being blown to pieces.

I heard the shooter pacing. I could see his feet right outside of our stall door. I didn't want to die, but each time I heard him click his gun, I lost hope.

I felt myself giving up.

Lying in excruciating pain makes you beg God to take the soul out of your body.

It makes you pray and ask forgiveness.

It makes you regret not saying all the things that you wanted to tell people, yet extremely grateful for the things that you *did* say.

Suddenly there was a loud boom. The entire building shook. Then there was another loud boom, even louder than the first.

I just knew that this was it. I knew that I was about to die.

I placed my hand in my mouth and clenched my fists in preparation for death.

Then out of nowhere, a voice over a speaker shouted, "Get away from the walls."

The shooter ran into our stall and began firing at people.

I didn't move.

I didn't breathe.

I just held my breath and clenched my fists.

I felt the man next to me move closer. I felt his body pressed on my arm. And then the gunman shot again, and I heard the man on top of me scream.

Then there was another loud boom. The wall came crashing down. Debris covered my face, but I could still see a light shining through the hole in the wall. The police shouted for the man to put down his weapon, and then the room erupted with gunfire and lit up like a night sky on July Fourth.

Then there was nothing.

There was silence.

When the police came in through the hole in the wall, I remember looking up at the officer with his armor and gun in complete shock.

I was alive.

I can still see the image of my legs on the stretcher, against the backdrop of those closed ambulance doors. It's engraved in my mind forever.

The hospital was a blur, but I do remember the nurse handing me the phone. I memorized my father's number just in case I ever lost my phone, and today I was glad I did.

The doctor explained the situation to my father. I had been shot in both legs, and the bullet that entered my right thigh had shattered my femur bone, so I was being taken into surgery.

They handed the phone to me. I could hear how confused my father was, and I tried my best to remain calm and clear. I didn't want him to hear the fear in my voice, like I heard the confusion in his.

He kept saying, "You're going to be fine."

My dad was no doctor, but I believed him. I kept those words with me as I rolled into surgery, and they were the only thing that gave me hope.

Tiara survived a gunshot to her side, but Akyra didn't make it. Earlier that night, we were celebrating all of her successes, and now she was gone.

It was the first time I ever felt the sensation of someone just suddenly being *gone*.

It's been three years since the shooting.

I remember my first time walking again.

I remember my first time going to school again.

I remember my first time going to a club again.

And I remember my first time being happy again.

But no matter how happy I am, or how much stronger I feel, I always ask God, *Why?* Even now I can't believe that I survived.

Forty-nine people were killed.

I think about the odds of the gunman not shooting me for a third time, or the police not coming in when they did.

And I can't stop thinking about, *Why me?*

Every day I think of that, and every day, I'm living to figure out the answer to that question.

PATIENCE MURRAY is an accomplished young woman who wears many hats: author, activist, entrepreneur, inspirational speaker, artist, poet, podcaster, and Pulse survivor to champion. Patience is the founder of Pages of Poetry, a self-publishing consultancy, and the Gun Violence Champion Awards, a financial assistance program for survivors of gun violence. Despite the horror she has faced, Patience turned her pain into purpose and uses her massive social media following to share important stories, build confidence, and inspire resilience in others.

This story was told on February 6, 2020, at the Anderson Theater, Memorial Hall in Cincinnati. The theme of the evening was Between Worlds. Director: Meg Bowles.

DANCING IN THE BAZAAR

MANIZA NAQVI

Back in December 2016, I was sitting in my office at the World Bank in Washington, D.C., feeling unmoored and disheartened. Every day, I walked through Lafayette Park in front of the White House to get to my work. But lately, the noise had been so loud and ugly about the Muslim ban and building a wall. I was beginning to panic. *What's a person like me even supposed to do about this? Why am I even here?*

I came from Pakistan thirty years ago for my job. I absolutely love my job. I get to work with national and local governments and villages to build social safety nets in order to reduce poverty. I get to design and supervise projects. I don't actually do anything with my own hands, but I'm on the ground in many different countries, and I travel a lot. And now—as if flying while Muslim wasn't fun enough—they're going to ban me too?

I feel scattered all over the map. My writing helps to ground me. But still, I feel like I need a change. I need someone to throw me a lifeline.

That day, while I'm sitting at my desk, munching a salad at lunchtime, an article pops up in my newsfeed. It's about one of the oldest bookshops in Karachi, Pakistan: Pioneer Book House. Never heard of it.

But a long time ago, for a short while, I lived and worked in

Karachi. I had a car of my own, and I explored the whole city—particularly the old part of the city—which has these buildings that are decaying but are beautiful to me. They're in this Indo-Saracenic, European architectural style. I think I've lived longer in Karachi in my imagination than I have in reality. But isn't that the way it is about the places you leave behind? They're more magical in memory.

Anyways, this article says that Pioneer Book House, which has been open since 1945, is about to be sold by the owner, Zafar Hussain.

He says, "No one buys books."

There's a photograph of the bookshop in the article, and I look at it, and I feel like I'm fusing with the photograph. There's even a sound in my head like a *whaaaa*. I feel like, *Oh my God, this is one of those old beautiful buildings. And what would happen if all the bookshops in the world start to close down? Hate is going to rise.*

I can do this. I can save a bookshop.

I think the universe is throwing me a lifeline.

The next thing I know, I've taken all my accumulated leave, and I'm on a flight to Karachi. I've catapulted myself from the heart of Washington, D.C., to the heart of old Karachi.

And now I'm standing outside Pioneer Book House in the clattering, clanging, busy bazaar, and I'm looking into the shop. I can see that inside, it's dark, and there's a man sitting, hunched over. He's bearded; he looks to me like he's despairing. I ask him if I can come in. He nods, so I go in and sit next to him. This is Zafar sahib.

I introduce myself as a writer. I tell him I read this article, and I want to help him save his bookshop.

He's not buying it. He wants to sell the shop. He says he has a family to take care of—a wife, four children, a mother, and a brother.

He says, "No one buys books."

His grandfather opened this shop seventy-one years ago.

He says, "Now someone will buy this bookshop and turn it into a biryani shop or a mobile phone shop because biryani sells, and mobile phones sell, and nobody buys books."

I look around me. There are wires hanging from the ceiling. In one corner, there's a broken fan and a broken chair. In another corner, there are two car doors—dented—and car tires. *Car parts?!* There are books spilling out of bookshelves, covered in one-inch-thick dust and grime. There is crumpled newspaper lying in heaps and heaps all over the floor. And this tiny little bookshop is lined by bookshelves.

Zafar sahib says, "These are made of teak."

When I ooh and aah, he says, "Well, if you think this is beautiful, wait until you see the upstairs."

And he points to the stairs in the back.

I go up the stairs and suddenly, I'm in this large, cavernous space of three huge rooms lying in the dark. The condition here is like the bookshop downstairs, only worse.

But it appears magical to me. It's a quiet space, a silent space, a waiting space. I feel like it's a waiting-for-*me* kind of a space.

In the back room, there's a gigantic table, just groaning under piles of books, pamphlets, cloth, and paper—all covered in dust. I think, *This room could be a book reading room, and that one could be an art gallery.*

I go rushing downstairs, and I sit next to Zafar sahib, and I say, "Zafar sahib, you might think you're invisible. You might think no one sees you or sees your shop here. But just think—what would happen if all the bookshops close down?"

Something about my impassioned plea moves him, apparently, because he agrees for me to come back the next day and talk to him some more. So, I go back the next day, and the one after that, and the one after that, until Zafar sahib relents and agrees for me to sort out his whole shop and show him that it can work as a bookshop.

Oh, I'm just overjoyed! I'm so appreciative and grateful for his kindness, for his generosity, for his indulging me this way and letting me into his shop in this manner. That night, I email back to Washington, D.C., and request and receive permission to telecommute.

The next day, I show up at Pioneer Book House with brooms and dusters in hand and ask Zafar sahib which books, which bookshelves, and which floors I can start cleaning.

I do nothing without his permission, and as soon as it's granted, I get started. Dusting and cleaning and sorting. And as I do this, I talk and talk, while Zafar sahib sits, staring out at the street glumly. But I ask him a hundred questions about the Pioneer Book House's history, the history of his family, and the history of the city, until he finally melts and starts answering them.

As he talks, and as I clean and sweep, I begin to realize and appreciate even more the troubles that Karachi has gone through, the troubles this city has faced. There's a war going on in Afghanistan next door, and the fallout has been on the city. It's a wonder that shopkeepers have been able to keep their shops open, let alone hold on to their properties. And there's so much distrust.

I know I must seem like an oddity here. A woman of my background sweeping and dusting and cleaning in the bazaar. I would have seemed like an oddity under any circumstance. But I just ignore that and ratchet up my clueless, can-do spirit. I'm going for endearing.

Even so, one day a shopkeeper in the neighborhood comes in, points a finger at me, and says, "American agent, FBI!"

I'm so startled.

I say, "FBI? Wouldn't CIA make more sense here?"

Everybody in the shop bursts out laughing. In the coming days, I make friends with that shopkeeper and other shopkeepers, as well as street vendors and a traffic cop or two. Every day, at least two people come in to have lunch with Zafar sahib. And everybody eats out of a communal plate, so that if there are four hands dipping into the plate, the fifth is mine.

And this means the world to me. I feel so welcomed, so appreciated. Like I matter here. I'm getting to do things with my own hands. And as I sweep and dust and clean in the shop, I feel like I'm spinning and dancing in the bazaar. I mean, what could be better than this? I'm a World Banker by night and a sweeper in a bookshop by day.

But I know I could show up here tomorrow, and Zafar sahib could tell me that he's sold his property, and the Pioneer Book House is destined to become the Good Luck Biryani Shop. But, until that happens, I'm going to try my darndest to keep this shop open.

It takes me about twenty days to sort through the whole shop. Every day, I'm covered with dust and grime, from the top of my head to the soles of my feet. But I want to do everything with my own hands. I'm lifting loads and loads of bags filled with paper and books that need to be discarded and sent to the recycler. But I can't do everything myself.

I need to get an electrician, for example, to fix the wiring. And to put in new lights and new lamps. I get these embroidered caps from the bazaar next door to put in between the books on the bookshelves. I get these glass bottles—green, red, yellow, blue—from the old bottles bazaar nearby to put in glass shelves in the window to catch the light. I get chairs to put around the reading table.

And those car parts? Zafar sahib never let me throw those out. But, shoved in the corner under the right light—modern art?

When the lights go on, oh, when the lights go on, the place is bathed in golden light. It has such great bones. It looks so beautiful, even Zafar sahib is smiling, and he's amazed. And I think maybe that's all it takes—for someone to come in and turn the lights back on.

In the coming days, we plan to have a book reading; at least twenty-five people will come. We plan it down to the snacks and the tea we are going to serve. I scrub the floors as much as I can upstairs. I scrub them and scrub them until I learn this important lesson: that dust is a reality in Karachi. I can dust and clean all I want, and it's going to come back.

When the book reading begins, I ask Zafar sahib to sit and enjoy the guests in his house, to enjoy the book reading. I tell him that I will go downstairs and mind the shop with his son.

I go downstairs, and I sit there looking out at the street. I feel so overwhelmed. What could be better than this? The house is full of people. There's a book reading going on here for the first time. And I think, *This boat might be afloat. This bookshop stands a chance.*

It's been five years, and Pioneer Book House's doors are still open. The bookshop is in the hands of the family that has owned it for seventy-six years now.

And me? I feel like all my scattered parts came together. When the noise and ugliness got so loud, I focused in on a point of beauty. I may have rescued a bookshop, but I'm pretty sure the bookshop rescued me.

* ⊙ *

MANIZA NAQVI is a Pakistani American novelist and short story writer. Her five novels are *Mass Transit* (1998), *On Air* (2000), *Stay with Me* (2004), *A Matter of Detail* (2008), and *The Inn* (2021). Her book of short stories and poems is called *Sarajevo Saturdays* (2009). Her short story "An Impossible Shade of Home Brew" is included in the anthology *And Then the World Changed.* Her short story "A Brief Acquaintance" is included in the anthology *Neither Night nor Day.* Her short story "Muse" is included in the anthology *Shaping the World.* Her play "That Sara Aziz" is included in the anthology *Shattering Stereotypes* and was produced at the Minneapolis Fringe Festival. Her book *A Guest in the House* chronicles her time at the Pioneer Book House in Karachi and provides a lens into the history of the city. She is a

Monday columnist for 3Quarksdaily.com. She has thirty years of experience in social protection and social development; managing the preparation, design, and supervision of social safety nets; community development; and job creation programs. Maniza is the founder and CEO of the e-book start-up The Little Book Company, Pakistan's first e-book platform.

This story was told on November 10, 2021, at St. Ann's Church in New York City. The theme of the evening was Terra Firma. Director: Chloe Salmon.

IT'S YOUR JOB TO HOLD YOUR BABY

WARREN HOLLEMAN

My mother believed that it was wrong to hold a baby. She said holding babies makes them soft, it makes them weak, and it makes them dependent. She said cribs were much better. They fostered independence and self-reliance.

To her, life was hard, and parents did their children no favors by coddling them. The job of the parent was to toughen up the child. If we went out in public and she saw a young couple kissing and cuddling with their children, she would get so irritated and agitated.

If she was at someone's home and saw them holding a baby for more than two or three minutes, she'd say, "They need to get a crib for that baby."

She didn't believe in kissing either. I never saw her kiss my dad. If she kissed me, it was just a peck on the cheek. (If you've been pecked by a chicken, that's what it felt like.) But it didn't exactly feel like a kiss—what I later learned was a kiss. She thought kissing was bad for your health because it spread germs.

As for my father and his side of the family, there's a very telling story about my dad's return home from World War II that pretty much says it all.

He's been away for three years. He's anxious to get home. The war ends. He has to take this long boat ride across the Pacific Ocean.

Then he has to take the long train ride across the United States. And on top of that, he has to walk forty miles through a snowstorm.

He was supposed to take the bus, but the buses weren't running because of the snowstorm. He wants to get home. So, he picks up that big duffel bag and just starts walking, and two days later, after dark, he arrives at the home place.

The family doesn't realize he's about to show up. They're eating dinner. The door flies open, and there stands my dad, Carl Holleman, and here's how his mother—with her rich North Carolina accent—welcomed her son home from the war.

"Why . . . there's Carl.

"We got plenty of food in the kitchen. Put your stuff down, and go in there, and get yourself a plate, and come join us."

And that was it. There were no hugs. There were no kisses. No nothing.

Now, don't get the wrong impression. My parents, my grandparents, had many fine qualities, but they were not the warm and cuddly type.

And I think the way that affected me is that, as I went through adolescence especially, I had a lotta trouble with hugs and kisses, a lot of embarrassing moments, a lot of awkward moments. And I found myself longing for this *something* I couldn't even name at the time. I later learned it was warmth and tenderness.

My friends, it seemed to come easily to them—not so easily to me.

But I made it through that adolescence. I got lucky and met this wonderful woman. We got married.

A few years later we're in the delivery room, and she's about to give birth to our first child.

The midwife turns to me, and she says, "Get ready. As soon as I catch this baby, I'm handin' her to you because"—and then of all the things she could have said to me—"it's your job to hold your baby."

So, my head is spinning. Part of me honestly wants to give it a try. I'd seen my wife's family do it, and I thought it was one of those life experiences everybody should have, but those tapes of my mother and my grandmother were still playing in my head.

I muddled through. That's about the best I could say. And of all the names we could have chosen for that little girl, we chose Annie. I'm sure it was influenced, to some extent, by the musical, but the real reason was, that's my mother's name.

So, the nice thing about having your baby birthed by a midwife is that you get this special private suite for the next twenty-four hours in the maternity section of the hospital. And it had some nice name like the "Family Bonding Room" or something like that. And that was the perfect place for me. I got twenty-four hours of practice learning to hold that baby, defying my mother every single minute.

But what my wife and I knew is that once that twenty-four hours was over, we would have to leave that cocoon—that world of wonderful new beginnings—and reenter a different world I haven't even yet told you about. A world of incredibly sad *endings*.

This was 1987. The AIDS epidemic.

We lived in Montrose, the so-called "gay neighborhood" of Houston. And at that time it seemed that every young man we knew was wasting away and dying, and it just seemed so wrong. I'm talking about young men who were in their twenties and thirties. There was a Walgreens pharmacy on Montrose Boulevard. It's still there. Over the next few years it would sell more AZT than any other drugstore in the entire United States.

So, we were in the middle of what would be recognized over the next few years as one of the worst epidemics in American history. Of course, many of our friends and neighbors were dying of this disease, but the one we knew and loved best was named Chelsea.

Chelsea shared an entryway with us in our apartment enclave. And we spent many great times together.

When he got sick, he moved into a home hospice arrangement

that was a few blocks away, but we continued visiting, and at first even going out to dinner together. He was so supportive when he found out that my wife was pregnant. Honestly, I think he was more supportive than *I* was.

He was so emotionally connected to the whole thing in a way that I didn't even comprehend at the time, but looking back, he was a mentor for me through that process. And he was so excited about the baby and getting a chance to meet the baby.

Well, there was a rule that after the baby's born, there's a period in which the baby needs to develop its immune system. And we were nearing the end of that when one day the phone rang.

This was our friend Martha, who was coordinating Chelsea's home hospice care, and she said, "I got some bad news. He's taken a turn for the worse."

I said, "Well, we'll be there tonight."

She said, "I need to warn you. Something's happened with his mind. He won't even recognize who you are. That's particularly bad because he was so looking forward to meeting your new baby."

That was a shock to me because I had just visited a week or two earlier, and we'd had a pretty normal conversation.

The other thing she said she needed to warn me of was, "His mother . . ."—she kinda whispered in the phone—"His mother, she's *here*."

And I knew what that meant.

So, we went that night, and this time we took our baby. Chelsea was in the center of his living room, lying on his back on a hospital bed which had been raised about forty-five degrees. His shirt was off, and in the corner of the room—as far from her son as she could possibly be—was his mother. She was sitting on a folding chair, and the chair wasn't even facing her son. It was turned sideways.

And if she ever looked our way, it was just to stare at the floor. And I tell you, that seemed so wrong too. Martha had told us that his mother was afraid to touch him because of the disease and because of her prejudice against him being gay.

As for Chelsea, it's true, he did not recognize us. But the thing was, we barely recognized him. Before he got sick he was six feet, five inches tall. He was the best-looking, friendliest, and humblest person you could ever meet—and the funniest. Everybody loved him. But now, as I said, he was lying there with his shirt off, and you could see every bone. He was as skinny as a person can be and still be alive. He had these awful sores in his mouth, and he was in constant pain.

And every breath was a struggle. It would take about three efforts to raise his chest, and then it would collapse down. And you just knew it would be the last, and you kinda hoped it would be the last, so he wouldn't have to suffer anymore. And as for his mind, it was clear that the Chelsea we knew was no longer there. He just sort of babbled. It didn't make any sense.

So, we stood around him and talked over him to each other. And after a while, though, he started doing this one thing that made some sense. I was standing there holding our baby (doing a good job). And he would look at her outta the corner of his eye.

And in time he started looking more. I could swear, it was almost as if he was trying to flirt with her. And one by one we started recognizing that. Our conversation ended because this was so much more interesting than whatever we were talking about. And then we got curious, *What does his mother think of all this?*

She was sitting over there staring at the floor. Her son is making this connection with our child, but his mother is making no connection at all. Even I, by that point—the only thing I wanted to do was to hold and touch our child, and she was afraid or unwilling to do that.

My wife and I were frankly offended by his mother. I mean, we felt sorry for her, but we were also offended. So, we had the same idea at the same time. It just was one of those things. We thought, *We gotta do something about this.* So, we laid our baby facedown, her chest on Chelsea's chest. Her face fit right in the cavity of his long neck. Her little arms dangled around his bony chest.

We stood close by because we really didn't know what would happen. And what happened was actually scary at first. His arms went into this spasm. He was trying to remember how to use his arms. He hadn't used them for a while. Then, those scarecrow arms stretched out wide, still jerking a bit, and then they started slowly rising.

And then he got control, and they formed this arch over our baby. And then his arms just relaxed—they relaxed around our baby. And as his arms relaxed, his breathing relaxed. The painful expression on his face went away, and we actually recognized that old Chelsea again.

He looked so content. And I've often said if that's all that had happened that night, it would still be one of the most amazing and memorable experiences of my life. But one more thing happened. This time Chelsea spoke, and his words made sense.

He said, "Annie!"—then he smiled, and he said, "Came to see me. Annie."

So, we went home that night and went to bed. In the middle of the night I woke up. I had this huge jolt of energy. It was four A.M. I couldn't get back to sleep. I went outside, sat on the back steps with our dogs. The sun came up, the phone rang, and it was our friend Martha again.

She said, "I wanted to call you earlier, but I thought I should wait till the sun came up. Two things. One, I'm so glad you came last night. That was amazing. And two, I wanted to let you know that at four o'clock Chelsea died."

Now, I've had thirty years to think about this, and I still don't understand how a young man who has severe advanced dementia awakens out of that and has a moment of perfect clarity just hours before he dies. But I know what I believe. I'll always believe that it has something to do—sorry, Mom—with the healing power of human touch.

*   ⊙   *

WARREN HOLLEMAN is a former professor of behavioral science at the University of Texas MD Anderson Cancer Center, where he directed a wellness program for physicians and scientists. His papers have been published in *Nature, Lancet, JAMA,* and other journals, and his workshop Nurturing the Spirit of the Healer has been presented in twenty-six cities throughout the United States. Warren is a two-time Houston Moth StorySLAM champion, and his stories have been featured on *The Moth Radio Hour,* The Moth Mainstage, TEDx, and the National Storytelling Summit. Warren has served many years as an editor of *Pulse—voices from the heart of medicine* and also as a co-host of *So, What's Your Story?,* a radio program devoted to live storytelling. Warren and his wife, Marsha, recently celebrated their forty-fifth year together. They are the proud parents of two grown children.

This story was told on April 6, 2018, at the Majestic Theatre in San Antonio. The theme of the evening was Standoff. Director: Catherine Burns.

YOU BETTER
GET THESE
CATTLE OUT
OF THE
KITCHEN

FINDING MY PLACE

IVAN MCCLELLAN

I was born and raised in Kansas City, Kansas. (Go, Chiefs!)

The neighborhood that I grew up in had many sides. It was urban and country at the same time. It was beautiful. And sometimes it could be terrifying.

My sister and I would run around in a five-acre field behind our house all summer long. We would play, and we would eat blackberries until our fingers were sticky. And then we'd run home through the thistle and have to pick thorns out of our socks on the front porch. Then at twilight, the lightning bugs would come out, and we'd scoop them up in mason jars, throw some leaves in there, screw the lid on tight, and poke holes in the top, so they could breathe.

At night, sometimes gunshots would ring out on the block, and my sister and I would look up as police helicopters flew up and down the streets, looking for suspects. There were a lot of gangs in the neighborhood, and they would walk around with pit bulls, and whenever they ran across a rival gang member they would fight their dogs.

I wasn't in a gang. I was a nerd and a church kid. But when I ran across this one guy, he would sic his dog on me, and I would go running. All the backs of my pants got eaten up. I got really fast.

My mom worked two or three jobs to keep us fed. We were

latchkey kids. Eventually, we determined that it was unsafe to go outside, and we quit going out in that field and playing.

As I got closer to the end of high school, my prospects were kind of slim. I could go be a delivery truck driver, I could be a pastor at my uncle's church, or I could go work at the assembly line at the Ford plant.

I didn't really want to do any of those things. I wanted to be a photographer. I decided I was gonna figure out a way out of Kansas. I never felt like I fit in there. And I knew somewhere there was a community where I belonged. So I saved up five hundred dollars that summer, and I just up and moved to New York City.

That money was *gone* in a week.

I didn't know anybody. So, I worked any job that I could get. I handed out flyers. Blew up balloons. I played guitar in the park—anything I could do for money. Until one day, through a bunch of luck, I got a job as a photographer and a junior designer at an ad agency. I didn't know anything that anybody was talking about. They would say ROI, SEO, KPIs, and I would just nod my head "yes" and then google what they had said. I did that long enough that I actually started to get pretty good at my job, and I got promoted. I went from junior designer to designer; to senior designer; and finally, from senior designer to art director.

Every time that I got promoted, I saw fewer and fewer Black colleagues. Until I got a job as a creative director, moved to Portland, Oregon, and I hardly ever saw Black people at all.

I was in the sea of white men at work, and I was never a culture fit. I understood their culture, but they didn't understand mine. They had no clue who Luther Vandross was, had never stayed up till two A.M. watching *Showtime at the Apollo*. They had no idea why I might be afraid of dogs.

This led to a case of imposter syndrome. I was in rooms where I felt I didn't belong, and I feared that I was going to be found out, thrown out in the street, forced to move back to Kansas.

One day I was at a party, and I didn't know anybody there except for the person whose birthday it was. And so, I was just drinking by myself and sulking in the corner. Somebody tapped me on the shoulder, and I turned around and there's a tall Black man with a salt-and-pepper afro. He introduces himself. He says his name is Charles Perry. Says he's a filmmaker.

I said, "Oh, I'm a photographer. What are you working on?"

He said, "I'm working on a movie about Black cowboys."

I said, "What, like a Western?"

He said, "No, like a documentary."

I kind of laughed and said, "There's not enough Black cowboys to make a whole documentary!"

And I knew a thing or two about cowboys. I grew up watching *Bonanza* and *Gunsmoke* reruns. My school choir used to sing the national anthem at the American Royal Rodeo in Kansas. I viewed the cowboy as the archetype of American independence and grit. But Black cowboys? The only Black cowboys I knew were Sheriff Bart in *Blazing Saddles* and Cowboy Curtis on *Pee-wee's Playhouse*.

So we kept talking, and he said, "Well, you gotta see it for yourself, man. Come with me to a Black rodeo in Oklahoma this summer."

I said, "Absolutely."

It was exactly the opportunity that I had been looking for. I had never felt more separated from Black culture. And going to a rodeo seemed like the furthest thing from working at a computer that I could think of. So I went home, and I bought my plane ticket. And I just sat there for the next few months, anticipating what this could possibly be like. In my head, it would be like *Soul Train,* but everybody would be on a horse.

So, August came around, and I caught my flight to Oklahoma City. I drove an hour and a half to Okmulgee, parked my car, got out, and was suffocated by the heat. It was 105 degrees, and it was 100 percent humidity. As I was walking through the grass, chiggers were biting my ankles, and there were grasshoppers jumping up on my clothes. There was just a haze of barbecue smoke over the entire lawn. I couldn't breathe.

Everywhere I looked there were white horse trailers glistening in the sun. And there was R&B music and gospel music and hip-hop coming out of the trailers. And everywhere around me, there were Black cowboys. Thousands of them.

I saw young men riding their horses with no shirts, gold chains, basketball shorts, and Jordans. And they were walking around, laughing, hitting on women, and talking trash to the other riders. I saw old men just sitting stoically on their horses with precise Stetsons and trim mustaches and pinkie rings. Their shirts were so starched you could hear them crunch when they moved their arms. And the women were bedazzled from head to toe—bedazzled hats, bedazzled shirts with fringe, bedazzled jeans. They had long braids and acrylic nails, and they were busy settling down these muscular quarter horses that they would ride at forty miles per hour in the barrel race later that afternoon.

I couldn't fit in any less. I was wearing khakis and wingtips.

But I felt so welcomed by this group of people. Everybody was so eager to share a smile, share their stories, and let me take their photos.

I met a man named Robert Criff. Robert had this leather raisin of a face, and he had a beautiful horse named Summertime. He pulled on her reins, and she put her legs down on the ground like she was bowing. It was so elegant.

He shook my hand. He had these twelve-grit sandpaper hands—

mine almost started to bleed because I've got dragonfly wings for hands from working in tech for so long.

He offered me a bottle of water, which I desperately needed at this point because I'm like, soaking wet. There's not a bead of sweat on his face. In fact, nobody else at the rodeo was sweating at all. And I looked like I had just gotten baptized.

He was wearing a Kansas City hat, so I said, "Where are you from?"

He said, "I'm from Kansas City, Kansas."

I said, "*I'm* from Kansas City, Kansas. Whereabouts?"

He said, "Oh, I live just off of 58th and Georgia."

"I grew up off of 57th and Georgia!"

It turns out that he lived on the other side of the five-acre field next to where I grew up.

I never saw a horse back there. I'd never met Robert Criff, but he knew my grandma. He knew my pastor. We went to the same high school. In fact, he told me that half of the people at the rodeo come down from Kansas City every year for their family reunions.

I was embarrassed. I was shocked because this entire culture had been right under my nose my whole life, and I knew nothing about it.

And I felt kind of cheated because as a kid, I had been hiding out from criminals who chased me with a dog when I could have been hanging out with cowboys just a field away.

It immediately changed my perception of home—from a place of pain and poverty and violence to a place of independence and grit and cowboys.

Suddenly, I was proud to be from Kansas City.

The rodeo started and a rider circled around the arena carrying a Pan-African flag. It's the American flag, but it's red, black, and green. And a singer belted out "Lift Every Voice and Sing" with so much sincerity and so much energy that I felt like I truly heard it for the first time.

> *Sing a song full of the faith that the dark past has taught us,*
> *Sing a song full of the hope that the present has brought us.*

And to me, that was what this rodeo was about. What we had been forced to do in slavery—work the land, work with animals—we can now do in celebration for our own profit and our own entertainment.

I photographed the rodeo with absolute joy. And I got home, and I looked at my photos, and I was just blown back by all of the vibrance and all of the energy and all of the fashion.

It was like I had gone to Oz and then clicked my heels back to gray, homogenous Portland, but I had proof that I had been there.

My favorite photo is of this rodeo queen. Her name is Jazmen Marie. I asked to take her photo, and she's standing there with her chin up and her hair blowing back, and her crown is glistening in the stadium lights. She looks like actual royalty.

I love all of the photos. Whenever I'm feeling separated from the culture, I just look through them, and I'm immediately taken back to Okmulgee. And I go back every year. I've now taken my family with me to dozens of Black rodeos around the country.

My work has been featured in museums. It's been featured in magazines and published in a book, and I've seen the figure of the Black cowboy elevated in film and television. And it's become a part of a narrative about identities in the West.

I go to the rodeos and take photos so that my kids, when they draw a picture of a cowboy, they'll color it in with a brown face. And I'll keep going, year after year, so that I'll never again forget that this is a part of who I am as a Black man in America.

* ✵ *

IVAN MCCLELLAN is a photojournalist and designer based in Portland, Oregon. His work reveals marginalized aspects of Black culture and challenges broad assumptions and myths about racial identity in America.

This story was told on January 25, 2022, at the Center for the Arts in Jackson Hole. The theme of the evening was When Worlds Collide. Director: Jenifer Hixson.

A VIOLIN'S LIFE

FRANK ALMOND

In 2008, I received an email and the subject line was "*A Violin.*"

The sender went on to explain that they had in their possession a Stradivarius violin from 1715. It was part of an estate situation, and they were looking for some guidance.

I'm a professional violinist and have had the good fortune to play any number of Stradivarius instruments for decades, all over the world.

The mystique about Stradivari is not that they're three hundred years old or that they're worth so much money; it's that they're these amazing functional antiquities, and they're powerful, and they're sonically nuanced. They are perfectly crafted and engineered, and they have these amazing pedigrees and histories behind them.

This wasn't the first time I had received an email that someone found a Stradivarius, and it's always very disappointing to have to write them back and say, "No, your violin from 1982 is not a Stradivarius because Stradivari died in 1737."

This email was really different.

It was full of information and details that completely drew me in. It even had a reference to a violin that I had heard about called the "Lipiński" Stradivarius, named after a famous violinist in the nineteenth century who owned it.

This violin was from 1715, and it kind of disappeared for about twenty years.

I thought, *I have to check this out. This is amazing.*

I wrote back right away. It turned out that the owners, who were writing to me, were in the same city where I was: Milwaukee, Wisconsin. They wanted to meet me in a bank vault where they were storing the violin.

So, I'm driving down to this bank vault, thinking, *It's, maybe, three miles from my house. There's, like, maybe 250 of these things left in the world, more or less, and is it possible that one of these just dropped out of the sky into Milwaukee?*

It seemed very unlikely.

We got down to the bank vault, and somebody brought in a violin case.

I opened it up really slowly . . .

. . . and it's the "Lipiński" Stradivarius.

I was absolutely dumbfounded.

It was like I had stumbled on some lost Rembrandt or something.

Over the next couple of months, this dialogue starts between the owners and myself.

"This is what happens if you keep it; this is what happens if you sell it. This is what happens if you leave it under your bed."

One day, I get a phone call.

The owner says, "What if you play it? What if you look after it? You've had these things before, and we could come hear and see it if we're around, and it'd be great for the city. What do you think about that idea?"

And I said, "I think that's an *excellent* idea. That's a really good strategy going forward, and we should *definitely* make that happen."

A couple of days later, I'm driving home with the "Lipiński" Stradivarius strapped into the backseat of my car with its little seat belt.

I get home, and I take it up to my practice studio. I open it up and start playing, and there's that sound and this power and nuance.

I set it down and started thinking about it.

It was a little intimidating.

It's not just the Lipiński thing. Nobody knows who Karol Lipiński is now. But in his day, in the nineteenth century, he was a hugely important cultural figure and virtuoso violinist who is often compared to Niccolò Paganini, who was sort of the Eddie Van Halen of the violin.

I knew that, on at least two occasions, on this actual violin, Lipiński and Paganini had done these giant spectacles where they would play one right after the other, and then the whole audience would vote on who was the better violinist—like this nineteenth-century violin smackdown.

It wasn't just that; Lipiński knew Mendelssohn, and he worked closely with Robert Schumann, and all these other people who drifted in and out of my life as a classical musician.

Here it was, in front of me.

I started to spend hours and hours with it. This kind of odd relationship started, almost like a dating period, where I'm putting my best artistic self forward with the hope that the violin has some kind of adaptive quality back. My playing really did change a lot, and the violin changed a lot.

I realized very quickly that this object was capable of maximizing my artistic abilities to a degree I would have never possibly imagined. At the same time, it could brutally illuminate all of my weaknesses as a violinist.

I started to play it more and more publicly. We settled into this sort of odd marriage, and people knew about the instrument and would come and hear it.

It was almost a matter of civic pride, for all the right reasons.

In January of 2014, I was finishing a concert in a series I run

based in Milwaukee. The last piece on the program was this incredible piece of chamber music, called the *Quartet for the End of Time*. It
was written by a POW in France during World War II. It's about an
hour long, and it's unbelievably intense, not just to listen to, but also
to play.

We sort of tumbled out of the stage door, and I remember I had
been happy to get a parking space close to the concert hall because
it was really cold, like ten below zero, and I could get to the car very
quickly to put the violin in its seat belt.

As I'm walking to the car, directly in the space next to my car
was a van. It was backed in, and it was running.

This was a weird van.

This was not a quality vehicle; this was like a *Scooby Doo*–level
van.

I'm walking over and this guy gets out of the van, and he walks
around the front, and he's got this big fur coat on and a big fur hat.

He's getting closer and closer between where I need to be, and at
the very last second, he opens up his jacket, and he's really close, and
I see these little flashing lights.

I'm thinking, *Why is that guy taking my picture?*

Then I felt this unbelievable pain and paralysis, and I was on the
ground.

Then I wasn't on the ground because I was up, and I was running
in circles, and I was screaming.

I mean, I was *really* screaming.

I was screaming because as soon as I got up, I saw the *Scooby Doo*
van drive around the corner, and I knew the violin was gone.

It was like somebody had ripped off one of my arms.

I looked down, and there were these little fishhook things stuck
in my body. One on my chest and one on my wrist, and I realized
I'd been shot with a Taser.

So, I called 911 and said, "A multimillion-dollar instrument was just stolen, and they shot me with a Taser. Could you please send a car quickly?"

I waited and waited.

Finally this lonely little squad car comes into the parking lot, and these two incredibly earnest beat cops start their initial interview, with me sitting in the backseat of the car.

It was lots of questions back and forth:

"It's a violin, and it's worth *how much*?"

"How do you spell Stradivari?"

And finally, I was getting a little agitated, and I said, "Guys, there's kind of a time factor. So, maybe you could get on the radio and try to find the van that's driving around with the violin inside of it."

They sort of looked at me and asked more questions and everything just kept going like this, and I'm really going crazy.

I finally said, "Look, I know this sounds insane, but is there any way you could get in touch with the chief of police of the city of Milwaukee? He's a huge symphony fan—he goes all the time, and I've met him. He knows the whole violin thing, and he'll get it right away."

They looked at me, like, "Yeah, well, we'll get right on that."

Another car came, and there were more questions back and forth.

I'm sitting there, and somebody hands me a cellphone. It's the chief of police, Ed Flynn. And I swear within one minute, there was this explosion of activity on the scene—police cars, forensics guys, lights, an ambulance, and homicide detectives.

They threw everything at this case instantly.

There was a part of me that was like, *That's great,* but I couldn't get rid of this pit in my stomach, thinking that *it's gone.*

I didn't know what else to think, and I was tired, and I just wanted to get home.

I did finally get home early the next morning and made a phone call to the owners that I hoped I'd never have to make.

Then this whole other level of crazy starts at my house over the next couple of days with media people on my lawn, and *Good Morning America* calling my cell.

I did a polygraph test.

I'm doing hours-long interviews with these homicide detectives—everybody's into it, and they're going to solve it.

All I could think was, *The violin is just GONE.*

I still had this pit in my stomach.

But I decided I had to get my life back.

I had these concerts coming up in Florida, so I found a decent violin and decided I was going to go.

I fly down to Florida, and at the airport a TSA guy pulls me aside and says, "Hey, would you mind opening up your violin case because this guy got his violin stolen a couple of days ago."

He had a flyer with the "Lipiński" Stradivarius on it, like it was somebody's lost cat or something.

I went and played the concerts.

Afterward, I wound up in a strip mall bar in Florida with bad drinks and bad karaoke. I'm sitting there, and my phone's buzzing and buzzing, and it's all these unknown numbers.

I finally pick it up, and it's the chief of police, and he says, "We found your violin. It's okay."

It turns out that when you fire a Taser, all this stuff comes out, this little, like, Taser chaff. And these little bits of paper have all this identifying information on it for that particular weapon.

My *personal* Taser had been purchased a year earlier by a man named Universal Knowledge. His legal name.

He had bought it in his own name, with his own credit card, and he had it shipped to his business, which was a barbershop.

He bought it with his friend while they were deciding how to pull off their masterful art heist of stealing a Stradivarius violin.

The violin had been found in a suitcase, wrapped in a baby blanket, and apparently it was in pretty good shape.

Also in the suitcase was the driver's license of the person who stole the violin.

The next morning, I flew back to Milwaukee. I drove right from the airport to where the owners were. It was just the three of us, and there were some hugs, a few pictures, and some tears.

I put the violin in my backseat and put its little seat belt on, and I drove home.

I took it up to my practice studio, and we sort of stared at each other for a little while.

My thinking had really shifted, and I now understood that this thing is three hundred years old, and this crazy saga is now part of its history. It's going to be around for a long time, and I'm like this little blip.

The reality is, I'm just passing through its life, and not the other way around.

* ☉ *

Violinist **FRANK ALMOND** served as concertmaster of the Milwaukee Symphony Orchestra for twenty-five years. He held similar leadership positions with the Rotterdam Philharmonic and the London Symphony Orchestra.

Frank is the founder of his own chamber music series in Milwaukee, Frankly Music. The series is consistently recognized for innovative programming and its ability to attract leading performers from around the world.

His most recent series of three recordings, *A Violin's Life,* chronicles the extraordinary history and lineage of his current violin, the 1715 "Lipiński" Stradivarius. This instrument has direct ties to Giuseppe Tartini, Beethoven, Edvard Grieg, and Robert Schumann.

Giving back to the Milwaukee community is foremost at the heart of

Frank Almond's artistic priorities. He mentors young musicians of all performing levels and backgrounds, and he performs in nontraditional venues where classical music has a rare and unusual presence.

This story was recorded at a live performance at Alice Tully Hall at Lincoln Center for the Performing Arts in New York City on October 13, 2018. The theme of the evening was Out of the Blue. Director: Meg Bowles.

MEETING MILES

ANDREA KING COLLIER

We got married in 1982, and we were so cute, but we couldn't have been more different. I was a privileged little only child, and my husband was one of six.

But we did have something in common. We were Black kids of the sixties, and we did civil rights marches. We helped register people to vote. We knew about segregation, and we knew that our folks expected a whole bunch out of us. We were their legacy, and they had a script for us that we passed on to *our* two kids.

When we got married, our whole family unit was the Huxtables before there were Huxtables. In fact, our motto whenever our kids were getting out of line was, "I brought you into this world, and I will take you out."

We've now been married for thirty-seven years, and as many Black families of our age did, we aspired to stick to our parents' script even as adults: to raise good kids who go to college, who don't get into any trouble, who move out of the house, and who don't get anybody knocked up. If you have kids, you know that it doesn't always work out the way you planned.

My daughter took the cues. She went to school, she graduated, she got a good job. She married a man that she says reminds her of her father.

(And when he's doing stuff that she doesn't want him to do, I have to remind her, "You wanted a guy like your daddy.")

Now, my son, who's a good person . . . I can't get him out of the house. He is a human yo-yo. His "script" involves living in the basement and never coming out. And no matter how much we try to get him out of the basement, it isn't happening. We have bribed him. We've offered him first and last months' rent. We bought him a truck, so he could either sleep in it or get his shit out of our house. I have called the exterminator, and yet sometimes I go in the kitchen, and he's still there.

Except in December of 2013, he disappeared. He left, and he stayed gone for a couple of weeks. Now, you watch the news. As the mother of a Black child, you don't want them disappearing. But he stayed gone, and I really didn't get worried until he didn't come and get his Christmas present. He is *not* that child.

I called his friends to check to see where he was. Nobody knew.

Just as I was about to call the police, he called and said, "Mama, I have something to tell you. Can I come over?"

Well, if you've got kids, you know. If they say, "I have something to tell you," it ain't never good. *Never ever* good.

They've never hit the lotto.

In this particular case, they're never moving out on their own.

It's never, "I have met Beyoncé. We've fallen in love. She's leaving Jay-Z for me."

So, I said, "Okay, come on over."

He comes, and my husband says, "I don't know what's going on. Christopher is rehearsing something in the driveway."

It's going to be a doozy.

He comes upstairs, and he doesn't want to talk to everybody who is there. He just wants to talk to me.

He says what I think is, "My girlfriend and I are going to have a baby."

Now, this is the kind of thing that would make my head explode. But something told me, *Ask him again.*

"What did you say?"

"We had a baby *yesterday.*"

And I knew that wasn't right. Nope. The child did not tell me that he *had a baby yesterday.*

"Say it again."

"We had a baby yesterday."

So, all kinds of things are going on in my head. You know, things that could have gone all kind of wrong.

But instead, because I'm in shock, I say, "Oh, how nice."

I'm thinking, *Calm this down. Ask nice, basic questions.*

"Are mother and baby okay?"

"Yes."

"Everybody got all their feet and hands?"

"Yes."

"And what is the baby's name?"

And this becomes tricky because people, especially millennials, Black millennials, can name their kids some really interesting things. Like, *Do not name the baby Tommy Hilfiger, please, or Boone's Farm, or Red Bull. Don't do any of that.*

And don't name it Apple.

Well, the baby's name is Miles, and I like that. That was the only piece of good news out of the whole damn thing.

"We got a baby, and the baby's name is Miles."

My husband and I have colds, so we can't actually go see the baby. And we explain that, and then he's gone.

What does one do with that? He has a baby, the baby's name is Miles, and you are a grandmother, and you didn't know it.

So, I do what anybody would do: I get in the car, and I go to Target.

Because you can work out *a whole lot of shit* in the aisles of Target.

I'm in Target, and I decide to call one of my anchor people. Everybody's got a person, and my person was my mother, and when she passed away, her friends agreed to stand in the gap for me. And so, whenever I need advice, I call them.

I call Gussie. Now, Gussie is my mother's oldest friend. She picks up the phone. When I hear her voice, I start to cry, and I'm sort of hysterical. The more I talk, the more hysterical I get.

She says, "Okay, let me get this right. Baby, not named Apple. You didn't know. Baby's fine. Is the baby going to live with you?"

"No."

"Okay, that's really good. So, this is what you're going to do."

And I am still ugly crying.

"You're going to put on your big girl panties, and you are going to be the best damn grandma you know how to be, like your grandparents were for you."

And then all of a sudden I was like, *Oh yeah, that's exactly what I am going to do. Shit, I didn't need to call you for that. I could have figured it out.*

So, then I moved to other parts of Target, and I buy everything that has "baby," "might be a baby," "going to be a six-year-old" written on it. I'm buying everything in Target to the point that when I get home, my husband has to go back with the car and get the rest of the shit that I bought.

But on the way home, I start to get really angry. Not at my son, not at the girl, and not at the baby, but at my husband and his co-conspirator, my daughter.

"You all *had* to know that. *Who* knew that?"

"Not us, not us."

"You *had* to know. So, why didn't you all tell me?"

"We *didn't* know."

"Why didn't he tell me sooner?"

"Well . . . you are intimidating and scary."

Now, I don't believe that. So they have to, as Wendy Williams says, show me the receipts.

So, they start rattling off how I'm intimidating and scary and say, "You know Evilline from *The Wiz*? 'Don't bring me no bad news.' That's you."

"You know how Clair Huxtable looks at Theo? That's you."

"You know Oprah?"

Okay. So there's some hope in that, right?

"You *are* Oprah."

And I'm like, *Okay, I can live with that.*

"No. You are not, 'You get a car! You get a car! You get a car!' Oprah. Not *that* Oprah. You are Miss Sophia, 'You told Harpo to beat me' Oprah. *That's* the Oprah *you* are."

Sometimes you just gotta give it up.

I waited until we got well enough to go to see the baby. The day arrives and my daughter is texting me and texting my husband: "Please don't let her say anything crazy. Please don't say anything. Please don't do anything crazy. What are you going to say?"

So, we get there, and I've never met his girlfriend's parents. And in fact, I've only seen *her* one time, and she was in a car; that's why I didn't know she was pregnant. I had never had a conversation with her. We're sitting, and nobody's saying anything.

And then finally they bring the baby out, and the first thing that just comes out of my mind is, *Give me my damn baby.*

His other grandmother puts him in my arms. And all of the hurt that I had felt about not truly being the Huxtables just sort of melted away. I looked at this baby's face, and not only did I love him because he's beautiful, but I could see everybody else that I'd ever loved in my family, right in this child's face.

It went from heartbreak to my heart breaking wide open.

So, I started looking at my purse, and looking at the baby, and I thought, *How long do you think it would be after I put the baby in the purse and ran for them to figure out he was gone?*

When my kids were teenagers, I heard Toni Morrison say, "Your children need to see your face light up whenever they come into the room." (Well, they were teenagers, and nobody's face was lighting up when they came into the room. Nope, not happening.)

But in holding Miles, I could see how your face could light up every time *he* came into the room.

And I remembered the rest of what Toni Morrison says: "They look at your eyes to tell what's going on in your heart."

I promise you, my grandson's ten now, and when he comes into the room, my face lights up. And for the rest of my life, he will be able to look into my eyes and know what's going on in my heart.

ANDREA KING COLLIER is an independent journalist, photographer, and author based in Lansing, Michigan. She is the author of *The Black Woman's Guide to Black Men's Health* and *Still with Me . . . A Daughter's Journey of Love and Loss.*

This story was told on March 5, 2020, at the Culture Center Theater in Charleston, West Virginia. The theme of the evening was A More Perfect Union. Director: Catherine Burns.

IS LOVE WILD, IS LOVE REAL?

SARFRAZ MANZOOR

There were no photographs of my parents' wedding day in the house when I was growing up.

I grew up in a town called Luton just outside of London in the 1980s. My parents were Pakistani Muslims, and they'd had an arranged marriage. Apparently, it had been so uneventful that nobody could remember the day, the week, the month, or even the year that it happened.

My parents were many things, but the one thing they definitely were not, was in love.

The word *love* was never used in our house. It was completely taboo. You could almost say that *love* was a four-letter word.

I was never told "I love you" before I went to bed.

Nobody told me "I love you" before I went to school, and my parents never said "I love you" to each other.

My parents made out that this was a really good thing because their argument was that white people fell in love, got married, and then got divorced.

Pakistanis never loved the people they married, but we stuck with them forever.

My parents thought it was their duty to keep me away from the idea of love and any kind of intimacy.

One way they did this was by making sure that I had a haircut that was short at the top and long at the back, which acted as girl repellent. It also suggested that Michael Bolton was some kind of style icon rather than a terrifying warning.

They kept me away from any kind of intimacy on TV. If two people were kissing or even looked like they were going to kiss on TV, I had to run over and turn the TV off because there was no way I could watch that in front of my parents.

The one place they could not police was the radio. And so, pop music became the place where I learned about love, and I was taught by people like Lionel Richie, Motown, and Foreigner. All *these* people were saying that love was amazing. They were saying you should really go for it. And it was weird because my parents were saying the exact opposite.

The most important song during my teenage years was by the Pet Shop Boys, and it was a song called "Love Comes Quickly" and the chorus was:

Love comes quickly.
Whatever you do, you can't stop falling.

I don't know about you, but that sounds absolutely terrifying because that suggests that love is like an infection. It's like some kind of disease, and it doesn't matter what you do, you're not going to be able to stop falling or catching it.

In my family, I had an older brother, an older sister, and a younger sister, and they were a little bit more traditional than me. I was always a bit of an outsider—a dreamer.

I had three dreams: I wanted to get out of Luton, I wanted to do an interesting job, and I wanted to marry somebody who wasn't a relative.

None of those things seemed entirely possible.

But in my twenties I managed to get out of Luton, and I did get to do an interesting job, but the love and marriage thing still seemed completely elusive.

By now I'd evolved from Lionel Richie to Bruce Springsteen, and Bruce became the person I went to for all my wisdom.

There's a song called "Born to Run," and in it Bruce says, "I want to know if love is wild. I want to know if love is real," and that was a really important question to me.

Is love real for somebody like me?

There was also another line in that song where he says to Wendy, "We can live with the sadness, and I'll love you with all the madness in my soul."

I'll love you with all the madness in my soul.

I was like, *I want to meet someone that I could feel this way about, who I could say this about.* And something made me think that this was not the feeling I was going to get from an arranged marriage.

My mum started to gently hint that it was time for me to have an arranged marriage. And when I say "gently hint" . . . she went on a hunger strike.

I would come home, and she'd be on the phone, and she'd be talking to the parents of girls that she wanted to marry me off to.

I'd say, "Mum, what the hell are you doing?"

And she'd say, "I'm doing my duty."

In 2008, I was turning thirty-seven, and I went to the Hay Book Festival, which is this big book festival on the border of England and Wales. I was there for a week doing some work. The last day of the festival, on the first Sunday of June, I took a taxi to the train station. It was a really hot day, and I was sure I was going to miss the train.

I get out of the taxi and run with a suitcase along the platform.

The doors are about to close, but I manage to get in, and I plop myself down.

I look up, and sitting opposite me is the most beautiful girl I've ever seen.

She's got blond hair and wild green eyes.

She's reading a copy of *Mary Barton* by Elizabeth Gaskell, and I'm looking at her, and I'm thinking, *Who gets to be your friend? Who gets to know you?*

I'm not the sort of person who talks to strangers, so I didn't do anything. I just let the train carry on.

But something inside me kept saying, *If you don't start a conversation, you're going to regret this.*

Then I noticed that she had a cloth bag, which said Hay Festival. That was my opening.

I said, "Have you been to Hay?"

And she said, "Yes."

So, then we started talking, and she told me her name was Bridget. She's a speech and language therapist. She works with kids with autism. And as the train rolled on, we talked about life and holidays and family and what was missing from our lives.

I was really enjoying the conversation, but I was also getting really, really stressed because this train was rumbling its way to London. It was going to end, and I was thinking, *I don't want this to be an anecdote. What do I do?*

I knew I didn't want to be one of those people that imposes on somebody else.

As the train was nearing our destination, I said, "Look, I'd really like to see you again, but I totally understand if you don't want to. So, I'm going to give you my phone number, but I'm not going to take yours. I don't even know your second name, so there's no way we're ever going to hear from each other again unless *you* contact me."

Then I went home and stared at my phone.

And the next day, I stared at my phone.

And the next day, while I was staring at my phone, she sent me a text saying she'd had a really nice time, and she'd like to meet up again.

So, on Saturday we went for a date at Tate Modern, and that led to a couple more dates, that led to more dates.

We ended up in a relationship, and I thought, *This is amazing. This is what Lionel Richie was singing about.*

Finally, I had the answer to Foreigner's question from their 1986 hit, "I Want to Know What Love Is."

I go back home to visit my mum, and she's getting more and more worried about the fact that I'm still not with anyone, and she's saying, "It's my duty to see you married. There's nobody that's going to take care of you. What are you doing?"

And I'm thinking, *I know something you don't.*

But then I thought, *Sod it. I'm going to tell her.*

So I said, "Look, I have actually met someone."

And when you say something like that you can't just leave it there, so I had to give her some more information.

I thought, *Oh my God, what am I going to do?*

So I said, "She works with children. She's really good with her parents. She knows some Muslims."

And then I sort of threw in that she was blond and Christian, but I hoped Mum didn't notice that.

That evening I rang home just to see how my mum was taking the news, and she said, "You have absolutely, totally betrayed everything that I believed about you. And if you're going to have a relationship with this girl, you're not going to have a relationship with us. You've got to choose."

This was difficult. I'd met somebody I absolutely loved, who makes me happier than I've ever been, but my family are saying, "You've got to choose."

What do I do?

I do what I always do in situations like this—I turned to Bruce Springsteen.

In "Prove It All Night" from the album *Darkness on the Edge of Town,* Bruce has a line where he says, "If dreams came true, oh, wouldn't that be nice? But this ain't no dream we're living through tonight. If you want it, you take it, you pay the price."

If you want it, you take it, you pay the price.

I thought, *Maybe that's what life's about. Maybe, in the end, you take the things you want, and you pay the price. And maybe that's what maturity is.*

Bridget and I went on holiday to Rome, and we were having dinner, and there was this really full moon, and the stars were shining, and it was *Rome.*

And out of nowhere I said to Bridget, "Do you think we should get married?"

She said, "Let's do it."

We returned to Britain engaged, and I rang my family, and I told them the good news, and they say, "Well, that's great, but don't expect us at the wedding. We're not going to come. If you're going to choose her, go it alone."

The wedding date was set for the twenty-first of August, and it was so weird trying to do the seating plan, and all of Bridget's family are on the top table, but there's nobody from my side.

But you make your choices.

We're going through the planning, and I'm sort of steeling myself for the happy day, and then on the twentieth of August, the day before I'm supposed to get married, I get a phone call, and it's my younger sister. I haven't spoken to her since all this argument stuff had been happening, so I was a bit surprised to hear from her.

She said, "How are you doing?"

I said, "I'm not great. How are you?"

And she said, "I'm actually not that great either. I go to work from Luton to London every morning, and by the time I get there, I've got tears streaking down my face, and my boss is wondering why my mascara is running and whether I'm on the verge of having an emotional breakdown."

I said, "What's going on?"

And she said, "Well, I've been listening to Bruce Springsteen."

(That's one of the things I did well—I got her into Springsteen.)

She'd been listening to the album *Tunnel of Love*. There's a song on it called "Walk Like a Man," which is about getting married.

There's a line in it where he says,

Would they ever look so happy again? The handsome groom and his bride
As they step into that long black limousine for their mystery ride.

She said, "The reason I'm crying is that every morning I listen to that song, and I think, *I want to see my brother as that handsome groom.*"

I said, "Well, what does that mean?"

She said, "Well, you know, the family have decided that we're not going to turn up to the wedding, but I'm coming. I'm going to be at your wedding."

On the twenty-first of August, I woke up, I put my suit on, I put a flower on my lapel, and I went to the Islington Town Hall, where we were getting married.

I see another car pull up, and my sister gets out. But then I see that she's also brought my mum.

My older brother and sister didn't turn up, but I was really moved by the fact that my mum was able to overcome some of her concerns to be there for my big day.

The following year, my wife gave birth to our daughter, Laila. And a couple of years later we had a little boy, Ezra.

The great thing about having kids is that you get to tell a new story.

In our house, there are photographs of our wedding day. And I tell my kids I love them.

And kids being what they are, they love for me to read books to them. But even more than reading books, my daughter, Laila, loves me telling her stories.

Her favorite story is of how Mommy and Daddy met and the fact that, if I had not met Bridget on that train, those two children would not exist.

As a parent, you have a lot of dreams for your children. But if I have one dream for my kids, it is for them to grow up believing that *love* is not a four-letter word.

That love is wild, and *yes,* love is real.

* 🞯 *

SARFRAZ MANZOOR is a journalist, author, and broadcaster. His journalism appears in *The Guardian, The Sunday Times Magazine, The Times,* and many other publications, and he is also a familiar voice on BBC Radio 4. He is also the author of the critically acclaimed *Greetings from Bury Park,* a memoir about growing up in 1980s Luton as a working-class British Pakistani Muslim whose life was transformed by the music of Bruce Springsteen. The book was adapted into the feature film *Blinded by the Light,* which was directed by Gurinder Chadha—who also directed *Bend It Like Beckham*—and co-written by Manzoor. His latest book is called *They: What Muslims and Non-Muslims Get Wrong About Each Other.* You can follow him on Twitter and Instagram @sarfrazmanzoor.

This story was recorded at a live performance at Alice Tully Hall at Lincoln Center for the Performing Arts in New York City on October 12, 2019. The theme of the evening was Tug-of-War. Director: Meg Bowles.

MS. MARY

TIQ MILAN

I was my mother's fourth daughter.

The first, she had when she was fifteen years old. Years later, one of my sisters had a baby at fifteen years old. So when I was fifteen, and I sat my mother down at the kitchen table, I knew exactly what she thought I was going to tell her.

I said, "Mommy, I got to tell you something."

She said, "Aw shit."

I said, "Wait a minute, wait a minute, wait a minute. I'm not pregnant. I'm gay."

She was shocked. She was *shocked*—but she got over it quickly, and she became one of my fiercest allies. I remember seeing her when I'd be marching in the Pride parade in my hometown of Buffalo, New York. She'd be on the sidelines—her and her younger sister, Stella—waving their rainbow flags, drinking their wine coolers, having a good time.

We grew really close. Particularly when I moved here to New York City in my twenties to start my adult life, I really needed her so much. I needed her for everything.

I called her every day and twice on Saturdays—to help me make decisions about decorating my apartment, about school, about the beginnings of my career. I would tell her all about the beautiful women that I was meeting and dating, but I didn't tell her that I was their *boyfriend*.

My mother was a nurse for over forty years. So if I caught a case of the sniffles, I'm calling her to ask her what tablets to take, but I didn't call and tell her that I was taking one cc of testosterone every two weeks.

I didn't tell her I was transgender, but she knew something was up.

So one day I'm at work, and she calls me, she said, "Tika-boo"— that was her pet name for me—she said, "Tika-boo, I hate to call you at work, but I just got to ask you this question. I just got to get this off my chest."

I said, "Mommy, what's up?"

She said, "Why you got to be so *mannish*? Why can't you be a soft butch like Ellen DeGeneres?"

I said, "Because I'm not Ellen, Ma, okay?"

She says, "You know what? I should have never allowed this. I should have never accepted you! I should have NEVER accepted you. What would've happened if I had never accepted you?"

I said, "Well, Ma, I still would've been me; I just would've been me without a mother."

And she thought about it for a minute, and she said, "Well, you ain't got enough good sense to do anything without me, so I guess I'll stick around."

Um, thank you?

So, we laughed and went on about our conversation, but I still didn't take that opportunity to tell her because I was scared.

My mother had high expectations of me, and she used to say, "I'm raising you to be better than me," and I thought that me being trans meant that I was failing at that. And as a transgender person, one of the things we risk is losing everybody in this life that we thought loved us in order for us to find ourselves.

I was not ready to lose my mother. I just needed her too much.

And I just loved her too much. So, I kept it a secret. I didn't tell her for years. And our relationship definitely took a hit. I'm from Buffalo, so before this, I would go back and forth, just visit like four or five times a year. I stayed for a week at a time. But during these years, I would only go home maybe once and stay for a couple of days. It wasn't sustainable.

It wasn't sustainable particularly because now my transition is progressing, and now it's time for me to have surgery, and I still had no plans to tell her.

And my girlfriend at the time looked at me, and she said, "You are crazy. You and your mother are best friends. You talk to her every day. She's a nurse. She will never forgive you if you don't tell her that you are about to have major surgery."

So, I was like, "Ugh, all right, I'm going to tell her."

I called her; I said, "Mommy."

She said, "What's up?"

I said, "I got something to tell you."

She said, "What is it?"

And this is exactly how it came out to her.

I said, "Ma, I am having a double mastectomy, a chest reconstruction. *I'm a man.*"

She said, "What the fuck?"

She's like hyperventilating on the phone, right?

So, I said, "Listen, Mommy, I'm having surgery, and I'm having surgery in three days, and I would love you to be here for me, but if you can't, I understand."

And she said, "Just get off my phone, and let me think. Just get off my phone."

Click, and she hung up on me, and I didn't hear from her.

The day of my surgery comes around, and I'm all prepped, getting ready to be wheeled in, and the door opens up, and guess who it is . . .

It's my mom, Ms. Mary. And here she comes—and she has this plush Ralph Lauren robe, and she has a jar full of chocolates covered in blue foil, and she has a little blue plush teddy bear for me.

She was there with me the entire time I was in surgery and during recovery.

I get discharged, and we go back to her favorite hotel, which is the Marriott Marquis here in Times Square. And we're kind of just hanging out in the hotel room. And I look over and she's crying.

I said, "Ma, why are you crying?"

She said, "Because it feels like my daughter died."

That was one of the hardest things I've ever heard. But I understood it because my transition wasn't just mine alone.

I went from being a daughter to a son. I went from being the little sister to the baby brother, from the favorite auntie to the favorite uncle.

So, I grabbed my mother's hand, and I looked in her eyes, and I said, "Mommy, I'm yours, and you are still mine, and everything that you've taught me, all the memories that we have made as mother and daughter have informed me and fortified me as a man that I am today."

And we laughed, and we cried, and we talked. And I think it was then that she really started to understand me and accept me as her son.

But it wasn't necessarily a smooth transition.

She kept messing up my name. She kept messing up my pronouns.

And so one day I called her, and I said, "Mama, look, I'm not coming home anymore. I'm not coming home to visit if you can't get my pronouns right, and you can't get my name right, because not only is it humiliating, okay? It's unsafe. You could be putting me in a really unsafe position when you do this."

She said, "Oh my God, I'm so sorry. I'm so sorry. I'll be better."

I said, "All right, get it together."

A few days later she called me, and she said, "Oh, Tika-boo, you'd be so proud of your mother. You'd be so proud of me."

I said, "Why, Mommy? What's going on?"

She said, "Because I've been *practicing*. Me and Stella have been *role-playing,* practicing your name and y'all pronouns. You'd be so proud of your mother."

I said, "Mama, I'm always so proud of you."

She said, "Oh, I just love you."

I said, "I love you too," and we went on in conversation the way we had always done.

Three years pass. Our relationship is stronger than ever, and in June of 2014, I get a phone call from my mom. This time she is hysterical crying, hysterical.

I said, "Mommy, what's going on?"

She said, "Baby, you got to come home right now. You got to come home right now."

I said, "Mama, I'm coming home on the nineteenth."

And she said, "Baby, I'm not going to be here on the nineteenth because the cancer has mushroomed throughout my entire body. The tumors in my lungs and in my back are bigger than the initial tumor in my breasts. You got to get home right now."

Now, we knew Mommy had a cancer diagnosis, but I don't think we knew it was that bad. So, I got on the first plane back to Buffalo, but by the time I get there, my mother's in hospice, in and out of consciousness.

And one of my sisters is there, and she sees me, and she says, "Tiq is here. Here *she* is. Tiq is here. *She* finally made it. Here *she* is."

My mother slowly opened up her eyes, and she whispered, "*He.*"

That was one of the last words she spoke.

So, over the next couple of days, we had it set up so that she was never alone. Everyone in the family took a shift. And I had the morning shift.

One morning I come in, and it's pretty obvious that we're reaching the end now.

Every breath she takes is so labored. Her whole body moves, and there's this loud gurgle with every breath that just fills the room.

I come up to her hospital bed, and I take the guardrail down, and I get in bed with her just like I used to when I was a little kid. And I put my head on her shoulder, and I put my lips to her ear.

And I said, "Mama, you could go."

I said, "It is okay. I promise you I'm going to be okay. You did such a good job raising me. You can go."

Then I fell asleep. I fell asleep right there. And when I woke up, the room was silent, and my champion had died right there in my arms.

I'll tell you, there are no words to express how devastating that was for me.

The sun still doesn't shine as bright anymore.

I was lost because my mother, she was my moral compass. She was my guiding light. She was the only person in this world who could check me—so I'm like, who's going to check me now?

And as I processed my grief over time and really reflected on this idea that she was raising me to be better than her—in actuality, it wasn't about me being better than her. She was raising me to live in this world *without her*.

And not only am I living, but I am *thriving*, because I am the man that she raised.

* ☽ *

TIQ MILAN is a thought leader, storyteller, and media maker whose work on equity and inclusion has had an impact in the United States and abroad for over a decade. He travels throughout North America leading discussions on healthy modes of masculinity, intersectional leadership, and engineering environments of inclusion. He has lectured at several universities, including

Harvard, Stanford, and Brown, on the importance of inclusion as a tool of innovation, and he outlines concrete strategies for productive engagement. Tiq is a sought-after host, having moderated conversations on intersectional inclusion and human rights at HBO's NewFest Film Festival and the Tribeca Film Festival. His 2016 TED Talk has been viewed over three million times and continues to inform and inspire people all over the world. His memoir, *Man of My Design: A Self-Determined Life,* is forthcoming.

This story was told on April 25, 2022, at the Walter Kerr Theatre in New York City. The theme of the evening was Hell-Bent. Director: Sarah Austin Jenness.

FEEDLOT CALVES

JACKIE ANDREWS

In 1979, I was sixteen, standing in the dining room of our western Nebraska farmhouse, and I was crying. I was telling my mom and dad that I was pregnant. I wanted to keep this baby, but I didn't want to bring shame to my family.

It was my father who said, "If you want to keep this baby, then you pick up your chin, and you look the world in the eyes, and you move forward. You can't undo the past, and there's never any shame in a newborn baby."

I know that he believed what he said was true because you could tell it in the way that he cradled his granddaughter on the day she was born.

It was my father who brought my daughter to my bedside, and he placed her in my arms, and he said, "Jackie, here's your daughter, and you do the very best you can with her. But no matter how hard you try, you're going to mess her up."

He said, "We all do. But if you love her and you let her know how much you love her, she'll forgive you."

That was the easy part, loving this baby. From the minute I held her, I loved her more than I loved life itself. I knew that she and I were going to fight our way through this world, and the very first fight we had was just to get out of that hospital.

It had been a very difficult birth. My daughter was eleven days in intensive care, and I was eight days in the hospital, with a couple trips to the OR.

But we made it out, and I started the ritual of our life. I'd get up in the morning, and I would do chores, and then I would go off to band practice and to school. I would race home after school to see her before I went off to work at Wendy's. At night, I would come home, and I would do the chores for the night and start my homework. I would learn to sleep with that little baby right here in the crook of my arm.

It wasn't easy, but I felt like I was keeping my head above water until that wave of hospital bills hit, and they were *enormous*. I didn't see any way that I was going to get these bills paid off working at Wendy's.

So I went to my dad, and I told him that I thought I was going to need some kind of public assistance.

He said, "No."

He reminded me that my grandmother and my grandfather had nine children in the Depression, and they had never taken a penny from anyone.

He said, "You got one kid, and I think you'll find your way through this."

I really had some doubts about that because these bills needed to be paid, and that hospital was going to expect money, and we didn't have money. And I don't just mean that we were poor, I mean that we had decided to live *without money*.

My dad was the kind of man who loved democracy, and he loved children, and he respected people who made an honest living with their hands. But he hated capitalism, and he distrusted institutions, and he was scornful of a wasteful society.

So, he had said that we would live on this farm, and everything we needed would come from the farm. If we couldn't get it from that farm, then we would barter for it—we might fill a freezer with meat or build you something.

If we couldn't barter for it, and we couldn't grow it, then we would scavenge it. We would see a barn that was falling down, and we would reclaim that wood and pound those nails straight for the next project.

I can still see my father standing there with a piece of rotten fruit that he had gotten from a dumpster behind the Jack & Jill grocery store.

He'd say, "Jackie, look at this: 75 percent of this pear is good, and someone's thrown it away."

Then he'd cut off the bad part, and we'd eat it.

He just had this way of looking at the world, and right now he was trying to see a way that we could get those bills paid off before I graduated high school.

We had a little more than a year, and then I was going to be out on my own, and my family always said, "When a kid graduates high school, they need to leave home, because if you don't push a kid out of a nest, they're never going to learn to fly." I may have had a baby, but there weren't going to be any exceptions made for me.

My life was going to be hard, but it was going to be a whole lot harder if I didn't get rid of these hospital bills.

That's when my dad spotted a problem out there at the feedlot, and that *problem* might be our *solution*. You see, out in western Nebraska, they take all these beef cattle, and they feed them in a feedlot, and they finish them off to market weight.

Feedlots are specifically for beef cattle, and there's no place for a calf in there. So, if you get a young heifer in that feedlot and she drops a calf, well, that's a problem for that feedlot. They'll separate that calf off right away because there's no place to raise it.

But it's also a problem for that calf. Because if you separate a calf, well, it won't get that first milk from that mother cow. It's called colostrum. It's a real thick milk, and it helps that calf survive.

That calf needs that milk every three, four hours. That calf's going to die if he doesn't get it.

My dad figured if we could get to these calves quickly enough, we might be able to take them, raise them, make some money, pay off those bills.

So, he and I went to every single feedlot in western Nebraska, and we talked to these feedlot managers, and we said, "Hey, next time a heifer drops a calf, you give us a call. We'll come out and get that calf."

We left, and I wasn't sure if they would do this because the thing about farmers is they like to do the same thing, the same way, every time.

We got a call about a week later. We raced out to this feedlot, and there was this sickly little calf there. We picked it up, and I was afraid to put it in the back of the truck. So, I held it in the front of the cab, and I remember looking at this little thing and just praying that it was going to make it. Because if this little calf died, all my hopes were going to die with it.

We got it home, and I set it up in the kitchen. I put down this little heat lamp, and while I was taking care of this, we got a call for another calf. I went and got that calf.

By the time we got a call for the third calf, my mama said, "You better get these cattle out of the kitchen."

So we moved the cattle out to the shed, and then we kept getting calls. They just kept calling and calling. We got about twenty calves, and let me tell you, that's a lot of work.

When August rolled around it was time to start weaning these calves and put them on feed. It meant a lot less labor bottle feeding them, but it brought a whole new problem. I had no money to feed these things.

So, we went down to the farmers' co-op and the feed store there in Mitchell, Nebraska, and I said, "Look, I've got this herd of feeder cattle. You front me some feed till I can get them to market in the spring, and I'll pay you off then."

They agreed. And I remember bringing that feed home. I didn't have the physical strength to unload it, but I had two younger brothers. They weren't very big, but they were farm boys. They were strong as grown men, and they could throw those hundred-pound sacks around, and they helped me feed those cattle.

By the time that school started again in the fall, these calves were looking good. They were healthy, and they were putting on weight. With every pound that those cattle put on, I could feel that weight just coming off my shoulders.

But then that calendar turned from 1979 to 1980, and it was the beginning of the farm crisis.

First thing to happen was the price of cattle plummeted. I listened to those farm reports over the radio and just hoped that they'd come back up.

They weren't coming up. Every day they'd go down lower, and every day we fed those cattle, it cost us more. Pretty soon we had to bring them in to sell them.

The day that we loaded those cattle up for market, it was like a cloud of doom had settled over that farm. We loaded them up, and we took them into the sale barn. We ran them down these chutes, and they weighed them in, and they put them in the pens.

The other farmers are getting there early, and they're checking their cattle in, and they're getting registered for this sale.

After you get registered, you kind of stand around, and there's this big sea of bib overalls and ball caps and everybody drinking coffee. The farmers are talking, and most of them are talking about the crisis.

Because this part of Nebraska that I live in, it's not a rich part.

And before this farm crisis was over, some of these farmers were going to lose their farms.

Some of the farmers that lost their farms were going to take their own lives.

My dad was talking to the farmers, and he was telling them how we'd gotten these feedlot calves and how we were going to sell them and pay off these hospital bills. The farmers were listening, but they were not saying a lot.

If you've ever been around a Nebraska farmer, they're not really a talkative bunch, okay?

That sale starts, and herd after herd is just coming through this sale ring, and the price is so low that they're practically giving these cattle away.

My stomach is tightening because my fate is marching toward me.

My herd comes into that ring. And those farmers started bidding. And then they kept on bidding. They bid on those cattle like they were some kind of prize breeding stock.

That price, it went so far beyond what those cattle were worth because those farmers were voicing their approval of my ability to try and pull myself up with my bootstraps and pay off those bills.

They voiced that approval with wallets that had been emptied in this farm crisis. They didn't give to me from their surplus, they gave to me from their hearts.

I walked away with enough money to pay that hospital bill off in full. I paid my dad back for that milk supplement, and I paid back the farmers' co-op for the feed that they fronted me.

And I had enough money left over to buy these two baby blue leisure suits with wide lapels for my brothers.

A couple weeks later, I graduated high school, and my daughter and I took off out of western Nebraska. I went on to earn a college degree. I joined the army, and I was awarded a Bronze Star for my actions in Desert Storm.

I have been able to travel the world, and I have seen magnificent things, but a part of my heart has never left western Nebraska. It will always remain with the farmers who gave me a chance in life.

* ⊙ *

JACKIE ANDREWS was raised in western Nebraska in the 1970s. After college, she served as an army officer and currently works as an art teacher. Jackie is a glass artist who enjoys storytelling and gardening. She and her husband, Steve, live in Grove City, Ohio, next door to her daughter and grandchildren.

This story was told on April 11, 2019, at the Victoria Theatre in Dayton. The theme of the evening was Carpe Diem. Director: Larry Rosen.

THIS PLACE
WAS HOME

LITTLE PINK GENERAL LEE

SAMUEL JAMES

My parents used to drop me off at my grandmother's house every Friday afternoon. Grammy was a tall, regal woman. She stood five foot ten, with ballerina posture, even into her seventies. She kept her hair in that semi-short, curly style popular amongst grandmothers.

I'd spend the night on Fridays, and she would let me stay up late and watch our favorite show, *The Dukes of Hazzard*.

She even gave me a little car that I would drive through the air and mimic the sounds of its Dixie car horn:

Na-na, na, na, na-na, na, na, na na na na . . .

My car was not anything like the car from the show. The car from the show was called the General Lee, and it was bright orange. It had *01* racing numbers on its doors. And its entire roof was one Confederate flag.

My car, *my* little General Lee, was one solid color: carnation pink.

It was a hollow shell made from a mold. It had no moving parts, but to my small child's mind, it was *exactly* the same.

Every Saturday morning, she would bring me back to my parents' apartment, and she would come in. We'd all have breakfast together, and she would get up to leave, and I would start to cry.

She would come over, make sure I had that little pink General

Lee, and she'd say, "Hang on to this, take good care of it, and I'll see you on the weekend. We can stay up late and watch our favorite show."

And she would leave.

And then twenty-four hours would go by, and I would have lost that car.

Come Friday, I would get to Grammy's, and somehow she would have found it, and I would have it in my hand, ready for when our favorite show came on.

This little pink General Lee is in all of my memories of Grammy.

There was the time I lost it under her couch, and I jammed my arm under to get it and got my arm stuck and *really* freaked out. But then along comes Grammy with a smile and one arm lifting up the end of the couch, saving the day.

Then there was a time that I was simulating one of the General Lee's famous jumps by throwing the car across the room, where it landed perfectly between Grammy's left eye and her glasses.

Then there was the time that I was five years old, and I was lying on my stomach on the floor between my parents' kitchen and living room, and Grammy and my parents were having breakfast at the table. Grammy liked to have a little sip of whiskey in the morning. She took a little sip, then took a little bite of banana, and she started to say something, and then she fell backward out of her chair.

My father jumped up, caught her, and he laid her on the floor, and I ran over. Her glasses had fallen off, and she looked so strange without her glasses. Her mouth was open, and her eyes were wide, but they had rolled back so they were entirely white, and I started screaming.

My mother picks me up, and she brings me to the other side of the room. She has the phone cradled in her ear, and she's talking to 911—but the ambulance did not arrive in time.

Grammy willed her house to my mother, and we all moved in.

This was a very old house. It was built by Grammy's father, who had been a veteran of the Spanish-American War. Everybody who'd ever lived in this house was still kind of there. You'd open up this closet and there'd be threadbare, monogrammed uniforms, and in this drawer there'd be old sepia-toned photographs of people forgotten to time. And in *this* drawer, you'd see old rusted tools, probably used to build this house.

When my mother died, she left the house to me, but I moved away, and my father stayed. I think the ghosts comforted him because he never changed anything about the house.

Every time I would come to visit, it was *always* the same.

I would bring a guitar, and he would sit in front of the piano. We'd trade songs, and we'd swap stories, and then we'd sing old songs, and we'd swap more stories. On and on, until I would go home.

But this one particular day, he gets up to get a glass of water, and I get nostalgic. I go up to my old room. My old room had also not changed.

My pretentious music and movie posters were still on the exact same walls, that were painted the exact same color I painted them in high school—black.

The bed was still in the same place.

This had been Grammy's room before it had been mine, and the bed frame had been Grammy's, and it was the white-and-gold set from Sears, with a matching dresser that was also still there.

Opening the drawers to the dresser, inside, you'll find Grammy's jewelry, old letters, and hundreds and hundreds of photographs. At least a hundred of which were of her and me. And they perfectly reflected my memory of Grammy.

I'm taken right back to this perfect moment of Grammy joy.

She also had a closet. Now, I never spent very much time in this closet, because it always felt like Grammy's. But on this particular day, I walk over to the closet, and it smells musty. There's cobwebs, and there's old coats hanging up, and my grandfather's tuxedo, and Grammy's wedding gown.

This is a walk-in closet. It's built under one of the eaves, so you kind of have to duck down if you're going to go all the way in. And on the floor, there's a plastic bag. It's an old degrading plastic bag, but it's the only thing plastic in this room, so I walk in to look at it.

As soon as I set foot in here, I feel like a kid again. Like when you're a kid and you're afraid you're going to get caught. Like any minute, someone's going to come around the corner and say, "HEY, what are you doing?"

I kneel down, and I open this bag, and inside are probably a hundred and fifty little pink General Lees.

It's like somebody gave me the setup for the joke and then waited twenty years to give me the punchline.

I'm just laughing.

I thought that she had found the one, singular, perfect toy, for only, singularly, me.

She was probably at a church rummage sale, and saw a bag of pink cars for a dollar, and thought, *Kids lose stuff.*

I grab this bag, full of Grammy joy, and I run downstairs.

I'm like, "Dad. Dad, do you remember the little pink General Lee? Because here's a hundred and fifty of them!"

And he does remember them. But there is no Grammy joy for him.

He's not laughing.

He's not smiling.

He looks half disappointed and half confused.

And he begins to tell me how his relationship with Grammy had been *very* different than my own.

Grammy's family has been in New England as long as there has been a New England. She was a pillar of her community. She was a sheriff's widow. And she was a very proud, and protective, white mother of a white daughter who had brought home and married, and had a *child* with, a big, Southern, Black man.

She was never forthright in her expression of her opinion of my father's race, but she let him know in other ways—in more passive-aggressive ways.

For example, she would introduce his small Black child—*me*—to a television show that whitewashed, and glorified, and romanticized racist symbolism of the South.

She would go a step further by encouraging that same Black child to run around his house literally singing Dixie. And she did this knowing full well exactly how my dad felt about it.

And so, there I am, standing there with this nostalgic grin fading from my face, holding the world's worst time capsule. Thinking about how she had found the *one, perfect, singular toy, just for me.*

But it hadn't even been *for* me.

And then my father laughs, just the smallest amount, and he explains how, every Saturday night, he would wait until my mother was asleep, and until I was asleep.

He would come into my room.

He'd take the little pink General Lee into the kitchen.

And he would throw it into the trash.

I took this bag of little pink General Lees back up to Grammy's closet, and I put it back where I found it. I stopped and looked at those pictures of her and me again, and they still reflect a grandmother's love for her grandchild.

It's still true.

But I also know that, digging through the house a little more, you will find a Barry Goldwater campaign pin and a little personal-size Confederate flag.

She was a loving grandmother, there was no doubt about that—it's absolutely true. But she was also a cruel person, who would manipulate her own grandchild in order to make his father suffer for their race.

Both things are true.

I'm standing there, thinking about how it's easy to love a child, while I am now the exact same size, and shape, and color as my father.

I move through the world how he did, and it reacts to me how it reacted to him.

I went back downstairs, and my father and I played some more songs, but we didn't talk about Grammy ever again.

About ten years after this, my father died.

I went back through the house, and it was still the same.

The closet still had those threadbare uniforms, and the drawers still had the sepia-toned photos and the old, rusty tools.

And up in my old room, those photos of Grammy and I were still in that dresser.

And her closet still had my grandfather's tuxedo and her wedding gown.

But that bag of little pink General Lees was nowhere to be found.

* ⊙ *

SAMUEL JAMES is an internationally touring musician, storyteller, and journalist living in Portland, Maine. He primarily covers local and national issues as they relate to race. He is also the creator and host of the podcast *99 Years*.

This story was recorded at a live performance at Alice Tully Hall at Lincoln Center for the Performing Arts in New York City on October 12, 2019. The theme of the evening was Tug-of-War. Director: Meg Bowles.

A COMPLETE, CORRECT HUMAN

JOHN ELDER ROBISON

There I was. Fifteen years old. I didn't have any friends. I was failing everything at Amherst High School. I was a misfit kid. I never knew what to say or do, and I couldn't tell what other people were thinking. I always seemed to say the wrong thing. I thought I said something nice to make them smile, and instead I pissed them off.

It was the same with my schoolwork. My teachers would give me work to do, and either I didn't understand it, so I couldn't do it at all, or I understood it all too well and frankly, thought it was stupid. I got to the point where I was getting straight F's, and it was just a question of whether I was gonna drop out of school, or they were gonna throw me out.

I could see I wasn't getting anywhere, so I resolved to drop out and do something else. This was the seventies, and I had a guidance counselor.

In his supportive way, he says to me, "Boy, you drop out of school, and even the army isn't going to take you because Vietnam's coming to an end, and they won't take high school dropouts and losers."

Encouraged by that advice, I decided to follow a common dream at the time, a career with a rock and roll band. Millions of young people dreamed of being that guitar player or being a singer up on stage. But I was really lucky because, as a boy, I combined my interest in music with an interest in electronics. I had started taking apart radios and TVs, sacrificing them in pursuit of knowledge, all with this dream that I was gonna be a star in music. But I wasn't gonna be a guitar player or a singer. I was gonna be the *engineer*.

I taught myself how to repair, modify, and, eventually, build guitar amplifiers and sound effects. Other kids thought they could become rock and roll superstars, I thought, *I'll be the guy who makes their amplifiers work.*

I joined a local rock and roll band, and they paid me eighty dollars a week to help set up the equipment and keep the sound systems running. I always had work! We traveled all over New England doing shows. And I was so proud of myself, you know, being self-employed and being independent. I started working for bigger and bigger bands. I got hired by a company called Britannia Row. Back then, they were Pink Floyd's sound company. I started to do shows with The Kinks and with Talking Heads and Roxy Music and one English act after another.

One day in the studio this fellow comes in, takes out a guitar, and starts digging at it with a chisel. I had always been unable to deal with people, but I had a great love of machinery, and I couldn't stand to see him destroying that guitar. I wondered what was the matter with him. I went over, and I asked him. He told me he wanted to make the guitar blow fire. I thought, *I better get it out of his hands before he destroys it.*

I said, "Well, I could do that. I could do it professionally."

I couldn't make friends or ask a girl the time of day, but somehow I could tell this famous musician that I could fix his guitar professionally. The fellow was Ace Frehley, the lead guitarist of KISS.

After talking to me for a few minutes, he turns to his roadie and says, "Tex, have Gibson send this guy a guitar right away."

And so they did.

I took it home, and me and some of my friends, because I had a few friends by then, we got together, and we made that guitar blow fire. We went on to make all the guitars for KISS that blew fire, shot rockets, lit up, or exploded. We made them all in Amherst, Massachusetts.

Anyway, there I was. I was in my early twenties, and I'd been labeled a total loser in school, but the world of musicians had welcomed me. It didn't matter what I looked like or what I sounded like. It didn't matter that I couldn't talk to girls, because I could talk to guitars. If you could help make beautiful music, you were welcome in that world.

One night we were setting up at the Silverdome, this huge arena that holds a hundred thousand people, for a concert. I stood on the stage, and I looked out, and it looked like it was five miles to the back seating. And I thought to myself how far I had come from being that loser kid.

People started inviting me to do other projects. They invited me to start making stuff for movies. Eventually, I got asked to go interview for a job as director of research at this new company called Lucasfilm. It sounded like a real great opportunity. But when I looked to see where they were located, I saw it was Los Angeles. And there I was in western Massachusetts. I thought to myself, *These people don't know that I'm a high school dropout. They don't know that I've been lying about my age since I was sixteen because you have to be twenty-one to play bars. And I'm going to go get a job out there? They're going to discover that I'm a loser and a total fraud. They're going to fire me, and then I'll starve to death out there in California.*

To tell you that today, I know it seems crazy, but that's what I believed. I thought to myself, *Well, boy. You can't keep this going. You've blown it. You'll be found out, and you better start doing something else.*

So, I turned them down, and I decided that I should just do something local. I thought I would start a business fixing cars. And I wanted to fix cars people really cared about, so I decided I would fix Bentleys and Land Rovers, cars like that. I figured fixing automobiles, nobody cared where you came from, and I could just do what I wanted.

I turned out to have sort of a touch with automobiles, just like I did with guitars and electronics. But fixing cars forced me to learn how to talk to people because, for the first time in my life, I had to talk nicely enough that they would want to come back a second time—that's the nature of being in business. My car business prospered, and I got friendly with some of the customers.

I got to know this one fellow who came in over a few years. He was a therapist. While his Land Rover was being fixed, I would tell him stories. I told him about being sort of lonely and isolated and that I always felt like I was on the outside looking in.

I'd complain that sometimes customers would come in and say things like, "Don't you know how to talk to somebody like me? Don't you realize the customer's always right?"

I would think to myself, *What kind of crazy shit is that? The customer is not always right. If the customer knew the answer, they wouldn't be here.*

I thought I was just being truthful, but the therapist would explain that sometimes customers didn't see things the same way I did.

After a few years of these conversations, he comes in one day and says, "John, in the therapy world we've got this saying that therapists shouldn't diagnose their friends, or pretty soon they won't have any friends left, but there's this thing everyone's talking about in the mental health community."

This is in the 1990s, and he says, "I thought for a long time about mentioning this, because you're a successful guy, but you have told me about being lonely and all. It's this thing called Asperger's syndrome, and it's a form of autism. You could be the poster boy for it."

I was stunned. I had no idea what autism was.

I took this book he gave me, and I looked inside.

It said, "*People with Asperger's can't look other people in the eye.*"

All my life people had noticed that about me.

"*People with Asperger's can't read body language, and they get too close to people and scare them, or they turn away. People think they are rude.*"

People with Asperger's, we say inappropriate things 'cause we don't have any filters in our heads. Even if we *are* the experts and are right, the customers don't like to hear that.

I read that book, and I thought to myself, *By God, I'm going to teach myself to act different. I'm going to make myself normal.*

Well, of course, today the disability community won't say things like that, but this was a different time. I resolved to teach myself how to behave.

The difference was like magic.

I began to have friends and to be invited places. I started speaking out, because I knew that there were millions of young people growing up who had crummy childhoods just like me, because people told us we were losers or morons and other ugly things. I wanted to show them that you can have a good life as a person who's autistic. I wanted to be that example. When I started speaking out, people began inviting me to speak out more. People began asking me if I wanted to get involved in research.

Some folks from Harvard Medical School came to me, and they said, "We'd be interested in your autistic perspective in a study. We want to use a new tool to see if we can help autistic people read emotions in other people."

They were just sort of looking for me to endorse it, but I heard that, and I thought, *Boy, that's the thing that's been wrong with me all my life.*

I said, "Where do I sign up?"

They brought me into the lab, and they sat me down in front of a computer, and they said, "We're going to show you these faces on the screen, and you just have to push the buttons to identify: Are they happy, are they sad, are they jealous, are they angry?"

The faces flashed in front of me, and I had absolutely no idea what I was seeing.

I said, "I flunked it before we even started."

They said, "No, not at all. What we're going to do is, we're going to stimulate you with this machine. We're going to fire pulses of electromagnetic energy into your head with this, and afterward we're going to test you again, and we're going to see if the responses change."

They sat me in a chair, and they fired this thing called TMS into my head for half an hour. My brain was just kind of in neutral the whole time, and then it stopped.

And they say, "Hurry, come on. We gotta get you in, and we've gotta test you before it wears off."

I go over, and I sit down, and they show me the faces again. And it's exactly the same. I've got no idea what I'm seeing.

I thought, *What kind of a crazy fool was I to think I could go to a hospital, and these mad scientists could do something to me, and I would change?*

(Well, it *was* Beth Israel Hospital and Harvard Medical School, really good mad scientists. But still.)

So, I get in my car for the two-hour drive home, and I pull out onto the highway, and I turn on music from my iPod. I'd always play music from the bands I used to work with, driving places. And I put on a recording of an old performance by a band called Tavares. Back when I was younger, they were playing clubs, singing soul music in the places I had grown up working.

I turned it on, and, boy, it was like I stepped back into 1977. The music was so alive and so real. It was like all the years just fell away. It was like I could smell the cigarette smoke—I felt like I wasn't even in a car anymore.

All the years I engineered rock and roll, people told me I did such a great job of delivering beautiful music, but I could never feel it. It didn't make any difference to me what we played. But in the car that night, as the music played, I could *feel* that these were love songs. They were stories written for real people. I began to cry, and I cried all the way home—I wasn't crying because I was sad. I was crying because all of a sudden I could feel the emotion in this music. Before, I had never understood what was behind the words.

I listened to music all night, and gradually the feeling faded away.

And in the morning, I wrote to the scientists in charge. I said, "*That's some powerful mojo you got in that machine.*" I really thought it was a dream come true. I could see and I could feel emotions in people. I thought, *It's going to be magical. It's going to be beauty and sweetness and light.*

Some of those experiences were like a window into the soul, but the brilliance eventually faded away. It was the ride of a lifetime, but it was a rough one. I had always imagined that there was this world of love out there, but because I was autistic, I couldn't see it. I thought, *If only I could see it, things would be great.*

But when I *could* see it, I could see *everything,* and I saw that the world was *also* full of anger and fear and jealousy and anxiety and everything else that fills the newspapers. It was overwhelming, and I didn't want to have those feelings again.

This all happened to me years ago. Now it's clear that it was being different—it was being that kid who didn't have any friends but could talk to guitar amplifiers—that was the thing that made me special in the world.

I always thought what I wanted most in the world was to be "normal."

But being different took me to the top of the music world in the 1970s, and that gave me the confidence to do everything since.

Being like everyone else would've meant throwing away the one thing in my life that made me successful.

The most important thing I learned from that experiment was that people like me are complete and functional humans. We are not broken versions of someone else's normal. We are necessary parts of the world. And in fact, the world needs our diversity. We're okay exactly as we are.

* ⊙ *

JOHN ELDER ROBISON grew up in a world of machines. At sixteen, he was lord and master of a small tractor and a CDC 3600 computer. By age twenty, he'd moved on to more sophisticated devices and found himself in jail on a small Caribbean island. At twenty-one, he was the engineer for KISS, where he designed their signature special effects guitars. In search of greater challenges, John went on to design power system components for our country's last underground nuclear tests, which led him to establish a business restoring Bentley, Land Rover, and Mercedes motorcars. He continues to oversee that business today in Springfield, Massachusetts. He is also the neurodiversity scholar at The College of William & Mary in Williamsburg, Virginia, and neurodiversity adviser to Landmark College in Putney, Vermont. John is the *New York Times* bestselling author of *Look Me in the Eye, Be Different, Raising Cubby,* and *Switched On.* He has appeared on a number of radio and television shows and has written many articles and essays, including the definitive work on diagnosis of noises in Land Rover engines and a fine monograph on how autistic Polynesians may have colonized the southwest Pacific. He lives in western Massachusetts with his family, a bulldog, and an Imperial Chinese war pug.

This story was told on October 12, 2017, at The Wilbur Theatre in Boston. The theme of the evening was Balancing Acts. Director: Jenifer Hixson.

RICH CITY SKATER
JACOBY COCHRAN

I'm standing on the sideline of the largest roller-skating rink floor in Illinois. It belongs to Rich City Skate, my family's skating rink.

When I was fifteen years old, my stepfather and his parents decided to realize a lifelong dream that I had never actually heard of: to own and operate a skating rink. And so, they bought it, our entire family renovated and renamed it, and tonight is our inaugural national party. Now, if you've never been roller skating in your life, a national party is kind of like the Grammys of roller skating. I'm talking about some of the greatest roller skaters in America all in one place, showing off their moves, their music, their style—and the place is packed. The DJ starts the roll call, which means that folks from different cities or states come on the floor one by one to represent.

So, you've got people in there from Texas doing the slow walk. Folks from St. Louis doing the ballroom. You've got partners in there doing Kentucky throws and New York trains. They had come from all over the country, from California to Florida. The music is thumping, the synchronized lights are blaring, and the fog machines are humming. Then, all of a sudden, the sound of the Godfather of Soul—James Brown—fills the building. Now, when you hear those horns from the intro to "The Payback," you know it's time for Chicago to get on the floor.

Suddenly, my mother skates by me, and she throws me a wink. My mom is one of the greatest roller skaters in Chicago, which means she's one of the greatest roller skaters of all time. Everybody knows Sweet T. When she skates, it's like time stands still.

I'm lucky that she passed down some of her gifts and a little bit of her first love of skating to me and my siblings. My entire childhood I grew up in the skating rinks on the South Side of Chicago. I went on field trips, spent weekends, and attended juke jams in Markham and in Glenwood, at the famous rink on 87th Street, and now, at Rich City Skate. And I loved it.

When my family bought this rink, it immediately became a family affair. My stepfather was the general manager. My grandparents were CEOs. My mom, the CFO. Aunts, uncles, cousins filled myriad roles in various spots throughout the building, from the snack bar, where we had to cook the food and serve annoying birthday parties; to the Stuff Shop, where we sold light-up trinkets and candy; to the skate rental, where we had to collect, repair, and pass out skates.

And me? Well, shit, I learned how to do everything. You name it, I learned it, and I loved it—all the way down to cleaning the nasty-ass bathrooms. I threw myself into the rink. Every free moment I had, I was there. When I described myself, it was—"Coby from the South Side of Chicago, and I work in my family's rink." And, somehow, that was cool when it came out of my mouth.

It wasn't just my family's or my love that made the place, but the community's as well. Black-owned skating rinks are far and few between. And these places have been a safe haven for Blacks dating all the way back to the Great Migration. From the very beginning, our community supported us. They showered us with love as we threw bigger parties and political rallies, as we were on the radio, and as we skated at Bud Billiken parades. Every day at the rink, I thought I had never seen so much joy in one place.

We were still flying high a few years later when I went off to college. I only moved like two hours away, but college was an opportunity for me to define myself, for myself. For me to stop just being "Coby, who worked at the roller-skating rink." So I joined a speech team, joined Alpha Phi Alpha. I got a job on campus.

Of course, every waking moment I could, I would go back to the skating rink. I would just fall into things, like I never left. I'd skate with my homies till four A.M. and—let me be clear—I was still a badass motherfucker on them skates.

But the distance I put between myself and the rink gave me a new vantage point. I started noticing things on my visits. My mom and my stepdad were fighting more, but they were putting on smiles for the people. The growing pressure of running a family business was starting to heighten the tensions and the egos as people positioned themselves for more control. My younger siblings, who were now in high school, had put a lot of space between themselves and the rink—which was a complete 180 from how things were when I was in high school. I noticed all of this, but I just figured, hell, this is just part of the business.

Things don't really crystallize for me until about midway through my junior year, when I get a call from my mom.

She says, "Coby, I called to tell you that I'm finished. Me and your stepfather are splitting, and I'm leaving the rink."

Sweet T wasn't really one for small talk.

I was shocked, and I just wanted to hold on to that fantasy, that family affair.

So I begged her, "What can I do? What can the family do? How can we turn back the hands of time?"

And she said, "We can't. Coby, this was never my dream. And now, I don't even feel the love."

I knew she wasn't just talking about love of the rink or her marriage, but her first love of skating, which had become my first love.

After that phone call, my visits started becoming a little less frequent. Family members felt like they had to choose sides, and so when I would go back to skate, the rink felt like a ghost of itself. When I graduated, I just wanted to hold on to that fantasy, so I ran. I went from living two hours away to twelve hours away. But I told myself that even though I was throwing myself into something new, I would go back and visit, and I would help out at some point.

But a month became six months, which became two years.

And then, the summer of 2016 rolls around, and I look myself in the mirror, and I say, "I can't for the life of me miss another Rich City Skate National Party."

It's our ten-year anniversary. So I grab my skates, and I head there. I knew that things at the rink had changed. But when I walked through the doors, many of those synchronized lights and humming fog machines were out of order. A lot of those thumping speakers had blown.

Once again, I'm standing on the sidelines of the largest roller-skating rink floor in Illinois, and it now has humps and dips and a clear spot that's been roped off because that's where the ceiling leaks.

Yet somehow, this place is packed from side to side. The DJ starts the roll call, and my heart swells, and I see people out there from Texas doing the slow walk. Folks from St. Louis doing the ballroom. You've got partners doing Kentucky throws and New York trains.

When the sound of James Brown fills the room, I sprint on the floor. But I'm a little rusty. It's been some time, but with each passing song, as those horns go on and on, the magic returns to my body. The moves start flowing through me like I never left, and I think to myself, *This is what it was all about—the people. And the people are here.*

As the sweat pours from my face, and the music fades, my stepfather skates by me, and he throws me a wink. He grabs the microphone, and he thanks everybody for being there, for making this one of the best national parties that the rink has ever seen. He thanks them for their love and their support.

And then he tells us that this is going to be the last Rich City Skate National Party, because Rich City Skate is closing its doors.

I'm hearing this for the first time, and it feels like a punch to the gut. I'm looking around as people are sobbing and hugging.

He says, "This was always my dream. But now it's time to wake up."

I've never seen so much sadness in one place. It feels like a funeral, and I don't really know what to do. So, I just sort of do what comes natural, and I start cleaning up, from the nasty-ass bathrooms, to the snack bar, to vacuuming the Stuff Shop, to collecting skates. And I come across this wall that is filled with pictures. Ten years of my family's history, strung out in Polaroids. There are birthday parties and graduations, rallies and parades, homecomings and homegoings. I see this picture of my family during our inaugural national party, wearing our freshly pressed polos.

In the past few years, I had started to resent this place, wondering if it took too much from us and if it was worth it. I stared at these pictures, and I realized that, for so many people, this place was home.

So, before I leave, I go to my stepfather and ask him for one last favor. He walks into the DJ booth, and the intro to "The Payback" starts playing in the background.

And I hop on the floor, sweat intermingling with tears running down my face. I take one last skate around the largest roller-skating rink floor in Illinois, and I know: Building or not, I'mma always be a Rich City Skater.

* ☺ *

JACOBY COCHRAN is a writer, educator, and storyteller. He is the award-winning host of *City Cast Chicago,* Chicago's favorite daily news podcast! The podcast was named Best of 2021 and 2022 by the *Chicago Reader*. You can also catch Jacoby discussing politics, sports, social justice, and culture on Chicago's TV and radio stations. As a performer, Jacoby has led workshops and campaigns for Google, Spotify, AT&T, Chicago Bulls, Best Buy, and Kohl's. Check out jacobycochran.com to learn more about his work.

This story was told on February 17, 2022, at Aaron Davis Hall in New York City. The theme of the evening was Passing Go. Director: Chloe Salmon.

THE DAY TYLER PERRY CALLED ME

BRITTNEY COOPER

In the early 2000s, I became the first person in my family to graduate from college and to go on to pursue a PhD.

Now, when you go to med school, you become a doctor. And when you go to law school, you become a lawyer. But when you go to grad school in the humanities—you become a critic.

Imagine studying for six years for the express privilege of telling everybody who's ever written or said anything what is wrong with what they have said.

Imagine further explaining this to your family at Thanksgiving.

So, one of the ways that I would cope with this unfortunate turn of events was to go to the movies, typically a matinee on a Wednesday. And my favorite filmmaker at the time was Tyler Perry.

When I went to see *Diary of a Mad Black Woman,* I thought to myself, *Here's a man who understands Black women who have been done wrong.*

When Kimberly Elise's character slaps the shit out of the husband that has been abusing her, I'm in the theater hooting and hollering with all the ladies in there.

But at the same time, I'm also becoming a feminist. And, you know, I'm down for smashing the patriarchy and everything, but nobody tells you that the first casualty of a feminist analysis is movies.

You hate them. Because you see the patriarchy absolutely everywhere.

You become a feminist, and suddenly, you can't like anything anymore. You're a professional *unliker* of everything. Or as they say in the hood, "I'm getting a PhD—Playa Hatin' Degree."

It occurs to me, though, that I like these movies. So I keep going, but I just don't tell my feminist friends how much I liked the movies because every time I talk to them, they're using language like *tropes* and *representation* and how *problematic* the films are.

But what I'm thinking to myself is, *But in* Daddy's Little Girls, *Gabrielle Union's character snags fine-ass Idris Elba, and I don't know a straight Black girl that don't want Idris.*

And I'm also thinking, *This feels a little bit like home.*

Tyler Perry built his career making these *Madea* stage plays. And there was an underground economy of VHS dubs that you could get of these plays. I remember watching one of these plays with my auntie and her laughing hysterically, and I'm sitting there going like, *This play look a little low budget.*

But Madea is a pistol-toting granny, and my granny was a pistol-toting granny, so it kind of worked for me.

But I was also starting to see what my friends were saying because I went to see *The Family That Preys,* and the female character in that movie is so villainized that by the time her husband knocks the shit out of her, the women in the theater are hooting and hollering again.

And this time, I'm not hollering with them because, you know, I'm a feminist now, and that's domestic violence. So, I'm starting to think maybe me and Tyler might have to break up.

I finished my PhD, and I got a job as a professor at a big state school in the Deep South. Tyler and I have broken up, but his star has continued to ascend. And though I'm nowhere near his orbit, my little star has continued to ascend too.

I'm trying to figure out how to wear this big old title as both a PhD and a critic, even though I come from people that don't really have fancy titles. So, I call in my girls, who are mostly first-generation PhDs themselves, and we form a crew and a blog called the *Crunk Feminist Collective.*

Around this time, Tyler puts out a show called *The Haves and the Have Nots,* and like a good feminist, I tune in to hate-watch the show. And, as expected, he gives me something to hate.

The next day I go to the *Crunk Feminist Collective* blog, and I pen a post called "Tyler Perry Hates Black Women." Now, let me say that some high-profile feminists would come through and read the blog, but I don't really think any famous, *famous* people were ever reading it. So, imagine my surprise the next day, when I get an email with the subject line, "*Tyler Perry wants to talk to you.*"

I think it's a joke, right? But I opened the email, I called the number back, and it's not a joke.

His assistant gets on the phone, and she says, "Oh, he wants to talk to you."

So, we set up a time to talk the very next day.

And that day, I spend my time calling all my homegirls going, "What are we going to do?"

And the consensus among the feminist cabal is, *FINISH HIM!*

They're like, "We have been waiting our whole careers for this, and you have been chosen. So, you got to do that shit."

And I'm like, "But it's Tyler Perry, though."

So, the next day, I'm sitting in my one-bedroom apartment with peeling paint; the person that lives across the hall from me is a grad student because, it turns out, professor money doesn't go as far as you think it does when you don't come from generational wealth. And I'm waiting on a famous millionaire filmmaker to call my phone. I also have an intense need to pee, but I'm afraid to make a run for it.

Right on time, the phone rings.

"Ms. Cooper, this is Tyler Perry."

"Hi, Mr. Perry."

"No, call me Tyler."

"Okay, call me Brittney."

"Brittney, you wrote some things about me that I want to talk about."

"Well, Tyler, let me begin by saying that I've seen all of your films, and I really respect . . ."

"Nope. You said that I hate Black women. And I don't understand how you came to that conclusion."

Deep breath, he really wants to do this.

"All right. Let's begin with *The Haves and the Have Nots.* Why in the first three minutes of that show do we have a maid, a sex worker, and a rich Black bitch? These are tropes of Black womanhood."

He stops me and says, "Tropes? Let me explain something. You're talking to a man with a twelfth-grade education. So, I don't know anything about tropes. But when I was growing up, the person that lived next door to me was a maid, and her daughter was a sex worker. And they were, like, the nicest people ever."

And then I realized, like, *Oh wow—yeah, he's Tyler Perry, and he's rich, and I'm not rich. But I have a PhD, and he has a twelfth-grade education.* And so, all of a sudden, maybe the playing field is not as disparate as I thought. And I also think to myself, *My mother was a single mother with a twelfth-grade education. And my uncle, who Tyler Perry is starting to sound like, also had a twelfth-grade education. I am basically talking to a hometown boy who had done well for himself.*

So I say, "Tyler, you know, you and I have a lot in common. We're both from Louisiana. We're both raised in the church. We both had pistol-toting grannies; we both had an abusive parent."

And he said, "Oh wow, I didn't know that about you. I just

knew you were sharp, and now that I do know this about you, I don't understand why you don't understand what I'm trying to do in my movies."

And so I say to him, "Okay, here's my real question: Why are the educated Black girls in your movies such bitches to everybody?"

And he says, "Well, because there was a whole branch of my family growing up, they all went to college, and they treated everybody like trash."

And I realize, damn, that's exactly the thing that I feared—that having all of this education might make me unrecognizable to the people that raised me. Because the thing that I loved about Tyler Perry's movies is that he rides hard for working-class Black girls, the girls that work behind the counter at Waffle House, the church ladies. The grannies that press twenty dollars into your hand when you come home from school. Those are the kind of folks that raised me, and I wanted to be recognizable to them.

So, I'm thinking about all this, and Tyler breaks in, "Brittney, something urgent just came up. Can I call you back? I'll call you back in twenty minutes."

And I'm like, "Okay."

So, we get off the phone. I run to pee, and then I'm sitting in my house going, *Damn, he not going to call me back* because I was blowing this conversation and maybe being a little bit of a jerk?

But like he said, twenty minutes later, the phone rings.

"Brittney, this is Tyler. Where were we?"

So, with my twenty minutes of hindsight and hastily gained wisdom, I say, "Here's the thing I'm really trying to say, Tyler. Is it possible for you to uplift working-class Black girls in your films without throwing the educated sisters under the bus? Because educated girls love your movies too."

And he says, "You know what? That's profound. Can I uplift one group without demonizing another group . . . I'm going to think about that."

And so then, I said to him, "Now, if you want to keep talking about this, I'm a professional critic, and I'm happy to offer these—"

"Nope," he says, "I'm never calling your ass again."

And we both screamed because it was like the realest moment in this conversation.

But he said, "I always like to talk to my critics. I learn a lot from them."

And I said, "Fair enough," and we hung up.

The thing that connects Tyler Perry and me is that we're both working-class Southern folks who, in our respective fields, have "made it." And we want to do the kind of work that always honors the places where we come from.

Tyler's films forced me to grapple with my own insecurities about what it means to be a Black girl who makes it and who still loves home—even if she is, in some ways, changed dramatically beyond recognition to those who raised her.

I also thought about how I'm used to men dismissing me—because I have loud opinions, and I'm brash and unapologetic, and I'm a feminist.

But when this millionaire filmmaker read the little old blog of a not even thousandaire professor and heard me say that the way he represented girls like me in his movies essentially hurt my feelings—he didn't ignore me or act like he hadn't seen it. He picked up the phone, and he called me. And then he listened and called back and listened again, until he could find something useful to make his art better.

I had been so swift and sure to proclaim that Tyler Perry hates Black women. And I was left to consider that maybe listening is what love looks like after all.

* ◉ *

BRITTNEY COOPER is a professor of women's, gender, and sexuality studies and Africana studies at Rutgers University; co-founder of the Crunk Feminist Collective; and author of the *New York Times* bestseller *Eloquent Rage: A Black Feminist Discovers Her Superpower.*

This story was told on February 17, 2022, at Aaron Davis Hall in New York City. The theme of the evening was Passing Go. Director: Michelle Jalowski.

KEEPING THE FAITH . . .
AND THE FEMINISM
BLESSING OMAKWU

When I was five years old, my family moved back to Nigeria. My parents had come to America to study at Christian universities, but they always had this dream to start a church together. And so we moved to Abuja, and they did just that.

Growing up, that church became the center of my existence and our collective existence as a family. Weekdays were spent hanging around the church offices; weekends were spent practicing in the choir, going to weddings, funerals, and church picnics. In many ways, the people I saw week after week became more like family to me than my blood relatives.

Sometimes though, I resented the church. I resented the fact that we lived in modesty, with extra income going back to the church. Most of all, I resented having to share my father with the church.

My father was my hero and my very best friend. He made me believe that anything I wanted to do or be was possible.

Once, I went to my father and told him I had decided to be a global music star, and so my father bought me a keyboard, and he said, "If you learn to read music and play this, then I'll help you."

(I never did learn and quickly moved on to other dreams.)

Another time I went to him and announced that I was going to run a hair salon. I had seen one for sale in our neighborhood, and I was very convinced that I could run it after fifth grade every day.

My father sat with me, taught me how to write a business plan, and said, "Well, let's talk through this."

And he allowed me to come to the conclusion that perhaps between doing my homework and other activities, like seeing my friends, I might not have the time to do this just yet.

But most of all, no matter how busy he was, my father would sit down with me and teach me Bible lessons. He would also pray with me.

I went to my father when I had questions about the Bible.

I was probably in the seventh or eighth grade when I wrote in the margins of my Bible, *God, why don't you like women?*

See, I couldn't understand when I read some scenes why women were not counted in genealogies or named. My father explained to me that this had more to do with the history and context in which the Bible was written, and that God really did love women. So I took him at his word.

My father would often assign Bible scriptures to us to memorize whenever he went on work trips.

We used the time when he was away to learn those, and he always said, "By the time you're done memorizing those scriptures, I'll be back home."

But there was one trip that took longer than usual. This wasn't a work trip. My father had begun to experience these debilitating headaches, and he had gone back to America with my mother to run some tests.

I was thirteen years old when I got a call from him saying doctors had discovered a tumor the size of a golf ball in his brain. I remember not being worried at all when I got that phone call because my father had told me two things.

Thing one, he said, "Blessing, I'm going to be okay."

And my father had always kept his word to me.

Thing two, he said, "God will heal me."

My father had raised me to believe that God kept his promises.

And so, I spent the time when my father and my mother were away reading the Bible and memorizing every single scripture I could find on healing and God's promises. Eventually, my father came home, and for a while it seemed like he was okay, but slowly his health began to decline. He began to lose his sight, his speech, his coherence, his cognitive abilities. We still were not worried, because God was going to perform a miracle.

One night we were in our home when relatives and people from my father's village descended on us. I had never met most of these people before. They stood around my mother and screamed at her. They were screaming in the language of my father's tribe, a language he had never taught his American-born children.

My aunt and I sat on a staircase, eavesdropping. There was a church member, who came from the same tribe as my father, translating for my mom. We were able to make out that my mother was being accused of either not doing enough to keep my father alive or actively trying to kill him through juju.

My mother had spent the past two years traveling around the world with my father, seeking chemotherapy, radiation, and alternative treatments, and when the doctor said that there was nothing more that they could do, my mother spent sometimes hours and days at a stretch in the church, praying and fasting. She fasted her body into half its size.

As they screamed at her, my aunt looked at me, shook her head, and said, "I wish you were a boy. If you were a boy, as your parents' first child, you would've been able to intervene."

Anger welled up within me. It was the first time in my fifteen years I had ever been made conscious that my being female accorded me fewer rights.

It was also the last time my father was ever in our home. The next day, the relatives took my father away. A few months later, when I heard knocking on my door around midnight, I knew.

My mother walked into my room, sat on my bed, and just blurted, "They said your daddy is dead."

Within an hour, our home was filled with church members and relatives from my mother's side of the family. There was wailing and screaming and crying. Someone somewhere was threatening to throw herself in the gutter. It felt like a movie.

My theatrics were different, though. No tears, no words. I went to my room, took my Bible, opened it up to Genesis chapter one, and I began to tear it page by page, chapter by chapter, scripture by scripture. If this book was true, my father would not have died. The only premise that made sense to me was that this book had to be a lie.

I had made my way through the Old Testament, ripping the Bible into shreds, when a friend of mine who had heard the news walked in and stopped me.

I tried to bury my faith the day that we buried my father. But here's the thing: My father never left a will. He never left any instructions for a life without him. He never left any notes about funeral arrangements.

The only inheritance my father left me was his faith.

The only guidance he left me was the Bible.

But in the months following his death, I found my mother being subjected to all kinds of conversations. There was all this talk about the impropriety of a woman leading the church. It seemed natural to me that my mother would take over. They had built it together in every sense of the word.

But people pointed to Bible scriptures, and they said, "This is sacrilege," "This is improper," and so on and so forth.

Eventually, the board of the church ordained my mother lead minister, and when they did, many of our church members left. In those and many other ways, the church broke my heart.

But perhaps you can say I left the church too. I came back to America for college, went to law school, began a career in public policy and global development. I also found that my views about gender and womanhood were really evolving from the views of the church that I had grown up in.

I was walking through the New York Public Library one day when I came across a book, *A Year of Biblical Womanhood* by Rachel Held Evans. And in that book, she chronicled an experiment she had taken as a blogger to take what the Bible says about women literally for a year and see what kinds of conclusions that leads to.

Her book showed that we often have to read the Bible in context, and that when we read the Bible literally (as we do all the time) it leads to really absurd conclusions. Rachel's work opened me up to a whole new world. I began to find women writers who were writing about the intersection of faith and feminism. I found womanist theologians, feminist theologians. These writers made me feel less alone. They helped me find my voice.

One day, sitting in a coffee shop, I decided to write a blog series called *My Troubles with God*. I already had a blog where I wrote about gender, popular culture, and more, but I had never written about religion.

As I began to type, documenting my experiences, reclaiming my faith and my conviction that the Bible supports gender equality, I worried, *What will people say? How will the small but faithful online community I've built respond to me challenging conventional wisdom about God and gender?* I wrote it anyway, and I hit Send.

In the weeks that followed, many women reached out to me and said, for the first time, they were seeing it was possible to be both faithful and feminists.

There were also people who called my work blasphemous. There were times when the criticism hurt, especially when it came from family members and other people I loved.

But a few months after I first released this blog series, I found out that the Nigerian senate had refused to pass a bill called the Gender and Equal Opportunities Bill, and they had refused to pass this bill on the grounds of religion.

Senators who were both Muslim and Christian read from the Koran and the Bible, and they said, "This bill goes against everything that our faiths spell out."

In reading the tweets, in marching with activists, and in seeing the impact of this bill, I was reminded why this work is important. And so, I've continued to write, to speak, to think, and to strategize about the intersection of faith and gender equality.

Sometimes I wonder what kinds of conversations I would have with my father if he were alive today. I think we would disagree on a lot of scriptures. But I think he would welcome the disagreement. And I know that he would be proud.

BLESSING OMAKWU is a Nigerian American strategist, creative, lawyer, and writer whose work spans the intersection of global development, gender equality, popular culture, and theology. She is currently the head of the Goalkeepers initiative at the Bill and Melinda Gates Foundation, focused on advancing the United Nations Sustainable Development Goals. Blessing is passionate about the intersection of gender equality and faith. Between 2019 and 2020, she led the strategy design of the faith portfolio of Melinda French Gates's Gender Equality special initiative. The faith work Blessing designed is now part of a multimillion portfolio within the foundation's gender equality division. Blessing also served as co-chair of "Room 5" (for Sustainable Development Goal 5 on Gender Equality), hosted by the Brookings Institution and the Rockefeller Foundation. In 2022, she curated Room 5 around a simple question: How can faith actors be catalyzed to advance gender equality? This led to the Women Leading Change summit, funded by the Rockefeller Foundation and the Gates Foundation.

Blessing graduated summa cum laude from Oral Roberts University with a BA in government and international relations and earned her juris doctor degree from the George Washington University Law School. She serves on the board of the Perelman Performing Arts Center in New York, an initiative of Bloomberg Philanthropies.

This story was told at The Moth Ball on June 22, 2021, at Spring Studios in New York City. The theme of the evening was Bring on the Light. Director: Larry Rosen.

THE SKY IS THE LIMIT

QURATULAIN FATIMA

It was the twenty-third of March, and I was eight years old. My father entered the room in his air force uniform. His boots were shiny, and his buttons looked like gold. My little brothers followed him in, wearing their own little uniforms with gold stars tacked on their shoulders. It was the day of Pakistan's annual military parade. They were going to see the parade. I was not—I was sulking.

My father asked me to come, but when I said I wanted to wear the uniform, he told me, "You can't wear a uniform. Girls can't get into the air force."

I really wanted to go, but not in my ugly frock that showed my stick-like legs—not while my brothers looked all happy and young in their own little shiny uniforms.

Growing up, I was a small, stubborn girl. I had two younger brothers. I acted like their protector. I would chase the kids who harassed them. I would jump up, roll over in the mud, and dispense a few punches to teach them a lesson.

For a short, sweet while I held the title of *big brother,* before losing it when my brothers grew up and left me out of their fights and games.

We Pakistanis *love* cricket the most—probably after God.

I was an avid left-hander. I played cricket with the boys in the area because no girl played the sport. I was a star cricketer in the making.

I would put on my trousers and my T-shirt, much to the dismay of my neighboring aunties, who thought it was such an ungodly way for a girl to dress. They thought I was nuts because I played hockey and cricket with boys, scaled up walls, and kept my hair short.

I dreamed of being a star cricketer, but then the boys' captain said, "Oh, you cannot be part of the team because girls are supposed to look nice, learn to cook, and stay silent. Not play cricket."

I *really* wanted to be a boy because boys could do anything they wanted.

My father was my idol. We would take long walks along lush, green paths, my hand in his, and talk about things.

I would ask him, "Why can't I get into the air force?"

And he'd tell me, "Oh, it's for boys. You need to be strong to get in. We live in the Islamic Republic of Pakistan, and girls and boys can't work physically close to each other."

I would only do selective listening.

Stronger? That I could do.

So, I started running and swimming, and I was often found hanging from the monkey bars in the local park.

I dreamt of becoming a boy. Anything to get into the air force— such was my desperation.

When I was growing up, in Pakistan, women often became teachers or doctors and then went on to get married. But when I was seventeen, I decided I wanted to become a banker. Not that I knew anything about banking. But it was one of the few options available for women at the time. Banking was my available *different*.

Then, one gloomy winter evening, the kind that makes you sad, my father entered our home, beaming. He lit up the room.

He said to me, "Beta"—which means "my son"—"sit down. I have some news for you."

And then he showed me this white-and-black advertisement announcing the recruitment of women, by the air force, for the very first time. It was by order of the president.

He said to me, and I still remember his words, "You must have prayed *very* hard to make them recruit women."

So, I took the initial test, and I passed. But the final selection exam coincided with the date of my banking exam.

I was devastated.

I thought, *It's not meant to be.*

But my father, who believed in my abilities, made me write to the air force and ask to change the dates.

The air force *never* changes the dates.

But miraculously, they did!

And I took the selection exam and passed it.

I also passed the medical exam. But before the training, I fell violently ill. The doctor could not find anything wrong with me, except anxiety. I was ashamed to admit it, but I was afraid.

I was afraid to fail.

It was the first time I was leaving the warmth and comfort of my home.

The day of the training came. I met seven other girls at the gate of the academy, and a male trainer, who was pretty serious. We had a lot of luggage with us, and we were very happy.

In Pakistan, it is culturally expected that men would come and help you with your luggage. So we were waiting.

But then we saw boy recruits putting their luggage on their heads and running.

The military trainer looked at us and said, "What are you waiting for? Run!"

A girl objected, "Oh, we have a lot of luggage!"

To which he replied, it was not his headache. We were not at a wedding reception, and if we did not start moving, *now,* we would miss the attendance call of the academy. And if we missed it, we would have to do loops around the academy, all day, with the same luggage. It was how the military academy operated, and it did not intend to change for us.

So off I went, dragging my luggage, cursing the day I ignored my father's advice to not take too much.

It was the first time that the air force academy was seeing *any* women.

We were told not to speak to the male cadets because any hint of scandal, or romance, would jeopardize our chances of completing the training and would jeopardize the future of women coming into the air force.

So, we, a handful of unsure women, were given the task to clear the path for future women into the air force.

Boys were equally confused. It was as if the status quo of the academy was shattered. Since we could not interact with each other outside of supervised spaces, we were suspicious of each other.

Five days into the training, I was a classic case of someone with buyer's remorse. Waking up at four o'clock in the morning, doing mandatory punishments, disciplined life, no makeup, not being able to go home for four months, and eating tasteless, huge meatballs (not so fondly called grenades) was making me question my choice to join the air force.

I really wanted to run away, but I could not.

I could not let the patriarchal structure of the military say that women are not made for its rigor.

So I stayed. I completed my training and made friends for life.

I graduated as a commissioned officer in the Pakistan Air Force.

My father came to my graduation wearing his uniform, looking tall and handsome. I was in the uniform that was once forbidden to me. I saluted him. A salute that said, thank you for letting me be who I wanted to be. And he smiled.

On the first day at base, I had to walk fifteen minutes to my office. Everyone on the road stopped and stared at me. They had never seen a woman in uniform. It was as if a UFO had landed, and an alien had alighted out of it.

I felt naked, vulnerable—it was odd.

My subordinates, my soldiers, gave me equal respect as they gave to their male superiors. It was the superiors that were the problem. They thought the air force had just inducted women for a cosmetic change. They were reluctant to give me any real work. I had to try very, very hard to gain their trust.

When I was a flying officer, I had to work under a supervisor who was notorious for making advances towards women. During my one year at the base, he inappropriately touched me and made explicit sexual comments and jokes.

One time when I was supervising a war exercise in front of my soldiers, he came up from behind and put his hands around me.

When I protested, he said, "Oh, it's just fatherly affection," and gaslighted my protest.

I never reported him.

It's not easy to talk about sexual abuse.

Being one of the first women came with a lot of pressures and a lot of expectations. The way I fared in my training and in my service might make it possible for other women to enter the air force.

I regret that I did not report him. It could have stopped the predatory behavior.

Pakistan's air force now holds one of the largest contingents of women officers in the Islamic world—ranging from pilots, to engineers, to ground support officers.

I can proudly and safely say that my female peers and I did well.

On the twenty-third of March, 2002, I asked my father to join me on the Pakistan Day parade.

I was not a little girl anymore, and now I was in uniform. I saw a little girl looking at me—at my shining boots, at my gold buttons, at my blue uniform, and dreaming dreams to do the impossible.

With tears in my eyes, I stood under the shining spring sun, shoulder to shoulder with my father, and saluted the passing parade.

* ☉ *

FLT. LT. (RTD.) QURATULAIN FATIMA is a policy practitioner working extensively in rural and conflict-ridden areas of Pakistan. Her focus is gender-inclusive development and conflict prevention. She was one of the first women to join the Pakistan Air Force and one of the only Pakistani women to serve in public service and the military. Quratulain holds an advanced degree from Oxford and is currently working on the intersection of water, conflict, technology, and gender. She has saved twenty-four minority religion sites in rural Punjab from illegal occupation, and was a core team member for the UN–World Bank flagship study "Pathways for Peace: Inclusive Approaches to Preventing Violent Conflict." She was named Aspen New Voices Fellow 2018, Build Peace Fellow 2017–18, and Oxford Global Leadership Initiative Fellow 2016, and she is a proud graduate of The Moth's Global Community Program.

This story was told on September 20, 2019, at the Union Chapel in London. The theme of the evening was Fish out of Water. Director: Meg Bowles.

A HUSHED
KIND OF AWE

BETWEEN THE ROCK AND A HEART PLACE

MARGUERITE MARIA RIVAS

In the early 1980s, I was a typical Staten Island working girl—going back and forth to my job on Wall Street every day on the Staten Island Ferry.

And then I got pregnant. I loved that baby from the moment I knew she was there. I went out and bought a Walkman, so we could listen to music on the commute with two sets of headphones—one for me, one for my belly. Carly Simon's *Anticipation* played constantly. As my belly grew and the headphones stretched, they finally snapped, and I fixed them with some tape from the office.

The doctor called at just about my seventh month and asked me to come in for a sonogram, so I did. And then he said he wanted to see me afterward.

When I went in, he looked at me, and he said, "I have some news."

He said the baby had a fatal birth defect and that her condition was not compatible with life.

My baby's going to die? It was inconceivable. I was seven months pregnant. She was growing. She was moving. She loved music. I loved music. I loved her, and she was going to die?

He said that she would die shortly after she was born. And I felt as though I had swallowed a rock that just plummeted me right down to the bottom of the harbor, just as hard and just as cold, and I couldn't breathe.

I went home to my family and waited for her birth. Two months later, I had my daughter Maria. I gave her my middle name because I knew that when she left, she would take a big part of me—like maybe the whole middle part—with her. She was so beautiful. She was bathed, baptized, and brought to me with a little pink cap on her head, so I couldn't see her birth defect so much.

The nurse who helped with the delivery brought her to me and said, "Kiss her goodbye, girl."

And I kissed that cheek. It was like cool water, and her mouth was like a rose, and I recognized the curve of her nose. When I spoke, she looked at me. She was taken to the NICU, where she died later that day.

Eventually, my family left for the night. I was twenty-three hours post labor, pumped up on painkillers, full of sorrow, and alone. A woman came into the room with a clipboard. She said she was from the city. She wanted to know what I wanted to do for the burial.

She said, "The city usually takes care of things in cases like this."

I remembered that my brother's baby, who'd been born prematurely and died just before Maria, had a city cemetery burial. I had this little vision of Maria and Christopher together, side by side, in some pretty place, with a picket fence and grass. So, I signed the papers.

I went home to grieve. And then I wanted to see the baby's grave. That's when I found out, I could never see the grave.

I had signed the papers for my child to go to New York City's potter's field on Hart Island, a little island off the Bronx. It was administered by the Department of Corrections, and prisoners dug long trenches and buried bodies in mass graves. And for that reason, no one could visit, ever. It was against the rules.

It was like Maria had died all over again.

I had nowhere to mourn. I had no patch of land to say, *This is where my child is. She was born, she lived, and she died.*

I had nowhere to go. It was especially hard on her birthdays and on holidays. When my mom would have Thanksgiving, and my nieces and nephews would sit around the table and play, I would look at them, and I would always see a missing person.

Eventually, I was blessed with two beautiful daughters who took their places around the Thanksgiving table. But when I looked at them, I would always see three. Maria was always there, a presence.

Thirty-seven years after Maria was born and died, my niece Jayme called me up and said, "Aunt, did you know there was a lawsuit? Families can visit Hart Island now. You can go visit Hart Island."

And I was first, like, floating out of my body.

Then I said, "No, no. Uh-uh. No, thank you."

In those thirty-seven intervening years, my grief had been compounded by my guilt at having signed away my child to a place I could never visit. And that was exacerbated by these horrible headlines I used to see—"City of the Lost Souls," "Island of the Forgotten." She was *never* forgotten, not for one minute.

I remembered the images I had seen over the years of trenches and dirt and mud and gravel, and I remembered that last beautiful kiss, and I said, "I can't go see my baby here."

Jayme said, "It's okay. I'll come down and get you. I'll take care of you."

I remembered the rock I had swallowed on the day that doctor told me that Maria was going to die. I carried that rock for thirty-seven years, and I knew I had to do something to move it. This rock had to go.

So I went to the city's website, and I filled out the forms for us to visit. Soon we were on the dock. Hart Island is off the Bronx—in order to get there, you have to cross water. I was at the dock with

Jayme, my niece, and Miranda, my daughter. As we stood there, I could see other parents who were going to see their children.

The corrections officer in charge came out and said, "We'll be going to Hart Island soon. We're going to get there by an old Staten Island Ferry that's been repurposed."

My daughter's first voyages and her very last were aboard a Staten Island Ferry.

Soon, the ferry came. We got on it, and we started to cross. The fog was so dense that I couldn't even see Hart Island. It was like we were crossing the River Styx to the underworld.

As we got closer to the island, the officer in charge said, "Okay, here's the procedure. You see that white bus? We're going to get on it, and we'll take you to your loved one's gravesite, where a corrections officer will be stationed to supervise your visit. You can't take pictures, and you can't leave until the bus comes around again to get you."

We shuffled onto the bus and got under way. At one stop, a woman got out with red flowers and put them down in front of an old, weathered statue of an angel child. The bus continued on its way, and a family got out at the next stop. They had this beautiful bouquet, and the father was so composed. The officer in charge showed them where the grave was, because none of them are marked. And when they came to the gravesite, that father fell to his knees.

And I thought, *Oh my gosh, what's going to happen to me?*

We went round and round and round, dropping people off. Finally, the bus came to a stop, and I got out.

The officer in charge said, "I'm going to show you where your daughter's grave is and where your nephew's grave is."

When I looked around, there were no trenches, there was no mud. The beautiful Long Island Sound was right there, and gravel did not cover their graves, grass did. When he showed me where my daughter was and where my nephew was, they were adjacent to each other.

That vision, thirty-seven years before, that addled-brain vision I had, was true. Those cousins were on one of the most beautiful parts of the island.

We knelt at Maria's grave, Miranda and Jayme and I, and I cried.

And then Jayme said, "Do you remember when we went to an Eagles concert as a family?"

She took something out of her coat. It was a yellowed ticket stub.

She said, "Maria would have been the right age to go. I'm giving her my ticket," and she put the ticket down on my daughter's grave.

Then she said, "Maria would have gone to Vermont with us, and we would have spent every summer swimming in Sunset Lake and playing on the dock."

She took out a bottle of water and unscrewed the top.

She doused the grave and said, "This is Maria's Sunset Lake."

Finally, she said, "Maria would have been at every Thanksgiving at Grandma's house, and we would have played with her in the backyard till it got dark. And we would have had dinner with her."

She took out a little bag of dirt, all desiccated and dry, and she sprinkled it on Maria's grave and said, "This is Maria's Grandma's house."

I knew in that minute, that Maria had not only not been forgotten, she had been missed. She had been missed by her companion cousin all those years.

The supervising officer called us over and said, "Would you like a keepsake?"

He had an old Polaroid camera, and he said, "I can take a picture for you if you like."

We stood, the three of us together, holding each other—the beautiful Long Island Sound at our back and the mounds of grass in front of us. He took the picture.

As he did, I could see that the bus was returning for us. And I started to panic.

I didn't want to leave her again.

I knelt down on the grave one last time with that rock still heavy in me. I started weeping like I had not wept in thirty-seven years. Thirty-seven years of grief and guilt came pouring out of me. I was keening at her grave.

I heard some noise behind me, and I got up, and the officer in charge was there. He was such a wonderful, sweet man.

And he looked at me, and he said, "Will you make me a promise? Will you do me a favor? Will you come back next spring?"

See, it was December. And it was actually the last visit anyone could make for that year.

"You come back in the spring—it's beautiful here in the spring"—and he motioned with his hand—"it's full of flowers. It's full of wildflowers. Come back. You'll feel better."

But I already was feeling better. That rock I had carried was gone, and in its place was a widening channel for me to navigate.

A channel left for me to navigate by Maria, out of this darkness, and finally into the light.

* ⊙ *

MARGUERITE MARIA RIVAS, a native New Yorker, is a poet, scholar, and storyteller whose work touches on the way the world and the heart are broken and mended. Marguerite is a professor at Borough of Manhattan Community College, where she teaches writing and mentors first-generation college students.

This story was told on October 14, 2021, at The Wilbur Theatre in Boston. The theme of the evening was Who Do You Think You Are? Director: Chloe Salmon.

CHASING THE GOOD NOTES

QUIARA ALEGRÍA HUDES

As far back as I can remember, I was chasing the good notes. The first time, I was four years old. I was visiting my Aunt Linda and Uncle Rick, who were professional musicians. They showed me an album cover, Champion Jack Dupree. Well, I thought that was pretty cool because his name, Champion, was a little weird and wild, and my name, Quiara Alegría Hudes, is a little weird and wild. They stacked two Yellow Pages on top of the piano bench. (For those unfamiliar, Yellow Pages are books that contain phone numbers.) They sat me on top of the Yellow Pages so that I was high enough that my hands could reach the piano keys.

They dropped the needle on the Champion Jack Dupree album, and they said, "Play along," and they left me alone.

The first thing I did was listen. I had never heard him before; it was New Orleans blues piano. Then, I just tried pressing one key down with my finger, and it sounded really bad. I recoiled, like I'd touched a hot stove top, and I tried putting my finger on another key, and that note went with the record. I was like, *Oh, let me play that note over and over again, but let me find the rhythm.*

I spent the next half hour chasing the good notes, chasing the notes that *went*. It was kind of like an action adventure for my hearing. As I did that for half an hour, the weight of the world outside disappeared.

I was only four, but the world had already started to weigh a little bit. My parents were fighting a lot. But that didn't exist as I listened and played along and chased the good notes.

By the time I was in middle school, the world had begun to weigh a lot more. By that time, my parents were separated, and my life was torn in two. I had been to more funerals than was normal. It was HIV-AIDS days. It was crack cocaine days. A lot of those funerals were for loved ones in their twenties.

But the weight of the world disappeared when the Batá drums came into my bedroom. See, my mom is a priestess or a santera in a religious and spiritual path called Lucumí. For those unfamiliar, Lucumí originated in Yorubaland, Nigeria, and was brought to and syncretized with Spanish Caribbean Catholicism. The Batá drums are an Orisha. They are the voice of a spirit or a god. So when I heard the drums, I would emerge into the living room because I knew my mom was hosting and leading another ceremony.

My mom would introduce me to the players, and she would tell me their given, their birth names, but also their Ocha names—the names they carried from the time they were initiated in the religion. I really liked that they had chosen a path that added a new name to their life. I would listen, and my mom would proceed with her ceremony, whether it was an offering, a cleansing, a Bembé, all sorts of different ceremonies. The drums had a physical vibrational effect on me. I could feel the density and the intensity of my heartbeat shift. I could feel it inside my blood. I would be in awe, but a kind of hushed awe. If she couldn't afford the Batá players for a given ceremony or if they weren't available, she'd pop in a Babatunde Olatunji tape. That's a master drummer from Nigeria. Or, she'd pop in a Celina y Reutilio tape, which was Cuban folkloric music also in the tradition.

Now, by high school, *Bachata Rosa,* which was Juan Luis Guerra's seminal album, had come out, and my cousins at Abuela's house would pop in the tape and press Play. We had all been to those funerals together, and we were reeling, but once those songs came on, my cousins became so embodied, and they would take little timid me, little timid Kiki, and drag me onto the linoleum floor of Abuela's living room, from whatever corner I'd been hiding in. They'd slap my ass until I loosened up, and I would join them. I would join the dance. Again, the weight of the world would just disappear.

When I got into Yale University to be a music composition major, I was pretty blown away. I was the first in my family to go to college. I thought, *Okay, here we go.*

My path, all these doors just opened in front of me. *I'm going to take this musical thing. I'm going to chase these good notes to places I can't even imagine.*

I got into those handsomely wooden paneled seminar rooms. They start playing Bach; they start playing Brahms; they start playing Schubert. I discovered that the word *music* actually had a different definition at Yale than it had in my life previously.

It meant Western classical without having to say so.

This little *uh-oh* planted itself in my gut.

It meant white, male, and dead—oftentimes by more than a century.

I tried to say, "Well, I want to do my project on Stevie Wonder."

I remember the students and the professor did actually laugh out loud at that one.

I also tried to say, "I want to do my project on Celina y Reutilio."

I remember the professor saying to me, "That's folkloric stuff; that doesn't really merit the level of attention that we're trying to look at in this classroom."

When dealing with Brahms and Bach and Beethoven, there is no dancing. This is how you listen to music. You sit still and listen—

that's it. Music is not about dancing. Music is not about the spirits. It's not about ancestry. It's not about body.

There's definitely no ass slapping happening in the seminar rooms at Yale.

I was pretty bummed out, but I thought, *Okay, well, I love this Bach so much. I love this Chopin so much. I love this Mozart so much. That's enough to sustain me for four years of really meaty investigation and playing.* But I was jonesing. I started jonesing for some Afro-Caribbean stuff, and I went to the listening library.

The listening library, like most rooms at Yale, is architecturally gorgeous. Wooden paneling, stained glass windows, and these floor-to-ceiling wraparound shelves of meticulously ordered boxed CDs and boxed vinyl sets. Entire catalogs of Bach—arranged just by certain individual performers.

I said to the listening librarian, "Do you have any West African stuff? Do you have any Afro-Caribbean stuff?"

She led me over to the ethnomusicology section. I was like, *Okay, here we go.*

The first thing I had to do was get on my knees, because the ethnomusicology section was basically down on the floor.

Unlike the wraparound collection, it was two shelves, about forty-eight inches wide, one shelf on top of another. I was like, *Okay, well, this is still really cool. I'm excited to see what they got.* But I noticed there weren't CDs, and there weren't records.

They were dub tapes.

The dub tapes didn't have names on them.

They only had place, locations. A tape might say "Senegal," for instance.

But there was no individual artistry acknowledged.

I remembered something Mom told me about the erasure of names that happened when West Africans were brought to the Caribbean.

The erasure of names that happened when Taíno and other native populations were decimated by smallpox and violence.

I had always thought the erasure of names was something in the past, something historic, centuries-ago stuff, but it was present tense.

My heart sank seeing those unnamed tapes, and the thrill was gone. I fell out of love with music.

The thing that used to remove me from the weight of the world now had begun putting the weight of the world on my shoulders.

So, I dragged myself like a good student into senior year, and I heard Wynton Marsalis was coming to town.

My aunt told me she knew the trombonist in the band, and she was like, "He's willing to sneak you into rehearsals."

So, I had to cut class, but I went to Woolsey Hall, and I sat in the very back row. Wynton was in town for ten days to rehearse a jazz oratorio that he was then going to premiere at his new endeavor in New York called Jazz at Lincoln Center.

Now, Woolsey Hall is the crown jewel of Yale architecture. It is massive and ornate, everything in gold leaf. The pipe organ alone looks like the Manhattan skyline. And I just disappeared in the back for about four days, cut class for four days straight, and listened to a different genre of music, a different practice of music.

On day four, he was like, "Hey, you, in the back row. All right. Come on, come up."

"Yes, Mr. Marsalis."

"I hear you're a music composition major. So, do you have good penmanship?"

Well, I *did* have good penmanship because my aunt had taught me musical calligraphy, how to be very meticulous and careful when writing a note.

He said, "Well, Cassandra Wilson is coming in ten minutes, and she's very unhappy with the state of her charts. So, can you copy this chart for her quickly?"

So, I did. I copied the chart quickly, but carefully, so that the calligraphy looked neat and pristine. I handed him back the corrected chart, and he gave me a twenty-dollar bill.

I return to my corner in the back, and Cassandra, this regal jazz vocalist—this woman is as centered and grounded and rooted as a tree—she gets on stage. And this is the first time they've run through this song because she hasn't arrived until today. The song is "God Don't Like Ugly."

It began, and it was a really ugly, conflicted, angry song. Her voice sank into that conflict and nastiness like thorns, like barbs.

The spirits in that song were angry.

My heart—the density, and the intensity of my heartbeat shifted.

The intensity of my pulse shifted, and I could feel that nastiness in me as music was restored to my body.

Well, the day before the dress rehearsal, Wynton Marsalis asked, "Hey, kid. Have you ever written a piece for trumpet?"

I lied and said, "Yes, Mr. Marsalis."

And he said, "Great, bring it tomorrow, bring a tape recorder, and we'll play it at the end of rehearsal."

I stayed up all night; I pulled the all-nighter of all-nighters at college.

I came the next day with my new/old trumpet piece and my tape recorder, and I gave him his chart, and he put his chart on a stand.

It was for piano and trumpet.

I brought my chart over to the piano. He adjusted his mouthpiece. My fingers were trembling. It starts with a two-bar piano intro, and I was really just trying to breathe into my fingertips so that they would just steady themselves and play the notes.

The tape player was recording. I play, and this note comes out of his trumpet that's like molasses.

It's so lugubrious.

I had written a very, very sensual piece.

Like, if you've ever run your fingers down velvet and seen the little tracks that leaves behind—

or if you've ever had someone you love run their fingers tenderly down your back.

That's kind of what the piece was like.

So, at the end, we finished; he said, "You know, that was really beautiful. You've got some talent, kid. What do you guys think?"

Because this whole jazz orchestra had been watching this thing. And they were like, *Oh, you've been looking at us all week. So, we're going to look at you now.*

His alto saxophone player said, "That girl's *bad.*"

I didn't walk back to my dorm room, I floated back to my dorm room. That was the best compliment I'd ever received.

I wanted to hear the tape, what had happened. It was almost like an out-of-body experience. So, I pressed Rewind on the tape player, and it didn't budge. It had run out of batteries. I got some new batteries, put them in the tape player, and rewound it, though I noticed it hadn't made it very far. I pressed Play, and I heard the first two bars of my piano intro with one or two note mistakes, but it was all right, and then, the tape had stopped recording—before he played his first note.

I feel like, in any other moment in my life, my reaction would've been like, *"No!"* But I swear it was this exhale and a little laugh, and I felt the universe just pushing my shoulder blade a little bit. I didn't know why; it had something to do with ephemerality and how nothing lasts forever.

Later that year, Wynton Marsalis premiered his jazz oratorio *Blood on the Fields* at Jazz at Lincoln Center and was awarded the Pulitzer Prize. Not to worry, my aunt and uncle, the musicians, they ended up recording my piano and trumpet piece later that year, and I still have that recording today.

Gradually, I stopped chasing the notes, I let go of music. And I started chasing something different.

I started chasing the stories I had been surrounded by all my life, and I started writing them down and putting names on them.

When my plays went to Broadway and won fancy prizes and went to Hollywood, people would ask, "Is that your dream come true? Oh my gosh!"

But the slightly embarrassing answer is like, "No, it's cool, but it's not my dream come true."

My dream was and still is to tell our stories. Name our names. Have them go on a library shelf that's eye level, and that's wider than forty-eight inches. A shelf that I know and trust—really deep in my heart—long after I'm gone, is going to keep getting wider and wider and wider and full of more names.

QUIARA ALEGRÍA HUDES is the author of a memoir, *My Broken Language;* the plays *Water by the Spoonful* (Pulitzer Prize), *Elliot, a Soldier's Fugue* (Pulitzer finalist), *In the Heights* (Tony Award); and other plays, musicals, and essays. She was born in Philadelphia in 1977 and studied music before moving to New York in 2004, where she continues to write and raise a family.

This story was told on June 30, 2021, at the United Palace in New York City. The theme of the evening was When You're Home. Director: Jodi Powell.

SWIMMER GIRL

HASNA MUHAMMAD

I learned to swim in summer camp when I was five or six years old. I held on to the cement edge of the pool; I put my face in the water and blew bubbles; I turned my head from side to side to breathe, lifted my feet, and kicked my legs behind me.

I had to let go of the wall to learn to tread water and to float first with someone's hand at my back. And then all by myself.

I moved my arms and legs to get from here to there, and "there" kept moving from someone's arms a few yards away, to the middle of the pool, and then to the end of the pool, where my feet couldn't touch the bottom.

In pictures of me as a little girl, I am in a bathing suit. I'm standing by a pool, jumping in a pool, diving in a pool, laughing and giggling with my brother and sister with my father's arms nearby. I wasn't really swimming, but I was having so much fun.

And now, I love to swim. Over time I learned how to *really* swim. And now I swim laps for fun and exercise.

I swim in open water, but most times I swim in pools. I swim in public pools, private pools, indoor pools, outdoor pools, twenty-five yards, fifty meters. I swim every chance I get in any pool that I can.

My dream swim is in the centermost lane of an outside Olympic-size pool. It's eighty degrees and sunny outside, there's a blue sky and wisps of clouds overhead, and I am doing the backstroke.

I am all by myself and completely naked.

I had to let go of the inhibitions about my body in order to swim. My breasts turn into my belly, my belly turns into my butt. I have a varicose vein down the entire length of one leg, and my thighs rub together when I walk. But I am out there in my one-piece competition bathing suit, letting it all hang out. That's because I am a swimmer girl, and I love to swim.

I live about fifty miles north of midtown Manhattan as the crow flies in Putnam County, New York, right outside the border of Westchester County and Fairfield County in Connecticut, near Danbury. And I swim three or four times a week at one of two Ys in Connecticut. And that gives me a choice of four pools.

When I swim, I don't ever see anybody who looks like me swimming laps for fun and exercise. I'm not talking about water aerobics. I'm not talking about wading in the water with your sunglasses on. I'm talking about swimming butterfly, backstroke, breaststroke, freestyle; back and forth, a mile at a time, counting yards, practicing drills, racing the clock; swimming long, hard, and fast for about an hour. I don't see anybody who looks like me swimming laps like that. Maybe I have to go to a different pool on a different day or at a different time, because Black women do everything everywhere all the time. I cannot be the only one.

I was raised by two hardcore artists and activists. And I was raised during the vortex of the Black Power movement, the Black arts movement, the women's liberation movement, and the civil rights movement of the twentieth century. Being Black and seeing Black and female is my lens for everything.

So, when I am in my car getting ready to go for a swim, and this Black man, driving a black Volvo SUV with a Black girl as his passenger, pulls into the space next to mine—I take note. We get out of the car together at the same time, and we say hello to each other. And inside I'm thinking, *Yes, Black people.*

I forget something in the car. So I go back, they go in the building, and I lose track of them. But when I get into the women's locker room, I see the girl. She's about thirteen, fourteen years old, she's tall, she's got a crown of hair over her head. And she's standing at the end of the bank of lockers frozen still. But she's wearing a bathing suit, looking down at the swim cap in her hand. This girl is going to the pool. This girl is going to be swimming. This girl better not take up my favorite lane.

I say hello to her again. And I make a mad dash to the locker and do a Superman change so that I can get to my favorite center lane. I close the door, turn around, and she's still standing there. But this time, she's stuffing her dry hair into her swim cap.

And I want to say to her, *Baby, you got to wet your hair before you put on your swim cap. That way the water gets in the cuticle, you put a little conditioner in there, and then you put on your swim cap. That way, the chlorine doesn't damage your hair that much.*

But I didn't want to embarrass her. She looked so uncomfortable, like she wanted to be invisible. So, I kept my advice-from-a-stranger mouth closed.

I said, "Have a good swim," and she mumbled something back.

And then I went on and took my shower. When I'm wetting my hair, I'm thinking, *You know, maybe I should have said something to her about her hair. But she'll see that my hair is wet, and then she'll learn that she should wet her hair too.*

I get poolside, and this girl is in my center lane. She obviously did not take the obligatory shower you're supposed to take before you get into a pool. All the other lanes are taken except for the one right next to her. So I claim that.

And I want to say to her how happy I am to swim next to her, somebody who looks just like me, albeit fifty years younger.

I wanted to ask her, *Did you know that there was a time when Black people weren't allowed to swim in pools? When even with the submersion of one toe, the pool was emptied. That most Black people don't know how to swim, and most people who drown are Black and brown.*

But I didn't want to interrupt. Her father was squatting on the deck, talking to her. And she was listening to her father.

She was listening to her father, but she was looking at me. And it's not the look that I get when I come on deck and all eyes scatter. It's not the look that I get when I talk about swimming in standard English. It's not even a look I get when people see that I tan. Like all over.

This girl was looking at me to see how I navigate this space. She was looking at me to see how I *be* in this pool. So, she watches me as I pull out my fins and my kickboard and my pull buoy and my paddles and place them on the deck. She sees me cup my forehead with my swim cap and tuck my wet hair in it. She sees me put on my goggles and straighten the strap. And then she watches as I slip into the pool and glide streamlined into the liquid cool.

My skin awakens all at once. My legs are straight, my toes are pointed, my arms are with my ears, my hands are stacked. The only thing I hear is my exhale as the water parts to let me through. I see the reflection of the water shimmering above me. I see the shadow of my body passing over the bottom of the pool that gradually deepens below me.

I start an underwater stroke. And when my body signals the need for air, all my chakras tingle. So I rise up and take a breath and come back down. Rise up and take a breath and come back down. And when I'm about a foot from the wall, I curl my body into a ball and flip over. Bubbles swarm everywhere. I'm upside down. My knees are bent. My feet are on the wall, and I push off, roll over, and start to swim.

By that time, the girl is swimming too. And we are swimming

laps peeking at each other over the lane dividers. She's faster than I am, but I'm steadier than she is. I see a lot of bodies in the water. But when I see her brown arms and legs piercing the water doing freestyle and flip turns, I feel like a proud mama bear. And she stops to watch me too. She stops, treads water, and watches as I pick up speed and start to sweat and focus on my workout.

When I take a break between sets, I notice that the girl and her father are gone. And once again, I am the only Black person in the pool.

I finish my workout, do my cooldown, then I play like that little girl in camp. I make angels in the water. Dive backward. Swim upside down. Do flips and handstands. And then I run to the shallow end, pack up my gear, and get out. And that's when I notice that the girl and her father are back. She's in her street clothes, and he's combing her hair.

And as I pass them, I want to ask, *Have you ever heard of the Harlem Honeys and Bears? Have you ever been to blackgirlsswim.org? Do you follow those Black Olympic swimmer girls?* But I don't want to intrude. So I just smile at them like I smile at everybody else on my way into the locker room.

When I'm in the shower, I am kicking myself for not saying anything to that girl. There she was. Somebody who looks just like me was swimming right there, and I didn't say any of the things that I thought to say. My mother would have said something. My grandmother would have said something. But neither of them knew how to swim.

I'm an educator, and I missed the opportunity to teach this child

As I dress, I'm thinking, *Well, maybe she didn't want to hear anything I had to say anyway. Maybe she's just a Gen Z teen unburdened by the racist history of Black people and swimming. Maybe she doesn't want to be seen as Black. Maybe she doesn't identify as a girl. Maybe she just wants to be a spiritual being, having a human experience swimming.*

I mean, isn't that what it's all about? Just being.

When I get to the parking lot, I see that black Volvo SUV, and I decide I'm going to tell her everything. And maybe she waited for me because she felt glad to swim with me because she gets those looks too. Maybe the lifeguard made her prove that she could swim before he let her into the deep end—that's what he did to me. By the time I get to the car, I see that the girl and the father are not in it, and even though I linger, they don't come before I pull out and drive away.

Every time I go to that pool, I look for that Black swimmer girl. I haven't seen her yet, but I know that she and other Black women and girls who love to swim are out there.

I know because I'm not the only one. And there will be more. I know because for about an hour on a Sunday morning at a Y in Connecticut, there were two Black swimmer girls swimming laps for fun and exercise. We were defying the assumptions about Black people, Black girls, Black women and swimming. And it didn't matter what I said or didn't say to this girl. She saw me and I saw her, even if no one else did. I wasn't alone.

We were together and *we both belonged,* even if just to each other. Have a good swim.

* ⊙ *

HASNA MUHAMMAD is a visual artist, writer, and educator whose work focuses on family, social justice, education, and the human condition. Her photography has been exhibited in various cities in the United States, and she recently published her first book, *Breathe in the Sky: Poems Prayers & Photographs.*

Throughout her career as an education activist, Hasna has served as an English teacher, a principal, and an assistant superintendent for curriculum and human resources. She taught executive leadership, diversity management, and community engagement. Hasna currently provides professional preparation for diversifying leadership forces.

Hasna received her BA from Sarah Lawrence College and completed her MA and EdD at Teachers College, Columbia University. Hasna is a 2018–2019 Schomburg Center for Research in Black Culture Fellow, a 2022–2023 Moth storyteller, and a member of the Harlem Writers Guild. Hasna is also a Scuba Schools International–certified scuba diver and a member of U.S. Masters Swimming. Hasna grew up in New Rochelle, New York, and now lives in Brewster, New York, where she and her husband raised three children.

Instagram: @birthmarkmedia

www.birthmarkmedia.com

info@birthmarkmedia.com

This story was told on September 22, 2022, at College Street Music Hall in New Haven. The theme of the evening was There's a Place for Us. Director: Jodi Powell.

DON'T GIVE UP
ON THE BABY
NICK ULLETT

I am a great believer in marriage. I myself have been married for fifty-six years.

Unfortunately, to four different women.

My present wife, Jenny, was also married previously, and when we got together, we did not want to make the same mistakes that had sort of ruined our lives before. So, we sat down and asked each other what it was that we wanted. The only thing that Jenny desired that caused me any apprehension was that she wanted to have children.

I already had a son from a previous marriage, and I knew how children could complicate a relationship, but I really wanted to make a life with this woman. So I agreed. And we leapt into the business of creating a family—which obviously involves lots and lots of sex . . . endlessly . . . everywhere. Delightful.

But after a year and a half, nothing happened—which was not only dispiriting, it also engendered a sense of inadequacy.

But we forged on into the world of fertility experts. The first thing they wanted from me was a sperm test. Which actually, that phrase alone almost defines the word *inadequacy*.

This is back in the mid-1980s, when these tests were sort of "do it yourself" affairs. You found a container, you put your specimen inside, took it to a fertility clinic, and they told you what was going on.

At the time, I was working as an actor in New York, doing a play. One freezing February morning, I had made an appointment at noon with a fertility clinic on the east side of New York. The same day, it turned out, I had a voiceover audition on the west side of New York at ten A.M.

The problem was, I couldn't carry this specimen around all morning because it has to be *freshly* delivered—if it's cold, it will die. So, I had to get this deed done between being in the voiceover audition and arriving at the fertility clinic . . . which is how I ended up masturbating in the men's room at Grand Central Station. A truly humiliating experience, and it was made no better by the fact that the only container that Jenny had come up with that morning was a Hellmann's mayonnaise jar. That's a big jar!

Anyhow, I did my duty, thrust the jar deep into my pocket to keep it warm, and I hightailed it to the fertility clinic, where I filled out the forms and then handed them in to the woman behind the desk, along with my specimen.

She took one look at it, and she said quite audibly, "That's it?"

I hastened to explain, "It's a big jar!"

She said, "What was the method of delivery?"

"I'm sorry, what?"

"The method? Intercourse with a condom, masturbation . . . ?"

I mutter *masturbation* under my breath.

She takes out a Magic Marker, and she writes this huge *M* right over the front of the form.

And I can see that *M* following me for the rest of my existence, a sort of shadow over my entire life. ("Oh, Mr. Ullett, you're perfect for this job. Unfortunately, there's the matter of this *M* . . .")

Two days later, the doctors tell us that my sperm has low motility—they don't swim well with others.

Now, my self-esteem, which had not been doing well since "the test," took another nosedive. I found myself feeling useless, emasculated, and truthfully worrying, *Is it really worth this bother?*

But Jenny was insistent, and so on we went. When nothing worked with the fertility doctors, we turned to adoption.

This was where my real fears began, because I already had a child. I understood how I loved that child, how instinctive that was. But how would I feel about one that was not biologically mine? That really worried me. But by that time we'd already engaged an adoption lawyer in California, who had in his practice a pregnant sixteen-year-old.

California is an open adoption state, which means that the birth mother gets to choose to whom she gives her baby. Our job was to write a letter explaining who we were, what we did, and why we would make wonderful parents to this as-yet unborn child. This letter was then sent to the young woman, along with letters from other prospective parents. The young woman reads all the letters, and then she makes her choice.

It started to feel to me in my anxious state rather like a weird reality show. Everything worried me. *We're both actors. Is that good, or is it bad?* Jenny at the time was on a weekly television show and had a kind of minor celebrity, therefore easily trackable. Might the young woman turn into a stalker, or even blackmail us?

And then, *she chose us!* And all that paranoia disappeared because we were absolutely thrilled.

Then the real business of adoption began. You have to register with Child Services. They send people to your houses. Two people showed up and went through our entire house—every room, wardrobe, closet. It's very intrusive. They took our fingerprints; they investigated our backgrounds for criminal activity. And through all this, this nagging doubt kept bedeviling me: *How am I going to feel about a kid that isn't biologically mine?*

I started freaking out and also doubting whether I really wanted another kid. But this was not a fear that I could share with Jenny. I had, after all, committed to this; I couldn't back out of it.

At the time, I was in the national tour of a musical, *Me and My Girl*. We were playing Pantages Theatre in Los Angeles, which is where I live.

One night, during the intermission, a friend of mine came to the stage door and told me that the young woman in question had gone into labor, and by the time I got home Jenny would be on a plane flying to Charlotte, North Carolina. (These were the days before mobiles, when people had to actually talk to you in person.)

The next day, a baby girl was born into Jenny's hands. The following morning she spent with the child and the young woman, and in the late afternoon, she got on a plane back to Los Angeles. That plane would get in at 11:15 that night.

So, I go to the theater, and I explain to my fellow performers what's going on.

And I say, "Listen, I have to meet that plane. I mean, this is a watershed moment in my life. I cannot NOT be there."

And they go, "Yeah, okay, fine."

I go, "Yeah, but to get there in time we've got to knock ten minutes off the show."

They go, "Sure, piece of cake."

So, the show starts exactly at eight o'clock, and we talk fast, we sing fast, we dance fast. We don't stop for any laughs—*Me and My Girl* whizzes by this bemused audience.

After the show, the stage door guy has my car outside and running, and I jump in the car and roar off to the Los Angeles airport. I arrive and, because these are the days before security, I run straight to the gate. But when I get there, the plane hasn't arrived.

I sat down, and every fear, every doubt, every apprehension, every worry that I had about this whole process and loving a child that wasn't biologically mine, everything formed itself up into a sort of cannonball and smashed into me. I was completely panicked. I froze. I couldn't move. I was covered in an ice-cold sweat.

Then the plane rolls by the window, and I'm thinking, *God, what if I don't have any feelings for this child? Can I fake it? And if I fake it, can I live with that lie for the rest of my life? And if I lived with that lie, what would that lie do to this child? I'm going to destroy somebody's life!*

Then the doors to the gate open, and instead of passengers coming out, flight attendants started coming out. First one, then another, then another. And they're sort of coming out and forming this V shape.

What has happened is that they made an announcement that, onboard the plane, they have this tiny baby, literally less than twenty-four hours old, whose father has never met her. And if everybody wouldn't mind waiting for a couple of minutes before they get off the plane, they would like to make this into a special presentation.

I don't know this; all I know is this phalanx of these flight attendants keeps coming toward me, and they're all smiling, with those gleaming American teeth.

I can't move, and I don't know what to do.

In the middle of the V is Jenny with this tiny baby, and she walks right up to me, and she places this child into my shaking hands, and she says, "Say hello to your daughter."

In terror I look down, and in that one moment, I am completely in love. Love literally suffuses my entire body. I am completely besotted by this beautiful tiny child in my arms.

Then, suddenly, I'm surrounded by passengers. They're all wishing us well, and they're patting me and her on the head. Some of them are bestowing blessings on us. And I think, *Wow, what a fabulous way to come into the world. To have your birth recognized in this public fashion.*

Jenny and I adopted another child a few years later, and we're still together. Our oldest daughter is thirty-four years old now, and I love her. She's terrific; she's a wonderful young woman. We've had our ups and downs, but there's one thing about her that has never changed—there's a part of her that is always that tiny child in my hands in the L.A. airport. Because from that moment onward, there was one thing I never doubted—that's my kid.

NICK ULLETT is an actor/writer. He's written plays produced in New York, London, and Los Angeles; a one-man show; several unproduced movies and pilots for television series that no one wanted. He continues to work on a novel and has been for twenty years. As an actor, he's done everything from Ed Sullivan to Shakespeare with a stop along the way for a Broadway musical. He thinks life is grand.

This story was told on September 26, 2022, at the Union Chapel in London. The theme of the evening was Holding On and Letting Go. Director: Michelle Jalowski.

HOME
ALISTAIR BANE

I was standing on a sidewalk in southwest Denver, looking up at a big gray house on a hill.

I was shopping for my first home, and I turned and said to my realtor, "This one's it."

She looked at the crumbling roof, the peeling paint, the shutter that had fallen into the mud, and the weeds that made up the front yard, and she said, "You know, this is what we call an extreme fixer-upper."

I wasn't worried. I had some average carpentry skills, and I watched a lot of HGTV.

Besides, the important thing was that this house had a huge yard for the dogs I rescued, and I could see its potential to be a *home*. And the work the house needed was nothing compared to the work that it had taken to get to this point in my life.

When I was young, I could never imagine having a home of my own, not just in terms of affording a house, but of having a home where I felt like I was safe and belonged.

I grew up with two very different parents—an Eastern Shawnee father, a strict Irish Catholic mother—and they married, despite seemingly disagreeing on every issue in the world. Their one commonality was a profound disappointment that I was queer, and I could feel that disappointment permeate every room of our house.

In the early 1980s, that feeling of being an outcast was something I felt throughout the whole society: If I was open about who I was, it meant doors were closed to the most basic things, like career, family, and a home.

I left my parents early, dropped out of school, and drifted without much feeling of it even being worth trying to build a life—until I reached the age of eighteen. Maybe there was something about being an autonomous adult that made me think, *If I did try, maybe something slightly better could happen.* So, I passed my GED and was accepted into art school. I attended classes during the day and worked at a bar at night.

I couldn't afford a proper apartment, but I did find a room at a rent-by-the-week transient hotel called The Adrian.

To be honest, some of the residents at that hotel scared me. Not in terms of them being tougher than me, because I was a pretty tough kid. But when I'd look in the faces of the older residents, sometimes I'd think that maybe once a place like this and the life it represented got a hold of you, it wouldn't let go. Maybe all my efforts were just in vain.

I mostly kept to myself at this hotel, but I did have one friend.

His name was Rex, and he lived in the room across the hall from me. I met him one hot summer night when I was coming home from work. It was about three o'clock in the morning, and he was standing in the doorway of his room, maybe so he could get a breeze from the hallway.

He was a tall, thin Lakota guy, and right away, I really liked him. He had his own fashion scene going on, where he dressed like he was straight out of 1972, and he reminded me of the pictures I'd seen of the American Indian Movement at the Wounded Knee siege.

When he saw me, he said, "Hey, Kola, where are you from?"

For Native people, when we say, "Where are you from?" we're asking, "What tribe are you? Who's your family?" We're looking for connection because relatives are what matter in life. Relatives are what make a person rich.

I told him I was Eastern Shawnee, and right away he seemed impressed. He started talking about our famous leaders, like Nonhelema the warrior woman, Tecumseh, Tenskwatawa, and others I didn't even know. He seemed to know more about my people than I did.

He said, "With ancestors like that standing behind you, I bet you feel strong. I bet you feel like you can do anything you want in life."

I'd never really thought of things that way, but I liked it when he said that. I fell asleep that night wondering if what he said was true—and if it was, what possibilities that put in front of me.

After that, I'd run into Rex a couple times a week, and there was something about him: I just felt like I could open up to him and tell him all my dreams, tell him what I was afraid of, tell him things about my childhood that I'd never told anyone before.

I remember one time I told him how it hurt to have my parents reject me for being queer.

He said, "You know, long before colonization, we considered people like you to be gifted. You were great healers, great artists. People even said you had power in battle where you wouldn't be hit by bullets. That you could talk to and see the spirits and help people. If anyone tells you you're less than, remember that. You have to believe in yourself."

He paused, and he said, "You have to get out of here. You're better than this."

I've heard it said that our words are medicine, and every day we choose to be good or bad medicine to each other. Rex's words were good medicine for me.

Every time we talked, it felt like I healed a little bit more.

And as I healed, there were better places to live. Jobs that had meaning to them. Rex's words carried me on a journey of reconnecting with my culture, becoming an artist who not only created our traditional arts but taught them to other people.

And finally, I found myself standing here in front of the house in Denver I was about to turn into my own *home.*

The day came, after a mystical process called *closing on a house,* when my dogs and I moved in. As I began working inside, the dogs began excavating the backyard. In dog terms, they had almost immediate success. They unearthed an old bicycle tire, a cow femur, a Barbie doll with tangled hair and mildewy clothes, and other valuable items.

If you rescue dogs, they love you so intensely. And the dogs would bring these items in and gift them to me, and I'd accept them gratefully because I didn't want to hurt their dog feelings. I'd wait till they went to bed and then put the items quietly into the trash.

Meanwhile, my work inside wasn't going quite as well. I was beginning to suspect that HGTV highly edits for time.

There was a lot of damage I hadn't seen.

I spent the first week just patching holes in the drywall. It seemed like in every room, there were these holes and dents about shoulder height. I'd worked my way through the kitchen, living room, dining room, and hall, and finally, I was ready to start work in one of the bedrooms that was painted a bright fuchsia pink that only happens if you tell a child, "You can pick the color out yourself."

On the inside of the door to this room were stickers of glittery unicorns and Hello Kitty, the kind that little girls often love to collect. And on the outside of the door, there were more of those holes and dents.

I said out loud, "What in the world caused all this?"

But as I stood there, this memory surfaced from when I was a teenager. I thought I met a man who was going to love me and keep me safe, only to find out that the opposite was true. I could remember ducking his fist and hearing it hit the drywall behind my head. I held my fist up to those holes and realized that every single one of them was a punch mark. I imagined somebody in this house raging and pounding on that door. I imagined a little girl in that room, fearful that if the door gave way, he would take his anger out on her.

I was angry, not only for what that child must have gone through, but because I had bought this house to be a sanctuary against all of the darkness in the world, and it was like that darkness was already there, just waiting.

I was determined that I was going to erase it, starting with that room.

I spent that whole weekend working—plastering, dry walling, painting, flooring, and hanging a new door—until the room looked blank and new. Finally, by Sunday night, I was almost finished painting the inside of the bedroom closet. When I got to the corner behind the door, near the baseboards, I noticed something.

It was the small, looping cursive of a child, and the words said, "Help me, help me, help me."

It was the kind of quiet, futile cry that somebody makes when they already know nobody is going to hear them.

I thought of that Barbie doll that the dogs had brought to me. Maybe that doll had been that little girl's only friend and comfort, and I had thrown it in the trash.

I felt almost an irrational panic. I ran outside, tipped the bin over, and began rummaging through construction debris for the doll—and I found her. I took her inside and began to wash her at the kitchen sink. I trimmed the ruined ends of her hair and gave her a short but stylish haircut. Then I got into my car and drove to Walmart, not caring how weird it was for a grown man to be Barbie doll clothes shopping at midnight. I found an outfit that was the same fuchsia pink as the paint had been in her room, so I knew the little girl would approve of it. I came home. I dressed the doll. She looked almost new again. I wrote on a piece of cardboard, "Give me a home," with a smiley face on it.

I carried the doll down to the retaining wall at the bottom of the hill that was next to the sidewalk. Every morning, kids walked past my house on their way to the elementary school up the street. I hoped one of them would find her and be happy to have a new friend.

That night, I couldn't sleep. I was anxious to see if the doll would be gone in the morning, but I also was thinking about the little girl—wondering what her life had become. *Had there ever been anyone who loved and cared for her the way she deserved?*

I thought back all those years ago: way, way back to when I lived at that hotel, and I needed a friend, and Rex was there for me. At the time, our short conversations in the hall meant so much to me. And sometimes, I thought maybe I should invite Rex to go down to the diner and get dinner or take a walk by the lake—things that normal friends do. But something had always held me back from doing that. So, I had decided the next time I paid my rent, I'd ask Bill, the desk man, what Rex's story was. Bill was a puffy-faced, gray-haired man of indefinite age who had worked at The Adrian since the late 1960s, and he knew every bit of gossip about everyone who had ever lived there.

So, as he counted my rent money, I asked, "Bill, hey, you know Rex, that tall, thin Native guy? Dresses real 1970s, you know, lives in the room across from mine? What's his story?"

Now, nothing shocked Bill—but at this point, Bill got really pale, his eyes got really wide, he leaned close to the plexiglass that separated him and the money from the rest of us.

He said, "You seen him?"

I was like, "Yeah, he lives across the hall from me, so I've seen him."

Bill kept repeating the question, and finally he motioned for me to come around the side of the office and come inside.

I did.

He pulled me real close with my jacket, and he said, "You actually seen him?"

I was like, "Yeah, I talk to him all the time when I come home from work. What're you trippin' about?"

Bill said that Rex lived at the hotel in the 1970s. He was a good guy, generous, kind, but he had a hard life, and he was an addict. One night, he ODed and died in his room.

Bill said that since that time, sometimes when other people would rent the room, they would come down in the middle of the night, freaked out, saying a tall, thin Native guy was standing over them, watching them sleep.

Bill said, "But you know what? People do anything to get out of paying for a room, so I never knew if I believed them, but you seem fairly sane, and you're saying you've seen him, and you've talked to him."

I said, "Yeah, he's my best friend."

That statement seemed to terrify Bill, but I had never felt so safe and loved in my life because it was true what Rex had said—that we never walk through this life alone. My ancestors and the spirits saw who I was, and they were always there and always loved me.

I was thinking of this all those years later in Denver—in my new home—when I woke up anxious to see if the doll was still there. I put on a coat, and I ran down the hill to see if she was gone.

She *was,* and that made me happy.

It might have seemed strange to some people that I cared that much about a doll that belonged to a little girl I had never met—but I believe that even a small act of love can ripple out across this world and touch someone. And maybe, it can even ripple from this world to the next and back again.

I looked up at my house.

It didn't have what HGTV calls "curb appeal," yet.

But I was proud of what it was becoming because I knew that no one would ever have to feel lonely or afraid again in my home.

* ❂ *

ALISTAIR BANE is an enrolled citizen of the Eastern Shawnee tribe of Oklahoma. He is a storyteller and writer, as well as a visual artist. He works in several media, including quilting, beadwork, regalia making, contemporary fashion, and painting. Alistair is a frequent Moth Mainstage storyteller and has been a guest host on *The Moth Radio Hour*. He still finds the time to foster dogs for local rescues and has fostered over three hundred dogs in his lifetime.

This story was told on February 29, 2020, at the Riverwalk Center in Breckenridge. The theme of the evening was Leap of Faith. Director: Sarah Austin Jenness.

Meg Bowles is a senior director on The Moth's Mainstage, co-host of the Peabody Award–winning *The Moth Radio Hour,* and co-author of the *New York Times* bestseller *How to Tell a Story: The Essential Guide to Memorable Storytelling.* Signing on as a volunteer in 1997, she had no idea where The Moth would take her. Over the decades, she has directed Mainstage shows everywhere from Anchorage to London. Although her background in television and film has served to sharpen her editorial sense and eye for detail, she is recognized for her ability to spot stories in the wild and to home in on what transforms a seemingly small story into something universal. For her part, Meg loves working with people one-on-one, witnessing and supporting their progress. She is especially excited to see people who never imagined themselves as having a story go on to proudly claim the moniker of storyteller.

Catherine Burns is a Peabody Award–winning director, storytelling doula, consultant, and public speaker. From 2003 to 2023, she was the artistic director of The Moth, where she was a host and producer of *The Moth Radio Hour.* As one of the lead directors on The Moth Mainstage, she has helped many hundreds of people craft their stories, including a New York City sanitation worker, a Nobel laureate, the

Tower of London's Raven Master, a jaguar tracker, and an exonerated prisoner. She is co-author of the *New York Times* bestseller *How to Tell a Story: The Essential Guide to Memorable Storytelling from The Moth,* and the editor of the bestselling and critically acclaimed books *The Moth: 50 True Stories, All These Wonders,* and *Occasional Magic.* Born and raised in Alabama, she now lives in Brooklyn with her husband and young son. Find her on Instagram: @thecatherineburns

Emily Couch is a producer on The Moth's artistic team, giving her the distinct honor of working on myriad creative projects. Having started at The Moth as an intern in 2017, she has worn many hats— meeting scheduler, associate producer of the Peabody Award– winning *The Moth Radio Hour,* resident grammar enthusiast, and beyond. She loves working behind the scenes to spread the beauty of true, personal stories to listeners and readers around the world. When she is not listening to a spun yarn, she is likely playing with literal yarn—knitting it into something that she may or may not finish. She lives in the Hudson Valley with her husband and cats.

Sarah Haberman has been The Moth's executive director since 2013. Prior to The Moth, Sarah held senior management and development positions at Jazz at Lincoln Center, Columbia Business School, the Whitney Museum of American Art, and the New York Public Library. Before embarking on a nonprofit career, she spent five years as an acquiring editor in Paris for Robert Laffont-Fixot, a major French publishing house. She is a member of the board of directors for the Herzfeld Foundation in Milwaukee and served on The Moth's board of directors until 2013.

Jenifer Hixson is a senior director and one of the hosts of *The Moth Radio Hour.* Each year she asks people to identify significant turning points in their lives—fumbles and triumphs, leaps of faith, darkest hours—and then helps them shape those experiences into story form for the stage. In 2000, she launched The Moth StorySLAM, which now has a full-time presence in twenty-seven cities in the United States, the UK, and Australia and provides more than four thousand individual storytelling opportunities for storytelling daredevils and loquacious wallflowers alike. Jenifer's story "Where There's Smoke" has been featured on *The Moth Radio Hour* and *This American Life* and was a part of The Moth's first book: *The Moth: 50 True Stories.*

Michelle Jalowski is a director and producer at The Moth, where she helps people across the country mine their lives for meaning, pinpoint the story of it all, and develop it for the stage. She loves the intimacy and connection involved in developing a story—of diving into someone's life with them headfirst and emerging with gold. Her work at The Moth allows her to combine her love of theater, documentary, and live events, and she is grateful. In addition to directing and producing, Michelle teaches Moth storytelling workshops for adults and young people in and around New York. She lives in Brooklyn.

Sarah Austin Jenness has a loud and distinct laugh that will make you smile. She joined the staff at The Moth in 2005, and as the executive producer she has had the honor of working with many hundreds of people to craft and hone their unique personal stories. She is a Peabody Award–winning director, is one of the long-standing hosts of *The Moth Radio Hour,* oversees *The Moth* podcast, and launched The Moth's Global Community Program, designing and coaching storytelling workshops for participants in the United States, South Asia, and Africa to elevate conversations around gender equality and human rights. Moth stories Sarah has directed in the past fifteen-plus years have been told on the floor of the United Nations, at the Sundance Film Festival, on rickshaws and buses—and in Dharamsala, India, during a two-day conversation between young peace builders from conflict countries and His Holiness the Dalai Lama. Closer to home, Elliot, Amelia, Evie, and Opal, her nephew and nieces, have given her the Best Aunt in the World Award. Sarah is also a co-author of the bestselling book *How to Tell a Story: The Essential Guide to Memorable Storytelling from The Moth*. She believes in challenging dominant narratives—and that stories change the world by creating connection.

Catherine McCarthy, LCSW, is the former senior manager of the Moth Education Program, which she helped to build from its first pilot workshop in 2012 into the nationwide program for young people and worldwide resource for educators that it is today. Through this program, Catherine directly helped hundreds of young people to build community, gain confidence, and reflect meaningfully on their lives. Her time in Moth EDU took her all over the country and world, leading workshops and directing stories with Lincoln Center Education, SXSWedu, the U.S. State Department, and the NYC Department of Education's chancellor's office, to name a few. She co-designed the first Moth Teacher Institute, developed The Moth's classroom curriculum guide, and co-wrote Penguin Random House's teacher's guides to *The Moth Presents: All These Wonders* and *The Moth Presents: Occasional Magic*. Catherine also directed stories on The Moth Mainstage, which can be heard often on *The Moth Radio Hour* and podcast. It was her experience of nearly a decade of working at The Moth—of watching the transformative power of sharing one's story within a supportive space—that inspired her to become a psychotherapist. She is currently the clinical director of Kip Therapy in Manhattan, where she helps clients to understand the stories that shape them, and helps train and support emerging psychotherapists. She regularly teaches courses for clinicians on how key concepts from personal storytelling can deepen their empathic listening and enhance therapeutic work. She is thrilled that she also gets to continue working as a teaching artist within the Moth Education Program that she helped create, as she never tires of witnessing the magic of people coming together to share and shape their stories.

Jodi Powell enjoys nothing more than getting lost in whatever the current situation is—be it listening to a story, cooking a Caribbean dish, or combing the neighborhood thrift store in Harlem. She also loves the theater, people-listening in NYC, and everything that happens in the sky. She vows to continue her search to discover the exact minute she was born so she can get a more accurate birth chart. She started as an intern on The Moth's Community and Education teams and then became, in turn, an associate producer, producer, *Moth Radio Hour* host, and director, who has helped dozens of people tell their stories on The Moth Mainstage. She is from Jamaica.

Larry Rosen has worked with The Moth since 2009 as an instructor, director, and story coach. He is proud to engage regularly with individuals and diverse communities throughout the United States and in selected cities worldwide. Larry has been teaching, directing, and producing storytelling, theater, improvisation, and sketch comedy for more than twenty-five years, in connection with such institutions as Second City, NYU, and the State University of New York.

Suzanne Rust is the senior curatorial producer and one of the hosts of the Peabody Award–winning *The Moth Radio Hour*. As curator, she enjoys the treasure hunt of finding exciting new voices for Moth stages around the world. Her triumphs include finding a sheriff who saved an abandoned baby from the wild woods of Missoula, Montana; casting a photographer who discovered the world of the Black rodeo; and bringing a beloved Broadway star to The Moth stage. A noted magazine writer and a Folio Award–winning editor, Suzanne has held positions at *Family Circle* and *Real Simple,* and her writing has appeared in *Essence, TheGrio,* and *Time* magazine. She was also a contributor to *How to Tell a Story: The Essential Guide to Memorable Storytelling from The Moth.* Suzanne, a native New Yorker who loves talking to strangers, is thrilled and grateful that a big part of her job includes listening to stories. She lives in Harlem with her husband.

Chloe Salmon is a director and one of the hosts of the Peabody Award–winning *The Moth Radio Hour.* The Moth first came into her life as a faithful driving buddy during long trips across her home state of Kansas. Now she takes great joy in her work behind the scenes that has set the stage for hundreds of stories to be told to audience members (and drivers) all over the world. She is ever grateful to each storyteller she works with for their generosity in sharing a part of themselves—whether that's their love for a family-owned roller-skating rink on the South Side of Chicago, their shock at being asked a question on *Who Wants to Be a Millionaire,* their hope to keep the doors of a bookstore open a world away in Pakistan, or countless other moments and memories that come alive in their telling.

ACKNOWLEDGMENTS

The Moth would like to thank:

The storytellers featured in this book—and anyone who has ever dared to share a story on a Moth stage.

Our audiences, and you, our beloved readers.

Our founder, George Dawes Green.

Our board of directors: chair Eric Green, Serena Altschul, Neil Gaiman, Gabrielle Glore, Adam Gopnik, Alice Gottesman, Dan Green, Courtney Holt, Lisa Hughes, Sonya Jackson, Mia Jung, Chenjerai Kumanyika, Maybel Marte, Joanne Ramos, Melanie Shorin, and Denmark West.

All those who bring our events to life and make the magic happen night after night—our talented musicians, incomparable audio and video recordists, photographers, and dedicated volunteers. And our Moth hosts, who bring their nimble wit, emotional intelligence, and fiery energy to audiences—you are our ultimate ambassadors.

Our Community Engagement, Global, MothWorks, and Education Program partners, storytellers, and instructors, who share themselves, listen with empathy, and demonstrate the power of storytelling every day.

The hundreds of public radio stations around the country who air *The Moth Radio Hour*, all of our national partners for both the

Mainstage and StorySLAM series, and all our regional StorySLAM producers and community for their tireless dedication.

Our collaborators, who challenge and inspire us: Jay Allison, Viki Merrick, and everyone at Atlantic Public Media and Transom; Ann Blanchard, Meryl Cooper, Kirsten Ames, Carla Hendra, Jordan Rodman, Michelle Elsner, David Schachter, and Kerri Hoffman, Jason Saldanha, and everyone at PRX.

Our foundation partners, incredible donors, and members, who make it all possible through their generous support.

Our unwavering agent, Daniel Greenberg—thank you for being by our side for five books! Your wise counsel, talent, and strong vision of how Moth stories could work beautifully on the page has taken The Moth to new spaces and audiences. None of these books would exist without you as our patient, humorous, and ever calm guide, and we are forever grateful.

And also: our gifted editor, Matt Inman. You were there to steady our nerves and problem-solve as we launched our first book over a decade ago and have (thank God!) been by our sides ever since. Thank you for your humor, sensitivity, steadfastness, and artistry. You always make us better.

The rest of the team at Crown: Gillian Blake, Annsley Rosner, Mason Eng, Melissa Esner, Gwyneth Stansfield, Jack Meyer, Julie Cepler, Dyana Messina, Michelle Giuseffi, and Fariza Hawke.

The incredible Moth staff at the time of writing:

Salma Ali, Melanie Avellaneda, Keighly Baron, Megan Bourg, Meg Bowles, Melissa Brown, Jonathan Cabral, Heather Colvin, Emily Couch, Travis Coxson, Estee Daveed, Aimee Davis, Ignacia Delgado, Jody Doo, Blaze Ferrer, Amanda Garcia, Brandon Grant, Lee Ann Gullie, Sarah Haberman, Jenifer Hixson, Michelle Jalowski, Sarah Austin Jenness, Sarah Jane Johnson, Aldi Kaza, Marina Klutse, Jen Lue, Isaiah McNair-Wilson, Nimat Muhammad, Chloë Muñoz, Charlotte Muth, Jodi Powell, Anna Roberts, Juan

Rodriguez, Alex Roman Peters, Larry Rosen, Edgar Ruiz Jr., Suzanne Rust, Chloe Salmon, Maria Seravalli, Marc Sollinger, Ana Stern, Gabriel Szajnert, Kate Tellers, Patricia Ureña, Manuela Velasquez, Vella Voynova, Zoe Walker, Devin Wilson.

Our former artistic director, Catherine Burns, whose creative leadership guided this book—and shaped The Moth into the organization that it is today.

And all of the other former staff and leadership at The Moth over the years, who helped make The Moth what it is, including our former board, artistic and executive directors, and board chairs: Deborah Dugan, Joan Firestone, Ari Handel, Kathleen Kerr, Anne Maffei, Alexander Roy, Judy Stone, Lea Thau, and Joey Xanders.

ABOUT THE MOTH

THE MOTH is an acclaimed nonprofit organization dedicated to the art and craft of storytelling. For twenty-six years, The Moth has presented over fifty thousand stories, told live and without notes to standing-room-only crowds worldwide. The Moth conducts eight ongoing programs: The Moth Mainstage, which tours internationally, has featured stories by Elizabeth Gilbert, Kathleen Turner, Malcolm Gladwell, Darryl "DMC" McDaniels, John Turturro, Molly Ringwald, Boots Riley, Krista Tippett, Damon Young, Mike Birbiglia, Rosanne Cash, Danyel Smith, and Tig Notaro, as well as an astronaut, a pickpocket, a hot dog–eating champion, and hundreds more; The Moth StorySLAM program, which conducts open mic storytelling competitions in twenty-seven cities: twenty-five in the United States plus Melbourne, Australia, and London, UK; The Moth Community Program, which offers storytelling workshops and performance opportunities to adults who are too often overlooked by the mainstream media; The Moth Education Program, which brings the thrill of personal storytelling to high schools and colleges in New York, and educators around the world; The Moth Global Community Program, which develops and elevates true, personal stories from extraordinary individuals in the global south; The Moth Podcast—the 2020 Webby People's Voice Award Winner for

Best Podcast Series—which is downloaded one hundred million times a year; MothWorks, which uses the essential elements of Moth storytelling as an empathetic communication tool; and the Peabody Award–winning *The Moth Radio Hour,* which, produced by Jay Allison at Atlantic Public Media and presented by PRX, The Public Radio Exchange, airs weekly on over 570 public radio stations nationwide. To date, The Moth has published four critically acclaimed books: the *New York Times* bestseller *The Moth: 50 True Stories* (2013), *All These Wonders: True Stories About Facing the Unknown* (2017)—described as "wonderful" by *NYT*'s Michiko Kakutani—and *New York Times* bestsellers *Occasional Magic: True Stories of Defying the Impossible* (2019) and *How to Tell a Story: The Essential Guide to Memorable Storytelling from The Moth* (2022). The Moth has released its first card deck, *A Game of Storytelling* (Clarkson-Potter). The Moth's second podcast, *Grown,* is out now on all major streaming platforms. Learn more at themoth.org.

Available from **THE MOTH**

"Stories that attest to . . . the shared threads of love, loss, fear and kindness that connect us."

—MICHIKO KAKUTANI,
The New York Times

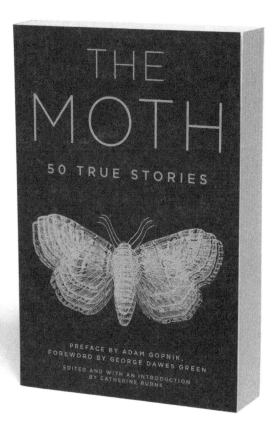